Smarter ventures

FT Prentice Hall
FINANCIAL TIMES

In an increasingly competitive world, we believe it's quality of thinking that will give you the edge – an idea that opens new doors, a technique that solves a problem, or an insight that simply makes sense of it all. The more you know, the smarter and faster you can go.

That's why we work with the best minds in business and finance to bring cutting-edge thinking and best learning practice to a global market.

Under a range of leading imprints, including *Financial Times Prentice Hall*, we create world-class print publications and electronic products bringing our readers knowledge, skills and understanding which can be applied whether studying or at work.

To find out more about our business publications, or tell us about the books you'd like to find, you can visit us at **www.pearsoned.co.uk**

PEARSON
Education

Smarter ventures

A survivor's guide to venture capital
through the new cycle

Katharine Campbell

FT Prentice Hall
FINANCIAL TIMES

An imprint of **Pearson Education**

London • New York • Toronto • Sydney • Tokyo • Singapore
Hong Kong • Cape Town • Madrid • Paris • Amsterdam • Munich • Milan

PEARSON EDUCATION LIMITED

Head Office
Edinburgh Gate
Harlow CM20 2JE
Tel: +44 (0)1279 623623
Fax: +44 (0)1279 431059
Website: www.pearsoned.co.uk

First published in Great Britain in 2003
© Pearson Education Limited 2003

The right of Katharine Campbell to be identified as Author of this work has been
asserted by her in accordance with the Copyright, Designs and Patents Act 1988.

ISBN-10: 0-273-65403-9
ISBN-13: 978-0-273-65403-2

British Library Cataloguing in Publication Data
A CIP catalogue record for this book can be obtained from the British Library

10 9 8 7 6 5 4 3 2

Designed by Sue Lamble
Cartoon illustrations by Roger Beale
Typeset by Northern Phototypesetting Co. Ltd, Bolton
Printed and bound in Great Britain by Bell & Bain Ltd, Glasgow

The Publishers' policy is to use paper manufactured from sustainable forests.

About the author

KATHARINE CAMPBELL is the former private equity correspondent of the *Financial Times*. She spent five years delving into the secretive world of private equity, and became one of the leading commentators on the sector. A weekly column on the Enterprise Page of the *FT* provided an outlet for her particular interest in entrepreneurship and venture capital.

Previous positions at the *FT*, where she spent a dozen years in total, included Frankfurt correspondent at the beginning of the 1990s, covering the early years of German unification.

She studied German and ancient Greek at Oxford University, and international relations at the School of Advanced International Studies, Johns Hopkins University, in Washington, DC.

She now works in the private equity industry.

Contents

PART THREE ◆ Working with venture capital

PART FOUR ◆ The future

Preface

SO WHY WOULD SOMEONE who is neither an entrepreneur with first-hand experience of extracting cash from a venture capitalist, nor a VC willing to dish the dirt about how the industry *really* works, think they can write a book like this?

First, let me explain how I got to know about venture capital.

My introduction to the industry and its occasionally paranoid ways came shortly after my appointment at the *Financial Times* to the curiously titled position of 'growing business correspondent' – a beat which, among other things, encompassed venture capital. Richard Lambert, the then editor, had received a letter from one of the most senior and sophisticated figures in European private equity who had heard there was to be a new reporter on the beat. He hoped, he wrote, that 'he' would be a 'friend' and 'supporter' of the industry. The editor found this odd, as did I. After all, when he appointed an aerospace correspondent, he didn't get airline chief-executives writing in hoping the new journalist would be a friend of their industry.

Venture capitalists can be a pretty self-important lot. They try and attach to the business of making (a very large amount of) money a higher purpose – as if their sole raison d'être were the greater good of job-creating capitalism.

At the same time, as I got to understand something of this distinctly opaque and secretive industry, I found it exciting. The best VCs are some of the brightest, most creative and energetic people. I also became convinced of the importance of the role of venture capital for funding high-growth young companies, something in turn that is indeed pivotal for the future health of every European economy.

Not that I was ever in much danger of being viewed as a 'supporter'. I have never met a corner of the business world that reacts so intemperately to a spot of healthy scepticism, never mind criticism. The industry has operated away from the public glare for too long, and developed a peculiar mixture of arrogance and hypersensitivity. One of the other challenges in writing in this area is the extraordinary pace of change. Even in the (relatively) short time since I was commissioned to write this book, venture capital has undergone a complete roller-coaster ride. At the height of the bubble, this was the sexiest corner of the financial markets. Yet in the latter months of work for the book, I was often driven onto the defensive as to why I was even still writing about the subject. But venture capital should not be viewed as a passing fad that, in Europe, came and went with the late 1990s excesses. Starting companies has to be a viable proposition at all stages of the economic cycle, not just in the course of a once in 50 years stock market aberration.

Europe desperately needs a more mature venture industry. VCs whinge about the lack of good entrepreneurs. Yet this is a vicious circle. The dearth is at least partly a function of the paucity of good VCs, who have the confidence and knowledge to invest throughout the cycle, rather than just at or near the top.

This book addresses you, the entrepreneur, raising capital – but will I hope say something to VCs too, and not purely out of curiosity to see who dishes the dirt on whom. The industry has plenty to think about in terms of its own development. And so many times, the VC–entrepreneur relationship falls apart, or is never cemented in the first place, because *both* sides make a poor job of understanding each other.

The idea is to demystify the process a little, and share as many of the dirty secrets of VC as the lawyers will allow. When an entrepreneur negotiates with a VC, the latter has probably done it countless times; for the former, everything is new. Few business situations are quite that unequal. What the book cannot do is to eliminate the unpredictability of a process that is anything but purely rational. If a VC likes a deal, weaknesses can be fixed. If a VC does not like a deal, weaknesses are weaknesses. Therefore, while I have not sat chewing my nails waiting to present to a VC, I hope I can bring a certain objectivity that the individuals either side of that negotiating table could not.

Acknowledgements

So many people have been most generous with their help and encouragement. Very special thanks to James Dobree, Mark Suster and Alain Falys, three entrepreneurs who spent many hours elucidating their experiences with great intelligence.

Chris Grew, Richard Eaton and Tom Kellerman steered me expertly through the complete minefield of the legals involved in a VC agreement.

Dimo Dimov did excellent work on preparing charts in a field where data gathering is a real challenge.

After I left journalism (for, yes, private equity) *Financial Times* managing editor Diane Summers most generously allowed me continued access to the newspaper database (a system cursed when I was on the paper for its unreliability at deadline time, but deeply appreciated as a wonderful and, strangely, almost entirely reliable, tool as soon as I left).

A very big thank you to the London Business School and Gordon Murray for access to its marvellous library.

Invaluable assistance came from very many others including Brett Allsop, everyone at Atlas Venture, Rod Attwooll, John Bates, Louise Ballard, Adrian Beecroft, Gordon Bonnyman, Geoff Bristow, Nigel Brown, Andrea Bonafe, Bengt Carlstrom, Danny Chapchal, Sir Ronald Cohen, Sir David Cooksey, Cary Cooper, Sherry Coutu, Charles Cotton, Simon Darling, Rolf Dienst, Nick Earle, Peter Englander, Stuart Evans, David Giampaolo, Hermann Hauser, Thomas Hoegh, Guy Kawasaki, Kenneth Ibbett, everyone at Index Ventures, everyone at 3i, Dominique Laffy, Michael Ledzion, Michael Liebrich, John McMonigall, Martin Mellish, Julie Meyer, Graeme Minto, Pierre Morin, Charlie Muirhead, Richard Muirhead, Alex Nigg, Diana Noble, everyone at Pond Ventures, John Pawsey, Jos Peeters, everyone at PolyTechnos, George Powlick, Lennart Ramberg, Doug Richard, Mike Risman, Stephen Ross, Bundeep Singh Rangar, Chantal Ligertwood, Falk Strascheg, John Snyder, Vijay Sondhi, Peter Tornquist, Adam Valkin, Katia Verresen, Nikko Waesche, Mark Weston, Marc Zuegel.

I should like to thank Richard Stagg, Editorial Director at Pearson Education, for his enthusiasm, ready grasp of the subject, and very valuable input. Many thanks also to Liz Wilson and the rest of the team at Pearson for all their help and patience.

But it is my partner Tony who deserves the medal. He performed the Sisyphean task of keeping up author morale. He never complained at the disappearance of the dining room table under the two-foot high filing 'system', not to mention the vanishing of the very concept of a weekend. And he seemed to know instinctively when to reach for the Alba white truffle (or whatever else might be in season) and an oversized bunch of flowers to unblock the latest impasse. T, I'm endlessly grateful.

OKAY, WE'VE ESTABLISHED THE SMART MONEY ISN'T GOING INTO START-UPS. WHERE CAN I GET SOME STUPID MONEY?

1

Introduction

With a banker, the appropriate question is How much money will he give me?
With a venture firm, the right question is How much money will he make me?
(Peter Wagner, partner, Accel Partners)

To be successful at venture capital there are three crucial rules. The only
problem is no one knows what they are.
(Kunze, 1990)

MANY EUROPEAN ENTREPRENEURS today vow they will never again take venture capital. Are they right? The late 1990s technology bubble briefly elevated the venture capital industry from the obscure corner of the financial world it had hitherto inhabited onto the pulsing stage of the so-called "new economy". The nascent market in Europe sprang to life. Founding a venture-backed start-up was briefly the height of cool and anyone who dared doubt the boundless prospects of any internet business simply failed to 'get it'. But experience was badly lacking and the buzz sucked in scores of people rushing to sup at the seemingly plentiful table with only the shakiest grasp of venture capital basics. Nor did the dotcommers much resemble true entrepreneurs. 'Is it only trust fund babes who get [venture] funded in Europe?' enquired a French friend of mine, recently returned to Europe after a decade in the USA, as she observed the roster of socialites and tycoons' progeny who seemed to be at the helm of half the London start-ups.

When the bubble burst in the spring of 2000, the European VC party had barely got going. A nascent industry was nipped in the bud before it had time to establish itself. But it has done plenty of damage. The pain of unwinding scores of ludicrously incompetent investments has pitted entrepreneur against venture capitalist, giving extra edge to the bitterness arising from the broader fall-out. When dreams evaporate, it is useful to have someone to blame, and the evil VC will do nicely. It helps that a good proportion of them deserve it. But as the European industry rebuilds from the rubble, it is down to each side to act smarter. Venture capitalists do an extremely poor job of understanding their core constituent, the entrepreneur, creating unnecessary tensions both entering into a deal and in managing the relationship thereafter. As a measure of the extent to which they are out of touch, many seem genuinely unaware of the disaffection and scepticism about venture capital in the entrepreneurial community that has been stoked by the multiple horror stories of the past few years.

At the same time, entrepreneurs in Europe need to become rather savvier about the venture process. Far too few make much effort to understand how VCs really work, and hence the tune to which they dance. Some people are taken by surprise even by the most basic requirements, such as an investor's need for an 'exit'. Meanwhile unprofessional venture capitalists survive (though the downturn is thankfully ridding the world of a good number of them) at least in part precisely because company founders failed to do their homework properly and genuinely research their prospective funders, as opposed to just listening to a bunch of scare stories.

Founders are also apt to set out with false objectives. I have lost count of the number of times entrepreneurs have said to me they would take 'dumb' in preference to 'smart' money – for which read 'no interference in my business because I know best'. That is a natural enough conclusion, given the incompetence of many practitioners who genuinely do not provide much worthwhile help, but it is also dangerous. VC money is far too expensive to be just that – cash. As Peter Wagner of Silicon Valley firm Accel Partners underlines, in making the distinction between picking a bank loan and a venture capitalist, the latter, if he is good, provides wisdom and perspective on the basis of his wide experience, and becomes a pivotal element in the development of the company. It is all down to building a functioning partnership. Granted there are still too few of these individuals and firms in Europe which genuinely do that, but you, the entrepreneur, need to know what you are looking for. Moreover, while dumb money may have the supposed merit of 'keeping out of your hair' when times are good, you may expect it to make a hasty reappearance the minute things start to slip (as they are bound to do in every start-up). The dumb money is likely to more than live up to its name in the way it then behaves in the crisis.

The world headquarters of venture capital is the USA. Sand Hill Road, in Menlo Park, Silicon Valley, northern California, is venture capital's Wall

Street. The industry began to develop in the late 1960s and early 1970s, and has been creating global companies more or less ever since. Almost every large US technology or tech-related company – Apple, Compaq, Dell, Genentech, Oracle, Cisco, Netscape, Amazon, eBay, Yahoo – is venture-backed. Venture capital, which rightly or wrongly seeks its high returns largely in the technology sector, has been a pivotal force in the US economy's capacity to innovate and create jobs, and over 30 years has developed a sophisticated infrastructure and deep pool of experience. The top-tier venture firms, such as Kleiner Perkins Caufield & Byers and Sequoia, achieved iconic status. Outside the USA, only Israel comes anywhere close in terms of sophistication; while struggling today on account of the political situation, the country has sustained a market roughly the size of that clustered around Route 128 outside Boston, the second most important venture funding centre in America.

In Europe, however, venture capital has developed very differently. Attempts to mirror the success of the US venture industry in the early 1980s largely failed, and many investors migrated into the less risky, more predictable game of backing management buy-outs (MBOs or leveraged buyouts, LBOs in US terminology). Established businesses, often divested from larger corporations, could be given a new lease of life with the injection of private capital, the gearing effect of a load of debt and generous incentives to managers by way of a slice of equity. MBOs came to dominate. Only in the second half of the 1990s was venture activity rekindled in a significant fashion, fuelled by the creation of stock markets for growth companies, rising levels of entrepreneurialism, government support – and then during the bubble briefly ignited. Still today there is no established 'top tier' of firms; certainly no equivalent of a Kleiner Perkins. The number of venture-backed companies that achieved global significance even briefly is tiny, while most of Europe's best known technology businesses – Nokia, Vodafone, enterprise software providers Dassault Systèmes and SAP, chip design company ARM – never had a cent of venture capital. As already indicated, the market is still very much maturing.

But what exactly do we mean by venture capital? The terminology is not helpful. The business of providing equity finance to unquoted companies in its broadest sense is labelled 'private equity' – encompassing venture and LBOs (and assorted other private financing tools). In the USA, the LBO industry and the 'classic' venture capital industry inhabit more or less separate worlds. In Europe, by contrast, the term 'venture capital' has historically been used to denote all forms of private equity investment. So buy-out shops which own mature businesses like pubs, publishing groups, and large chemical manufacturers get called venture capital firms. This sounds very strange to

American ears. They are entirely different industries – and this book addresses venture capital in the US sense only.

This is more than mere terminology. The dominance of the buy-out mentality has meant that many European firms have had a tendency to approach the subject of investing in early stage companies from a financial engineering standpoint, as if they were engaged in a banking transaction. It has not helped that, at least in the past, venture firms recruited heavily from the accountancy profession, a much more appropriate profile for a buy-out than for a venture investor. The dominant buy-out mindset can affect everything from investment priorities to the types of agreements signed, to the nature of the post-investment relationship. While the venture industry is now gaining more of an identity of its own, the conflation of the two has been a considerable impediment to progress.

Getting to grips with the venture market is no easy task. To begin with, it remains an anachronistically fragmented, often insular, cottage industry. During the bubble there were an estimated 400 early stage funds in Europe alone (out of a total of 1200 private equity firms). Plenty of firms have only two or three partners. In the concentrated Silicon Valley cluster that is one thing, but in Europe this has resulted in a multiplicity of fragmented networks. The VCs, let alone the entrepreneurs, do not have much of an overview of the sector. Moreover, contact between European and their more experienced American peers has been minimal. Hermann Hauser, an entrepreneur turned venture capitalist and Cambridge (UK) luminary, says his stint 'through quite difficult times' on the board of broadband chipmaker Virata, alongside partners from US firms Oak Investment Partners and New Enterprise Associates (NEA), taught him much of what he knows about venture capital. But he is the exception. Some European VCs are still extraordinarily ignorant about the US market – though mostly not as incompetent as the individual roped in during the bubble to head a new £100m venture fund (set up by a buy-out firm and an investment bank, caught up, like everyone else, in start-up mania) who had never heard of Kleiner Perkins.

Venture capitalists also revel in opacity. Their trade is at heart more art than rocket science (as Kunze, in the chapter-opening quote suggests), yet it is swathed in more than its fair share of jargon, and the inclination of many practitioners is to overcomplicate, not elucidate. In the early days of researching this book, I naively volunteered to one senior US VC in London my mission to demystify the industry for entrepreneurs. 'Why would it be in our interests to help you do that?' he enquired. When I first started writing about private equity for the *FT*, everyone tried to tell me that 'carried interest' – a version of performance-related pay and a mechanism to make its recipients (who are not necessarily the people who do the work) very wealthy indeed – was 'terribly complicated', hinting I would never understand it. Eventually, I persuaded one of the industry's resident mavericks to explain it to me, which he duly did, with some intricate diagrams. (It is actually very simple, essentially a 20 per cent share of the profits.) As I reached for the piece of paper for my files, he got there first and binned it.

Performance numbers have also been shrouded in mystery. A partner at one venture firm would typically have no idea of the returns of another firm, however often the two worked together. Firms report to their own investors, but not to anyone else. In 2001, Calpers, the Californian pension giant which has extensive exposure to private equity, posted the returns of individual firms on its website. The private equity community – those with good and bad returns alike – arose in uproar and forced the numbers to be removed from the site. More recently, there has been further pressure from various quarters in the USA for greater disclosure – and it will undoubtedly come, but not without a lot of resistance from an industry accustomed to operating well away from the glare of public scrutiny.

Another curiosity of the venture business is its extreme cyclicality. It can lurch from irrational exuberance to irrational pessimism in a matter of months, as investors part with excessive sums of cash close to the top of the market, only to withdraw to lick their wounds as the market falters, and their will and faith to make new investments seemingly evaporates with every further ten-point fall in the stock market index. The internet and technology bubble – during which US VCs invested $100bn at the height of the mania in 2000, now resulting in the most fundamental shakeout in the industry's history – is only the most extreme version of earlier cycles. A Harvard paper (Sahlman and Stevenson 1987) about the overfunding and unsustainable valuations in the Winchester disk drive industry was written 'to help investors and entrepreneurs avoid charter membership in the greater fool club'. It referred to events in the early 1980s.

One of the most devastating effects of the bubble has been the excessive capital that has flowed into the venture business, which highlights a more fundamental size paradox at its heart. The more successful a firm, the larger the fund it can raise (because investors have faith in its abilities and choose to park their money there). Large funds are desirable from the partners' point of view by virtue of the way the fees are calculated. In terms of carried interest, doubling a big number gives you an awful lot more loot than doubling a small number. Management fees are also based on a percentage of capital committed. Yet it rapidly becomes uneconomic for large funds to invest in chunks of €1m or €2m – investments which take more or less as much time and effort as pulling together a multi-hundred-million euro leveraged buy-out. Apax Partners provides a paradigmatic illustration of the problem. One of the first venture capital investors in Europe, and led by industry visionary Sir Ronald Cohen, Apax has graduated from its first fund of £10m in 1981 to a €4.4bn investing vehicle. While the official spin is that the firm still finances start-ups, advisory board meetings have apparently agonized over the conundrum of how the shop has now 'risen above the level of entrepreneurial investment'. Europe still desperately lacks sufficient VCs experienced in backing early stage companies; more than a handful of them are sitting at Apax doing large LBOs. Conversely, the tiny management fees paid on seed funds, which supply that all-important initial capital to a young business, but which by their very nature are small, make the game unattractive in the extreme for the individuals concerned. Yet which is harder – effecting a buy-out of an established business, or guiding an embryonic start-up through its initial growth?

Entrepreneurs think VCs are:

◆ Arrogant, young, self-obsessed

◆ A necessary evil

◆ Grossly overpaid – and yet they somehow genuinely believe they deserve it

◆ Risk averse, simply living off other people's money

◆ Cheeky enough to come into my business and believe they can make a difference

◆ Lacking in operational skills

◆ Never around/always interfering

◆ Incapable of adding value

◆ Liable to boot me out at my first mistake – when they make loads of mistakes and keep their jobs

◆ Clueless idiots (for turning down my wonderful plan/closing my fabulous business)

◆ Wielding power without responsibility

◆ Unaware that all my emotion is invested in this one business

Venture guys think entrepreneurs are:

◆ Arrogant, young, self-obsessed

◆ Stubborn and don't listen

◆ Liable to forget they couldn't get anywhere without our money

◆ Prone not to understand it's not their company

◆ Obsessed with valuation

◆ Wildly optimistic

◆ No good at giving us any credit – if it's a success, they did it all themselves and gave away too much of the business to us; if it's a failure, it's because we didn't understand the business

◆ Apt to forget it's an emotional roller coaster for us too

A cynic might say that entrepreneurs and venture capitalists are almost programmed not to get along. Yet both sides need each other. Understanding some of the tensions may be useful in managing them. The two groups cannot even agree how to refer to each other. Venture capitalists call themselves just that, or 'venture guys' – or in Europe sometimes just plain 'investors'. Entrepreneurs, meanwhile, almost invariably term them VCs – an acronym that can be enunciated in varying tones of disdain. Venture capitalists simply *never* call themselves VCs.

When things are progressing smoothly, of course, both sides are stroking each other's (ample) egos. Indeed almost every deal starts off as a full-blown love affair. The entrepreneur is starry eyed, having been let into the magic circle after months of toil, while the VC, who has championed the company through his investment committee, is on a high, convinced this will be the blockbuster investment that returns the capital of the entire fund.

But in tough times the two can work against each other. In the words of one jaundiced entrepreneur: 'VCs are a bunch of people, most of whom have never run a business. They believe they are clever. Most come from wealthy backgrounds. They won't dirty their hands, they think any fool can run a company. They think *they* know about money.'

The qualities of true entrepreneurs and today's VCs are arguably very different. Together with vision and drive, true entrepreneurs possess ruthlessness, a high tolerance of risk and the capacity to bounce back after strings of rejections. A US psychiatrist has diagnosed founding CEOs as suffering from a condition called psychological certitude; you know you are right, regardless of the evidence (a quality shared with dictators). As Professor Cary Cooper of UMIST notes, a high proportion of entrepreneurs have loss-related events in childhood – divorce, death of a parent, rejection by authority (teachers who thought they were thick). They are setting out to prove something, to gain control of a world which they could not control as children. They take quick decisions, often operating according to gut feel and instinct; it is not in their nature to dither.

Venture capitalists, on the other hand, are not paid to be risk takers and, aside from bubble era aberrations, are surprisingly risk averse. They are, after all, managing other people's money. They have time to (try to) get it right; unlike the entrepreneur, they are not in a hurry. Today's VCs in Europe tend to be part of the educational elite – mobile international types with multiple degrees and often moneyed upbringings. Too many are former investment bankers. They are trained to be thoughtful and analytical, and will be happier when surrounded by reams of data. Forming instinctive views of people, companies and markets is not their natural modus operandi and snap decisions are not their bag. VCs rarely say yes (to a deal) but, masters at prevarication, they rarely say no either.

VCs can be annoying to entrepreneurs, not least because they appear to be getting a risk-free buzz from the vicarious ride. They haven't sunk years of their life into a single endeavour. When the going gets tough and start-up companies are slashing costs and laying off staff, they continue their VC lifestyle of first-class travel and posh hotels. Despite their line of business, they are not psychologically prepared for failure. As Bill Hambrecht (1984) writes: 'Everybody likes to talk about risk taking but they really only want risk when it works.'

While entrepreneurs spend their days dealing with rejection – from funders, customers, potential employees – VCs are at the other end of the seesaw – rejecting proposals, fighting off demands on their time. Again, many company founders are temperamentally loners (even if they team up with a cofounder or two). One of the more thoughtful London VCs adds: 'Many entrepreneurs are paranoid loners, so it is actually difficult to form a partnership with them and build trust.' VCs, by contrast, tend to be buddy-buddy with each other and collude to a considerable extent. One affable entrepreneur, who regularly attended a VC networking event called The Chemistry while fund raising, says cliquish VC behaviour invariably managed to make him feel a complete alien. What the two groups have in common is that they are generally alpha males (or females) with ample egos. In Europe, it is more or less *de rigueur* macho for an entrepreneur to say: 'My VC is useless.'

While true entrepreneurs have typically bailed out of school or university early, there is another kind of company founder, particularly prevalent during the bubble but still significant, who attended business school with the VCs and comes from similar stock. In my experience, the tensions are no less – each thinks they can do the other's job and greatly underestimates some of the above differences.

VCs rarely admit it, but much of their job is about successful human inter-action – which is where the overeducated, analytical types tend to fall down.

Charles Waite, founder of Greylock, an eminent US venture capital firm, enunciates some of the old-fashioned principles of venture capital:

> *We try to hire mannerly personable people with a good education who honestly want to make a contribution to the companies they're involved in and are not focused only on making money. Most firms say they do but my experience is that many don't. They'll hire the smartest people they can get . . . but [who] are often devoid of people skills and the ability to help entrepreneurs.*
>
> (Charles Waite quoted in Gupta 2000: 232)

One of his first successes as a VC, he explains, was because he got along with the entrepreneur when other investors had not. His description of partnership depicts venture capital at its most effective.

It is often argued that former entrepreneurs make the best VCs – and that one of Europe's problems is that these are much rarer beasts than in the USA. But that formula is by no means fail-safe (as will be seen in later chapters). The transition is not invariably successful and, given some of the traits dis-cussed above, one can see why. Perhaps the best VCs are *near* entrepreneurs, or entrepreneurs who have mellowed.

Insufficient understanding of the nature of the interaction between VC and entrepreneur brings unnecessary tensions, as do much more basic forms of miscommunication. Investors often do a bad job of explaining to entre-preneurs their need for an 'exit' – which is how they return capital to *their* investors. Even the terminology is distinctly unhelpful, as the transition may well not be an exit for the entrepreneur (in the case of a public market listing, for instance).

Founder succession is another thorny issue that is often poorly communi-cated. Some of the confusion arises when VCs trumpet their investment deci-sions as based on 'backing management'. How come, then, they suddenly decide they want to turf out the founder and bring in a 'seasoned' chief exec-utive during the course of the investment? The answer is that management is a dynamic 'not static' concept, and that different people skills may be appropriate for different stages of the business. The idea of someone else running your business may well be abhorrent to you, but succession can be well managed. Some of the best founders often appreciate the need for change and make a smooth transition into a different role. Others have the skills to adapt and remain at the helm. But VCs are often not as clear as they should be and, far worse, many change management when they cannot think what else to do (another very good reason to research prospective funders). And don't ask about the venture capital firm's own plans on this issue; they are notoriously hopeless at managing their own succession.

Another common source of conflict is a mismatch of ambition. If the VC wants to make $100m and you are happy with $5m, there will be constant tensions over the type of business you are building.

Following the blatant excesses of the bubble, it is fashionable to knock the US venture capital industry. But plenty of lessons remain; for instance, the importance of the spirit of partnership. The ability to think big is another. Bruce Dunlevie, a partner of Californian firm Benchmark Capital, described trying to convince a British founder that he had the makings of a $1bn company (even in the downturn). 'But I'm quite content if I make £5m,' the entrepreneur kept saying, as one of America's best-known VCs stood there more or less with his cheque book open. 'That'll put the kids through university and buy me the second home.'

In the current climate, realism is essential but need not equate with capped ambition. As you go through the process, remember, whatever the VCs like to pretend, it is really not rocket science.

References

Gupta, U. (ed.) (2000) *Done Deals: Venture Capitalists tell their stories*, Boston, MA, Harvard Business School Press.

Hambrecht, W. (1984) 'Venture Capital and Silicon Valley', *California Management Review*, 26 (2): Winter 1984, The Regents of the University of California.

Kunze, Robert J. (1990) *Nothing Ventured: the perils and pay offs of the great American venture capital game*, New York, HarperBusiness, 1990.

Sahlman, W. A. and Stevenson, H. H. (1987) Copyright © 1987 by the President and Fellows of Harvard College. Harvard Business School teaching note 'Capital market myopia'. This teaching note was prepared by Associate Professor William A. Sahlman and Professor Howard H. Stevenson. Reprinted by permission of Harvard Business School.

Links

VC news sites/about the industry

www.privateequityonline.com
www.altassets.net
www.evcj.com
www.tornado-insider.com
www.vcexperts.com
www.ventureone.com
www.ventureeconomics.com
www.vcapital.com
www.privateequitycentral.net

Industry statistics:

For the industry bellwether, the USA www.pwcmoneytree.com

For Europe   www.evca.com

PART ONE

The industry

Inside the venture industry

If you want to succeed, you should strike out on new paths rather than travel the worn paths of accepted success
(John D. Rockefeller)

Something called the limited liability partnership

The search for effective ways of funding loss-making start-up projects dates back at least to Babylonian times nearly four thousand years ago:

> *During the era of Hammurabi, King of Babylon in the eighteenth century BC, a sophisticated form of private enterprise had grown up, namely the private partnership, where one set of individuals furnished the capital, and another carried out the trading enterprise and shared in the profits.*
>
> (Lutz 1932: 335–55)

The modern venture capital industry, however, is rather younger. Its roots are in entrepreneurial investment by wealthy American families in the late nineteenth and early twentieth century – the Rockefellers, the Phippses, the Vanderbilts. But the first real institutions were formed in the immediate aftermath of World War II, with the founding of American Research and Development (ARD) and, in the UK, the Industrial and Commercial Finance Corporation (ICFC), the forerunner of 3i, one of Europe's best known venture capital brands. Not that either outfit looked much like a venture firm of today. ARD, established by MIT and others partly with the aim of commercializing technologies developed during the war, became a publicly listed fund, its cash supplied mostly by private individuals (after it failed to attract significant institutional interest). ICFC's rather broader aim was to try and address the problems of small and medium-sized companies accessing long-term capital, and its shareholders were the large British retail banks and the Bank of England.

It was not until the 1960s or 1970s that the limited liability partnership, the classic US venture structure, became established. It is how all the famous Silicon Valley firms – Kleiner Perkins Caufield & Byers, Sequoia, Accel, Mayfield, Greylock – are organized. This model (see below) has also been adopted in Europe in its pure form by firms ranging from Amadeus Capital Partners in the UK, to Capricorn Ventures in Belgium. But the European private equity landscape is, at the same time, distinctly more diverse. Many venture firms have grown up as units of large financial institutions. There has also been more experimentation, with some firms for instance established as companies rather than partnerships.

One of the biggest differences is that, whereas the buy-out and venture industries are almost completely separate in the USA, they are heavily interlinked in Europe. Firms such as Apax Partners are 'multistage', meaning that they invest in both young and more mature companies from a single fund. Other structures include the so-called asset gatherer model found on both sides of the Atlantic. The Carlyle Group, the Washington DC based firm, has used this approach to become one of the largest private equity firms in the world – setting up a stable of funds, each investing in specific areas such as venture capital, buy-outs, real estate and so on. Doughty Hanson, which has a technology venture fund among its offerings, is a smaller European version of the same thing.

The basic principle of a limited liability partnership (LLP) is simple enough. Investors, known as limited partners (LPs) – institutions such as pension funds, insurance companies, banks, university endowments, foundations, corporations and wealthy individuals – subscribe to a fixed-life fund run by a venture capital firm, the general partner (GP). Well-known European private equity investors range from Wellcome Trust, the research charity, to Dutch pensions funds such as PGGM, to Allianz, the German insurer. Banks have also been one of the largest sources of capital for the industry in Europe (although a large number are now exiting the business, having discovered how highly volatile are the earnings from this asset class). European institutions have by and large been much slower into private equity than their US counterparts (partly because a number got burnt during the 1980s) but more are now dipping a toe into the water. Entrepreneurs who have made money with the venture firm in the past also get the chance to invest in funds – although that is more prevalent in the mature US market.

The LLP took hold, incidentally, not primarily because anyone alighted on the structure as the most effective way of helping build young companies, but because it addressed investors' tax issues. An LLP allows investors to be treated as if they are investing directly in the companies themselves, instead of paying twice, once when the fund makes its capital gain on the sale of the assets and once when they receive the proceeds. The partnership agreements themselves, meanwhile, remain a lawyer's paradise, particularly in Europe with the extra complexity of myriad different fiscal and regulatory regimes. From the general partner's point of view, the best thing about the whole affair is that it is deliciously private, with the partnership generally an offshore entity, tucked well away from the public eye.

LPs' limits

The LP/GP terminology is somewhat obscure and even confuses industry practitioners. The easiest way to remember it is that the limited partners are so called because they are at risk for the amount of their investments and no more – and their powers are correspondingly restricted. While they may sit on an advisory board, they have no rights to interfere in individual investment decisions, or in the running of the partnership. In theory they can sack the general partner – typically a 75 per cent majority is required – but, somewhat surprisingly, this rarely happens in practice.

Most funds have a ten-year life, with the majority of the cash typically invested over the first three or four years (much more quickly during the bubble) and the remainder set aside for later rounds of investment in portfolio companies. This is then harvested in subsequent years as the VCs achieve realizations or 'exits'. The proceeds – the initial sum plus profits (assuming all has gone well and there are such profits) – get paid back to investors, rather than being reinvested, and the fund is liquidated at the end of its life. From the investors' point of view, this arrangement exercises a degree of discipline on the GP, forcing him to deal with the investments that are drifting – 'the living dead', as industry jargon has it, which have neither gone bust nor managed to achieve healthy exits.

In the past, investors put up all their cash at the outset, which was then held on deposit until needed, hence severely reducing investment returns. Now venture firms draw down cash as they go along, leaving the LPs theoretically able to deploy the money elsewhere until their commitments are 'called'. Under this system, the VCs' performance certainly looks a whole lot better, though what it does for the LPs' bottom line is more of a moot point. Normally, firms raise new fund vehicles every three or four years, although, in the frenzy of the bubble, many went out fund-raising every 12 months.

So who's the client?

The entrepreneur, right? Venture firms compete, after all, for the attention of the leaders of the best start-ups. Silicon Valley firm Benchmark's mission, for instance, is 'to help talented entrepreneurs build great technology companies'. Bill Gurley, a Benchmark partner, says: 'We see venture capital as a service industry. We work for the entrepreneur, not the other way round.' If only it were that simple.

The cash, as we have seen, comes from the limited partners. So, loathe as some VCs may be to spell it out, these people are their real clients. The great irony is that when times are good – most particularly during the 1990s – GPs were high handed in the extreme with their LPs and paid them scant attention. Since the downturn they have had to start mending their ways. For an entrepreneur, understanding the way in which venture firms source their funds is important in determining their motivations and pressure points, and hence predicting how they are likely to behave.

At the most basic level, VCs have to be mindful of exits in order to deliver returns to their investors. The other client's agenda – that of the entrepreneur – may not always chime with that. During the downturn, meanwhile, venture capitalists have been keeping companies going – dripfeeding them cash – when they know they are not going to survive in the long term. Why? So as not to have to show investors all the write-offs at once.

There is also something of an irony when it comes to performance. In the good times, venture capitalists are producing glittering returns, which makes them look great to their LPs. But, viewed from the entrepreneur's seat, things may appear a little different. The more cash the VCs are making, the more they are effectively charging their portfolio companies for their money. The VC argument, which holds up to a point, is that if returns are really good everyone is making so much loot that such concerns become pretty irrelevant.

Raising the fund

If entrepreneurs – perfectly reasonably – complain about the time the fund-raising process consumes, they may derive some faint amusement from how long it takes VCs to secure their own cash. While many funds were assembled in a matter of weeks during the bubble, the process in more normal times takes a year or more for all but the very best firms as they trail around the globe talking to scores of potential investors.

And they loathe the process. After all, it is something of an infra dig role reversal. They find themselves on the wrong side of the table, with investors or their advisers grilling them and demanding answers to awkward questions. The stakes are very high, too. While failure to raise venture capital certainly often constitutes the difference between survival and failure of an entrepreneur's business, failure to raise a new fund is invariably terminal for a venture capitalist.

However, the exact nature of the process depends, as much else in the world of VC, on who you are. The top tier Silicon Valley VCs, many with a track record spanning eight or ten funds or more, command a historic performance record that allows them to call the tune. Their funds have long been 'invitation only', more or less closed except to existing limited partners, who tend to be the well-connected endowments and foundations rather than big state pension funds.

In August 2000 I visited Kleiner Perkins when they were putting together a new fund. While the dotcom bubble had burst, Silicon Valley remained on pretty ebullient form, with the telecoms sector riding high and the IT spending slowdown not yet visibly biting. Would the firm be letting in any new investors, I enquired? Yes, the alma mater of one of their new partners, I was told. Indeed the talk at the time outside the firm was whether Kleiner Perkins' next fund might be drawn entirely from the partners' own pockets. They had made so much money in the past, people said, that they could easily scrape together a billion or so in loose change without recourse to their LPs. The only snag was this might displease those loyal LPs, who would be needed at a – then remote seeming – time when cash was harder to come by.

Such firms could, in the good times, exercise a certain tyranny over their limited partners. Anyone who passed on one fund was unlikely to be allowed to participate in future offerings. When Benchmark was raising a $750m fund for investment Europe in 2000, a certain amount of strong-arming went on, according to one investor. It may have been the height of the bubble but some people, this investor included, were rightly questioning whether the group's success in the USA could be replicated in the very different European environment. He was told he would not be allowed into future US funds unless he ponied up for Europe. None of the indigenous European funds have acquired that sort of cult status yet.

In a downturn, when limited partners have lost large sums of cash from the GP's bubble investments, the tables are turned. Even the very best funds have to pay more attention to their LPs. The LPs' bile rises at the arrogant way in which they were treated in the good times. As one US LP was heard to remark about the partners at a more than averagely self-regarding venture

.rm: 'I hope all their trophy wives have to get cleaning jobs.' Hardly likely of course, because venture capitalists, at least in the USA, have mostly made an extraordinary amount of money – which in turn further heightens LP/GP tensions. Moreover, firms which had raised huge funds during the boom were still making their multimillions from their management fees while sitting on capital they were not investing – and showing abysmal performance on what had been committed.

An interesting dynamic to this is that the individuals with the power to commit capital are themselves often on pretty average salaries – as employees of state pension funds or universities – and they can be inclined to resent the GPs' largesse on a personal as well as professional basis. The GPs, meanwhile, have to flatter them if they want cash – while privately, or not so privately, making remarks about how the lavish annual investor meetings constitute a 'nice outing' for these impecunious individuals.

Alternative structures

A number of venture operations are still owned by financial institutions, par-ticularly in Europe. Some – known as captives – invest entirely off the parent's balance sheet, while others – semi-captives – raise a proportion of their capi-tal from outside institutional investors. Large financial groups have not on the whole proved terribly suitable homes for private equity operations – the pol-itics and bureaucracy tend to be inimical to the venture game, there are con-flicts of interest aplenty. As already hinted, the parent's commitment to private equity is also often highly cyclical. Hence the trend has been for a number of such groups to seek independence. The investment partners know they will generally earn a lot more money if they do not have to share the fees with the parent. More significantly, the extraordinarily generous remuneration struc-ture standard in an independent venture capital firm (see below) tends not to be implemented in a bank hierarchy – it would hardly do, after all, to have a thirty-something venture guy earning more than the boss of the bank.

From the entrepreneur's point of view, there are some advantages of a cap-tive fund, including the fact that banks investing off their own balance sheets may have less aggressive return requirements, making it effectively cheaper capital. On the other hand, the less attractive remuneration system for the investment executives may produce a second-rate team – and more bureau-cratic decision making is likely to prove a nuisance, or worse. Moreover, while the deep pockets of such institutions may superficially appear attractive, these players can in practice prove very fickle – rushing in at the height of the market and withdrawing just as suddenly when the climate turns and they discover they have made a host of ill-advised investments, or when other factors change, such as regulatory controls.

Meanwhile, the venture firm organized as a corporation – rather than partnership – is not uncommon, particularly in continental Europe. When setting up b-business partners, a hybrid arrangement backed by largely Swedish corporations, the then chief executive Hans-Dieter Koch observed simply that the firm was structured as a company 'because that is what we understand'. Outfits set up this way argue that they avoid the exit pressures of the limited life fund – though to date they are not yet exactly threatening the Silicon Valley model.

In many cases, it was the lure of the public markets that constituted the main driver to incorporation. During the late 1990s, as internet holding companies CMGI and Internet Capital Group soared to peak capitalizations of $40bn and $50bn respectively (at the beginning of 2000), the lustre of the limited partnership began to wane a shade. I remember breakfasting with an angst-ridden VC around that time as he fretted: 'My dollar is just a dollar, but their dollar is worth a multiple of that, how can I compete?' The exorbitant valuations the public markets were placing on such entities meant these firms could afford to outbid their private counterparts in start-up financing rounds. Most established venture firms gave at least some thought as to how they might restructure themselves to go public (though the markets collapsed before any established entities did so).

In Europe the bunch of new wave VCs set up as private corporations rather than limited partnerships included Emerging Technologies, the Swedish shooting star which was formed from the portfolio of angel investments made by Kjell Spångberg, and Europatweb, the €500m internet investment vehicle set up by prominent French businessman Bernard Arnault. Some even managed to go public – such as 2M in Denmark, which listed in 2000, and filed for bankruptcy in July 2002. Today, that breed has shrivelled, leaving only a handful of quoted venture firms. These are mostly the old stalwarts such as 3i – organized as an investment trust, listed on the London Stock Exchange since 1994 and, as a member of the FTSE 100 index of the UK's largest public companies, far the most prominent quoted venture firm in Europe.

On the whole, the public markets are pretty unfriendly places for venture firms, whose portfolios of holdings in private companies are exceptionally difficult to value, even for sophisticated investors. Overvalued in the boom times, they are then punished almost indiscriminately in bear markets – which then hobbles their ability to raise new cash. 3i is large enough not to need to raise money by public market rights issues very often, but its public status has certainly not helped as the group has struggled to regain its footing following its technology bubble misadventures.

Public sector funding sources aplenty also exist across Europe. Some of the biggest programmes – such as the European Investment Fund, part of the European Investment Bank – invest into venture firms' funds rather than directly. Others such as TBG and KfW, the two most active German agencies, invest alongside venture firms, but are also set up to deal with entrepreneurs directly. Other entities that invest directly range from Enterprise Ireland, to Industrifonden (Swedish Industrial Development Fund), to the government-sponsored regional venture capital funds set up in ten regions in England. The debate about the role of public sector support for venture capital is outside the scope of this book, but suffice it to say that quality control is a very real issue. Moreover, as an entrepreneur you are unlikely to get the calibre of assistance that you would from a good institutional venture capitalist.

Who's who

The classic Silicon Valley style venture capital firm is a small, entrepreneurial organization, driven by people rather than process. The structure is flat and lean – a handful of partners, some associates and a number of analysts (and some firms even dispense with the associates and analysts). There may also be one or two entrepreneurs in residence – individuals given house room while they are looking to build their next business (they have usually done it before) – and venture partners, more senior characters, often part time with the fund, who have an operational background and can help evaluate deals and sit on the boards of one or two portfolio companies. But that is it. The biggest names in the industry are in fact tiny firms – Kleiner Perkins, for instance, has just 14 partners. Much of the venture business is still a cottage industry. A fluid, non-hierarchical partnership clearly has many advantages for coping with the uncertain environment in which the early stage investor operates. Flat as the structure may be technically, a certain hierarchy often develops, especially if the founders are still around. While the decision-making process is invariably presented to the outside world as 'entirely consensual', there may in reality be a senior partner on whose say-so everything hangs. Many of the Valley firms have gravitated to a strong star culture, with one or two investors – such as John Doerr and Vinod Khosla at Kleiner Perkins during the late 1990s – dominating the show.

As long as this is a process of meritocracy, with the rainmakers who do the deals becoming the leaders, this may work well. Many professional service firms function along similar lines. But venture firms are actually notoriously bad at managing crucial aspects of their business, notably succession. A brilliant investor may be totally uninterested in building an institution that will survive him, and will quite possibly lack the patience to nurture the skills of an heir apparent. The division of spoils between partners often becomes a hugely divisive issue. If the founders hog too much of the rewards, then the younger ranks, who are actually doing most of the work, will naturally become disenchanted. Partners who have retired to the 80-foot yacht but are still hogging a large share of the profits constitute a further problem. More recently, the better firms have been making an effort to become rather more professional – recruiting chief operating officers and implementing better decision-making processes.

At the other end of the scale are the more institutional organizations, with 3i something of an unique animal insofar as it is best described as a financial institution specializing in private equity rather than as a private equity firm. It is a hierarchical global organization with some 300 investment staff and another 600 support people. There is scale and depth, but the calibre of the individuals is variable and investee companies will also often have to deal with a string of different relationship managers over the course of their involvement with 3i.

Somewhere in the middle is Apax Partners, another international group which has built a quasi-institutional structure – with a string of committees and a very formal investment process – but which in many ways preserves the private equity partnership arrangement and close personal involvement with its portfolio companies.

Can't scale, won't scale

VCs may spend their time advising entrepreneurs how to scale their businesses, but most have yet to figure out how to do it themselves – whether in size or in geographic scope. The venture business as it has grown up in the USA, particularly California, thrives on small informal partnerships and deep local personal networks. It used to be said that Valley VCs would only look at companies located in two or three telephone area codes (part, but not all of the Bay Area). Viewed through a west coast lens, Europe was a remote place and a byword for everything second rate (in technology and technology financing). When Benchmark was launching its European fund in 2000, one of its US-based partners stood up at a conference, in Europe, to boast about how he had only ever spent three weeks outside the USA.

To create a larger firm, more institutional structures have to be put in place. It is striking that the more institutional firms have largely been European – like Apax Partners. While American VCs are known by the deals they have done, Sir Ronald Cohen, founder and chairman of Apax, is known principally for the firm he has built. There are a number of reasons for this – starting with a more formal business culture. Not blessed with the font of innovative technology on their back doorstep that has fuelled the growth of Silicon Valley, European VCs have also had to cast their net wider. The multistage approach, mixing buy-outs and venture, lends itself to the creation of larger, more international firms, because the larger funds available to such firms means they can support the overheads of overseas offices and so on. The few US firms which internationalized early, such as Warburg Pincus and General Atlantic, were multistage firms and east coast based, so, in shorthand, nearer to the European business culture than freewheeling California. But then the larger funds find it very difficult to do very small deals – in turn reinforcing the problem of the lack of scalability of the industry.

During the bubble US VCs flocked to Europe with the dawning realization that the USA did not necessarily possess a complete monopoly on technological innovation – particularly in the wireless industry. Not short on arrogance, they were going to teach the Europeans the art of company building – the mantra of the US venture capital industry. The irony possibly escaped many of them that it was precisely during that era, when they were all prepping companies for IPO within 18 months, that they were doing less company building than they had ever done in their history. Not only were cultural sensitivities in short supply, but the scale problem was evident. Geocapital, one of the early arrivals in London, was one of the smaller firms but trying very hard to act big. A Powerpoint slide around the time of its European launch boasted that it had 'over $0.3bn invested in 85 companies to date (established in Fort Lee, New Jersey in 1983)'. This was a tiny firm that quite clearly lacked the resources to go international.

Even the firms with the best reputations in the USA made something of a hash of their European entry. Benchmark Capital kicked off in London in May 2000 with just two partners (one of whom had departed just over two years later) and a $750m fund. It took them 18 months before the third partner was on board – and gave them a correspondingly slow start to making investments. The jury is still out as to whether any of the handful of firms that remain will really make a success of their international endeavours, or whether they too will in time retreat back to the USA.

A VC's week

Monday is a terrible day to attempt to get the attention of a VC, for that is when most firms hold regular partner meetings – sometimes lasting six hours or more. Items on the agenda will range from a run-down of the current portfolio, to deal prospects, to firm-wide strategic matters. Some VCs will also invite companies in to present to the entire partnership – generally at an advanced stage of the decision-making process.

The Silicon Valley model eschews anything as formal as an investment committee – whereas other firms have much more of a process (which may or may not be part of the Monday meeting). Apax, for instance, has a formal investment committee (which convenes later in the week) whereas, reflecting the size of the firm, its Monday morning meeting is just an hour-long session with (in London) 60 people three deep round the boardroom table in a brief run-down of everything from executives' engagements for the week to exit prospects.

So what do VCs do for the rest of the week? The job divides into four principal activities:

◆ sourcing and evaluating the opportunity

◆ negotiating and executing

◆ on board

◆ exiting.

Sourcing and evaluating the opportunity

'Deal flow' is a pivotal aspect of a venture capitalist's competitive advantage. The very best opportunities will flow to the cream of the crop. But most VCs have to work at it – and cannot simply sit and wait for business plans to drop into the e-mail box.

Venture capitalists should be arch networkers – with entrepreneurs, with other VCs, and with intermediaries such as investment banks, accountants and lawyers. In the Valley, where all the firms cluster along Sand Hill Road, and all hang out at a handful of spots – Bucks in Woodside or Il Fornaio in Palo Alto – that is one thing. In Europe, where there is no Sand Hill equivalent, the process is necessarily much more dispersed. But trade shows, conferences and events around university hubs such as Cambridge and Munich all form part of the VC's habitat. Analysts at venture capital firms spend a good proportion of their time rooting out deals. Meanwhile, the ability to filter promising transactions from the welter of propositions received is a crucial aspect of the job. Effective evaluation ranges from deciding which entrepreneurs to meet, to performing detailed research – 'due diligence' in the jargon – on the company and its customers. For firms that genuinely invest at the earliest stages, months of work may be entailed in rewriting an entrepreneur's business plan, helping assemble a team, finding office space, and so on.

Negotiating and executing

Negotiating the right terms – the percentage equity share, the valuation and the terms – is a pivotal element of the future success or otherwise of an investment from the venture capitalist's point of view. Securing a lower average valuation than his competitors for deals across his portfolio can boost a VC's returns significantly. Likewise, overpaying (a danger not just during the bubble) has a severely detrimental effect on performance. As for terms, this is the point where entrepreneurs have to pinch themselves to remember that VCs are in the risk business. The investment agreement is a painfully lengthy affair (see Chapter 13) and too many investors, particularly in Europe, take great delight in negotiating unsuspecting entrepreneurs into the ground on these matters. As firms progress through the deal, many draw up a formal investment proposal – a document of some 50 or so pages for the consumption of the partners or the investment committee. Needless to say the company does not get to see it – containing as it may remarks about management's perceived shortcomings, for example.

On board

When the deal is closed comes the moment of truth for the entrepreneur as he discovers whether his new VC actually lives up to his promise of 'adding value'. Most VCs (at partner, not associate level) take board seats, and the best will use these as more than just a monitoring exercise. This is the whole point of venture capital. Recruitment is one of the most important areas where they can help. Persuading Meg Whitman to leave a successful, high-profile job as a divisional manager of toymaker Hasbro, based on the east coast, and to move her family across the continent to a no-name dotcom called eBay was probably Benchmark's most important contribution to that investment. ('You've got to be kidding' was her reaction when she was initially approached.) Other areas where VCs should be contributing range from strategic input into product development decisions, to customer introductions, to help with negotiations of large sales or licensing agreements. They can have significant input into a range of nitty-gritty practical issues such as setting up options schemes, or arranging seminars for portfolio companies on how to obtain government grants and tax breaks, such as the UK's generous credits for research and development costs. Meanwhile VCs face a constant dilemma as to where they should spend time: should it be on the companies doing well or those that are struggling? Anne Glover at Amadeus says: 'Individually we are bad at it. We force ourselves to have a quarterly discussion, where we forecast each company's value at exit. We reckon we should be spending time with those with the big potential.'

Investors more naturally devote their energies to those that are struggling – because no one wants to admit they have made a mistake. Moreover they get criticized for the ones that fail, whereas the input to success – helping a company to get from a valuation of €20m to €75m – is rather less immediately visible. Christopher Spray at Atlas, for instance, is of the view that by and large really good companies require much less attention: 'If it's a basket case, then it should have been buried by now. The ones in the middle that are not quite there is actually where you spend your time – helping on recruiting, getting the product into the market, fund-raising.'

Exiting

Venture capital is only exceptionally a short-term game in the manner seen in the late 1990s when 18-month-old start-ups were being primed for initial public offering (IPO) or sold to large technology companies. But it is not a long-term game either. Before the bubble the standard exit time frame – from when the VC made the initial investment to realizing their cash – was three to five years (although some investments took rather longer, such as IT infrastructure services company Computacenter, in which Apax invested in 1985, and finally exited some time after the IPO on the London Stock Exchange in 1998).

Conventionally there are three sorts of exit – a flotation or IPO; a trade sale, namely acquisition by another, generally much larger company; and receivership. (It is an old industry adage that the lemons ripen before the plums, namely the bad companies fail first.) Selling well is a crucial part of the business, as John McMonigall, formerly a senior director specializing in telecoms at Apax Partners (now retired), points out. During the bubble he put all his 'emotional energies' into selling during a period when he thought valuations were really 'crazy'. One of his best deals was to dispose of Apax's entire stake in Teles, a German telecoms company, a week before the Neuer Markt peaked. The other venture capitalist in the deal sold down only half of its holding.

And who does what?

In a firm like Benchmark where there are no associates and analysts, the partners do everything. Indeed, most VCs take a particular pride in claiming to do just that, though in the larger firms this is a bit of a myth. I came across one transaction where, from the company's point of view, it had been the associate who had done almost all the work, and indeed kept the deal alive. Yet the senior partner described the process to me entirely in the first person, with not a single mention of the associate.

IRRs and all that

When it comes to performance records, the industry is opaque in the extreme. Every private equity fund you will ever meet claims to have a performance record that is upper quartile – in other words in the top 25 per cent of the league. Where the other 75 per cent of the industry is remains an eternal mystery. And don't expect anything in the way of hard numbers to back up such claims.

General partners report on a more or less regular basis – though many in a surprisingly amateurish and tardy fashion – to the investors in their funds, but not to anyone else. Industry-wide performance numbers published by the likes of the European Venture Capital Association and Venture Economics, the private equity research group, tell you nothing about individual funds. So-called private placement memoranda are put out by most firms when they are fund raising (unless they are a top-tier US venture capital firm, for whom such things would be infra dig). In this obsessively secretive industry even these documents, which are essentially marketing material and heavy on spin, are highly confidential and hard to get hold of. (A sort of samizdat market does exist.)

One of the private equity industry's great coups in preserving its opacity is its deployment of the internal rate of return, one of the principal measures of performance. Getting a venture capitalist to give a coherent explanation of what an IRR is is something of a challenge, but technically it is a discount rate – the rate at which all the fund's positive and negative cash flows (commitments by investors and disbursements back to them) are discounted so that the net present value of the fund amounts to zero. The trouble is, IRRs can be calculated in many different ways. For instance, a fund can claim at least three different IRRs – say 80 per cent, 29 per cent and 19 per cent – depending on what is being measured. The highest number applies to the gross return on realized investments, namely those which the venture firm has exited and returned cash to investors. But it takes no account of investments still in the portfolio, which the second number does. Then again, valuing the portfolio is a controversial issue in itself, consisting as it does of privately held companies with uncertain prospects. One reason why the full impact on returns of the technology crash was long delayed is that it is common practice to leave investments valued at the price paid in the most recent funding round. If that financing occurred before the market crashed, that price clearly no longer reflected reality. On the whole, the better the firm, the more likely they were to take the write-offs early because they could tolerate it. The weaker ones tended to be a lot slower facing up to reality. The third and final measure expresses the return to limited partners net of the hefty slice of fees earned by the firm along the way.

Just to complicate matters, the IRR does not tell the full performance story. The other measure to which investors pay close attention is the cash multiple achieved. A quick hit produces a high IRR. But a very high IRR over a few months may be less attractive than a lower IRR over two years, because the latter gives the investor a more substantial outright capital gain. An investment which returns five times the initial capital is dubbed a '5x'.

Bottom of the class

While more or less every fund boasts upper quartile status, the truth is dramatically different. The spread between the performance of the best and the worst funds is actually wildly more extreme than in any other investment asset class. David Swensen, chief investment officer of the University of Yale's endowment, produces some sobering numbers in his book (Swenson 2000). Venture capital funds formed between 1980 and 1997 produced a median of just 8.1 per cent, he calculates. The best produced a 'stellar 498.2 per cent' and the worst 'a much more terrestrial' minus 89.7 per cent.

Success?

Venture capital is a roller-coaster game at the best of times. One huge win (or, in American baseball parlance, a 'home run') can return the capital of the entire fund, or more. As a rule of thumb, VCs used to say – everyone had slightly different versions – that out of ten investments one would be 'on fire', two would do pretty well, two would go bust and the rest would fall into the 'living dead' category. The riskiness of early stage investing means that the portfolio effect is very important. A former 3i executive described trying to persuade the group's Spanish office to do more early stage investments in the mid-1990s. He had looked at 23 investments 3i had made between 1990 and 1995 with an overall return of 35 per cent. But all the return had come from three of the 23, and the bulk from one of the three. So the rather sceptical Spanish office said, logically enough: 'You are telling me I want to do 23 or none.' VCs with a more hands-on approach than 3i would claim a higher hit rate, but all are undoubtedly greatly reliant on the portfolio effect. How these metrics are changing in a period with much more uncertain exit scenarios is something over which VCs are still very much puzzling.

What stays constant is that, in pure financial terms, the performance of any individual fund is considerably influenced by the year in which it was raised. Like wine, it is the vintage year that matters more in determining quality than the producer. If the weather is bad one season, the most exclusive vintner operating on the best *terroir* will turn in a relatively poor show. But in a good year even an average producer will come up with something pretty drinkable. Hence even the very top tier, the 1999 and 2000 vintage venture funds, invested at the tail end of the bubble, are expected to show dismal results – probably barely returning original invested capital. By contrast, the average annual IRR for funds launched in 1996 was 88.9 per cent, according to Venture Economics.

Beyond vintage, the single most important differentiating factor between the best VCs and the rest is brand. Success in venture capital is a virtuous circle (Figure 2.1). The most talented entrepreneurs want to work with the

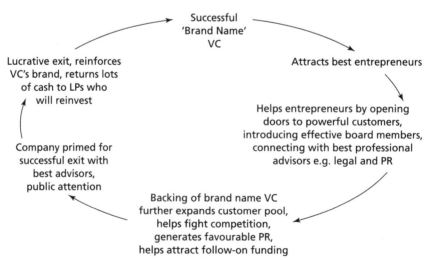

Figure 2.1 ◆ The VCs virtuous circle

best venture capitalists. In a mature market like the USA, the top-tier VCs see the best deals, the second tier see the next tier and so on (see Chapter 5). The power of the VC brand in turn helps drive the success of the venture. It opens doors to the best suppliers and customers. It brings access to the best intermediaries from lawyers, to public relations advisers to investment bankers. And it helps drive a successful exit, with brand name VCs, certainly in the USA, carrying clout with public investors in the case of an IPO.

High profile exits are in turn the main drivers of brand building. Benchmark stormed into the top tier with extraordinary speed – the firm was founded in 1995 – on the back of essentially one investment, eBay. Really solid reputations take a lot longer to build. Kleiner Perkins, for instance, was founded in 1972 and has been through many VC cycles since. Brand creation in a downturn has been a real challenge for younger European VCs when the opportunities for exits have shrivelled. Michael Elias of Kennet believes it is 'partly about the deals you *don't* do'. The few who genuinely avoided dotcoms (as opposed to the multitude who just said they did) may have enhanced their reputation – especially if they were heavily criticized at the time for not partaking. But in the much younger European market, where awareness of venture capital is much lower than in the USA, the virtuous circle still has some pretty shaggy edges.

Success is, moreover, a slippery concept in venture capital. Can an individual VC be regarded as highly successful after one really big hit, or does he have to earn his spurs by riding through a cycle or two, and making money in the down periods too? It is certainly true that the VC business takes a long time to learn. Adrian Beecroft, a seasoned Apax partner, describes venture capital as 'a business where lots of aspects are not initially obvious'. For instance, VC investors get gradually better at interpreting the way customers will react to different sorts of products. 'The entrepreneur will inevitably tell you customers are terribly enthused. And if you just ring them up they will indeed sound very enthusiastic. But you have to get them to buy the product. Until you have been led up the garden path a few times, you simply won't get it right.'

Coping with failure is an entirely separate dimension, and the beasts that prosper in a downturn may not be at all the same breed that thrived in the bullish times. Then again, to what extent are venture capitalists measured by the size of the financial win, and to what extent by the durability of the companies they create? One former judge of the British Venture Capital Association's Entrepreneur of the Year competition recalled countless arguments between the VCs and industrialists on the judging panel. The VCs wanted the winners to be among those that had achieved cash exits, while the industrialists pushed to support those at the helm of companies with the best future growth prospects.

Successful investments are by no means synonymous with successful companies. Excite@Home, the merged Excite portal business and @Home broadband access, for instance, went spectacularly bankrupt in 2001, but is said to have made $1bn for Kleiner Perkins and its investors. Lastminute, the UK travel site that listed in early 2000 just as the dotcom bubble was bursting, caused a storm among investors that bought the stock at the initial public offering, but the VCs were keeping quiet because it had been a perfectly respectable investment for them, because they had invested early at a much lower price. Technologieholding, a German VC, gained its reputation from its investments in Intershop and Brokat, making its two founders wealthy (though not quite as wealthy as did their canny sale of the entire firm to 3i at the top of the market in February 2000). At the time, these start-ups were beacons for the nascent German venture capital scene. But Brokat is now bankrupt and Intershop trading at a fraction of its former worth.

The billion dollar benchmark

The measures of success have also changed dramatically since the downturn. During the 1990s, building the 'billion dollar' company became the industry benchmark, at least in the USA. The billion dollar company is, of course, a special sort of VC speak. It did not apply to revenues, and certainly not to profits, but rather to market capitalization; the value of the company when it got to the stock market. During the bubble, the billion dollar benchmark was extended as it came to refer also to a big hit by a venture capital firm, namely turning an investment of a few million dollars into a billion dollar gain for the firm and its investors. In a few cases, it also became a measure of the (paper) net worth of the entrepreneurs, and then of a few individual venture capitalists.

Conversely in Europe, it was for a time the benchmark of failure. When on earth would Cambridge create its first billion dollar company, people fretted. The answer was Ionica, the local loop wireless company that was, like so many technologies, ahead of its time. Its iconic status was limited, as it went bankrupt in 1998, the year after it listed on the London Stock Exchange. There then followed a clutch including ARM Holdings (not VC backed) and Autonomy Corporation, the latter managing to hit three separate 'billion benchmarks' – market capitalization, net worth of founder Mike Lynch (on paper) and an estimated billion pounds in return for Apax and its limited partners.

Today the billion dollar benchmark is largely a historic curiosity. In the downturn, exits have been more or less non-existent and VC firms are readjusting their expectations to count companies worth €75m upwards at the time of realization as being successes.

Who earns what

Venture capitalists inhabit some of the most expensive pieces of real estate in Europe, around St James's and Mayfair in London, or the Theatinerstrasse in Munich. There is nothing in the slightest bit risky or venturesome about the compensation structure of the venture capital business. Remuneration comes in two ways. VCs earn both a management fee and carried interest or carry, a fancy term to denote their share of the profits. Management fees are typically 2 to 2.5 per cent a year (3 per cent for the funds with the very best track records). Surprisingly to the uninitiated, fees are charged on the entire fund; namely, the sum committed by investors rather than the amount drawn down. Towards the end of the bubble, at least 25 US venture funds raised funds of $1bn or more, each of which would be collecting an annual fee of $20m to $30m on that fund (in addition to fees from earlier funds). This alone can keep the relatively small bunch of partners quite comfortable.

Meanwhile, for no reason that anyone can explain, the typical carry divide is 20 per cent to the VCs and 80 per cent to the LPs. This arbitrary split arguably dates right back to the rates extracted by Venetian and Genoese merchants setting sail on trade missions in the twelfth and thirteenth centuries (Gompers and Lerner 2001) – 'carried interest' in the sense that the merchants earned dues from the merchandise they were carrying. To see how it works, imagine a $300m fund with a 20 per cent carry is invested to produce $900m, or a three times multiple. The profit would be $600m, $120m to the VC firm, the balance to investors. This is a simplified example; for instance carry is sometimes only paid only after investors have received back their initial capital plus a so-called 'hurdle rate' of around 8 per cent. The funds with the best performance have in recent years been able to charge 'premium' carries of 25 to 30 per cent.

The carry is supposed to be where the venture capitalist makes his money. Management fees pay the firm's overheads (including the fancy real estate leases), but the profit comes with the carry – so aligning the interests of the firm and its LPs. That is the theory. But as fund sizes ballooned in the late 1990s, investors rightly became concerned that some firms were getting pretty comfortable on the management fees alone and were perhaps not quite as driven to leap out of bed in the morning to further the success of their portfolio companies. It is the nature of this management fee structure which also helps to explain that while VCs' investments may fall like flies during a downturn, the VCs themselves are not subject to such immediate Darwinian forces. They can stick around, at least for a while, living off their fees – before they find they cannot raise another fund.

In the downturn, one way in which venture capitalists are paying attention to their institutional investors, vast amounts of whose capital they have lost, is by reducing the size of existing funds. In releasing LPs from a portion of their commitments, they argue that investment assumptions have changed since the bubble and that they are now investing at a much slower rate. Benchmark Europe, for instance, reduced its fund from $750m to $500m. In the USA, Accel Partners returned about half of a $1.4bn fund raised two years previously. These moves are of course presented by the firms as purely a gesture to their investors, reducing the management fees they are drawing, and so on. But the cynic might point out that it is very much in their own interests to do so too. The VCs realize they are unlikely to see any carry from the funds invested at the tail end of the bubble, so, from their point of view, the sooner they can start a new fund (assuming they can raise one) the better. Investing the old voluminous fund over a much longer period would also depress performance.

Institutional investors are certainly becoming more restive about fee levels too in the current climate, but change may be slow. They will be much less likely to thump the table at the best funds, for example, where there remains fierce competition to get investment allocations in the first place. Moreover, a significant part of the institutional investing community is made up of so-called fund of funds – firms which themselves raise money from institutions and invest in a portfolio of private equity firms. Their own compensation structure is similar to the underlying funds – fees and carry – so they face a certain conflict of interest.

Venture capitalists have certainly made staggering sums of money, especially in the USA. The partners at Benchmark are reputed to have made around $200m each on their investment in eBay alone. There has been nothing of that scale in Europe. Assessing the true net worth of venture capital partners is, luckily for them, impossible for outsiders, given the secretive nature of the limited liability partnerships. But it is amusing to note that John Doerr and Vinod Khosla both sat in the Forbes Rich List at a cool $1bn each in 2000 and 2001, whereas the *Sunday Times* puts Sir Ronald Cohen in at £50m. Both sets of figures were almost certainly underestimates at the time.

Other types of organization pay less. 3i for example does not have a traditional carry scheme in most parts of the business – and the 'university of venture capital' has often been a fertile hunting ground for other private equity firms because of its uncompetitive compensation scheme. A friend of mine living in California commented to me one day how 'outrageous' it was that Brian Larcombe, 3i's chief executive, had earned £10m over the course of his career. (I have no idea about the truth or otherwise of the figure in question.) I was puzzled. It didn't seem to be an excessive sum to me in the context of the industry. Then it dawned on me she meant outrageously little. Conditioned by the British view of executive compensation, I had automatically interpreted outrageous as excessive.

The downturn has taken the gilt off the gingerbread. There are even stories in the USA of bankrupt venture capital partners – those who took carry on early deals in a fund and spent it in anticipation of future successes. It then transpires that the fund will not return all its capital, so they owe that money to investors. But it remains the case that the industry continues to be extraordinarily lucrative for even quite average performance.

So there is the venture business, in all its contrariness. It appears to serve entrepreneurs, when its real customers are the investors. The game is supposedly about risk, when much of the time is taken up with mitigation thereof. Investors in growth businesses with international aspirations, VC firms themselves are often parochial and insular, operating a business model that is almost impossible to scale. While seeking to persuade company founders of the merits of 'moving on', they rarely manage succession deftly at their own firms. Understanding such contrariness will be helpful throughout the process of fund raising and living with VCs after the deal.

The next chapter has something to say about a further element – notably how finely developed is the herd instinct in an industry whose job, one might naively think, was to make bold independent judgements about the prospects of embryonic companies.

References

Gompers, P. A. and **Lerner, J.** (2001) The Money of Investion; how venture capital creates new wealth, Harvard Business School Publishing, Boston, MA.

Lutz, H. F. (1932) 'Babylonian partnership', *Journal of Economic and Business History*, 4: 335–55.

Swensen, D. (2000) *Pioneering Portfolio Management: An Unconventional Approach to Institutional Investment*, The Free Press, A Division of Simon & Schuster, Inc, New York.

Links

It is never too early to start studying the VC firms' websites. Most, but not all, firms are members of national venture capital associations. Glean as much information as you can – although it is a source of constant surprise to me as to how pedestrian, unimaginative, generally unhelpful and often out of date, most VC sites are.

www.evca.com
www.bvca.co.uk
www.BVK-eV.de
www.afic.asso.fr
www.ascri.org
www.aifi.it

Public sector sources of funding:
German funding for young technology businesses at www.tbgbonn.de, the site of the Technologiebeteiligungsgesellschaft, an excellent website, with anything from help on business plans, to extensive links to VC sources, business angels, business plan competitions etc.

The other major sources of official funding in Germany is Kreditanstalt für Wiederaufbau, www.kfw.de

UK regional venture funds etc	www.businessadviceonline.org
L'agence française de l'innovation (A great starting point, with plenty of links for France)	www.anvar.fr

Other national providers/initiatives include:

Industrifonden, the Swedish industrial development fund	www.industrifonden.se
Enterprise Ireland	www.enterprise-ireland.com
Scottish Enterprise	www.scottish-enterprise.com
Finnish national fund for research and development	www.sitra.fi

3

Cycle psychology

The four most dangerous words in a fund manager's lexicon are:
This time it's different.
(Sir John Templeton)

ONE OF THE SHIBBOLETHS of the late 1990s putative 'new economy' was that it had abolished the business cycle, which is a touch ironic, powered as the new economy was by a glut of venture capital. Venture capital is, after all, one of the most cyclical industries in existence. For supposedly professional investors, venture capitalists do turn the spigot on and off with remarkable force. While the internet and the telecommunications investment bubble exemplified the most extreme form of boom and bust – you might call it a bubble on top of a cycle – the venture industry has always been to a certain extent a caricature of Schumpeterian creative destruction. Or not so creative. Joseph Schumpeter, the Austrian economist writing in the first half of the twentieth century, talked of 'the perennial gale of creative destruction'. He saw innovation as the main engine of economic growth in a free market economy, occurring in 'discreet rushes' as entrepreneurs pursue new ideas that destroy existing, weaker businesses. The excesses of the late 1990s bubble were so great, and the subsequent crisis of confidence so damaging, that there was not much creativity to the destruction on this occasion, as potentially good start-ups withered along with the dross in the ensuing funding drought.

Entrepreneurs will find it useful to understand something of the inherent cyclicality of the industry and the way venture investors behave at different points of that cycle.

The VC cycle

The cycle starts far below the radar screen, with the best venture capitalists making early investments in obscure start-up companies. But capital really begins to flow into the industry with the first public signs of success – a stock market flotation. Eye-catching investment returns suck in new investors, but soon the glut of capital pushes up prices in the private as well as public markets. Too many bad, me-too companies get funded at excessive valuations and eventually the effects of the glut become clear. The market crashes and investors withdraw.

The pull of public market success is not just a venture capital phenomenon. 'The success of the issue was like a firing pistol,' writes Charles Kindleberger (1978: 33), referring to the success of brewer Arthur Guinness going to the stock market in the 1880s and unleashing a flood of more than 80 private brewers listing in the next few years. But its effect on venture activity in the USA was already clear when Digital Equipment – backed by American Research & Development – went public in 1968, encouraging a host of venture-backed companies to rush to the market later that year. After the peak of that first US venture cycle, there followed a prolonged slump in public markets. The industry, in danger of disappearing altogether, raised just $10m in 1975.

It recovered in the late 1970s, to experience multiple cycles – spurred by, among other innovation waves, personal computers and disk drives at the beginning of the 1980s and biotechnology in the early 1990s – before the arrival of the internet boom, kick-started in 1995 by the IPO of Netscape. The period between 1989 and 1991, meanwhile, saw the most significant contraction until the post-2000 downturn, with plenty of venture firms unable to raise further funds, and withdrawing.

In Europe, the dynamic has been rather different. The catalyst in the early 1980s for the first wave of venture firms was the huge returns seen in the USA as the early personal computer companies went public. But conditions were hostile, particularly because of the lack of stock markets to facilitate exits, so investment returns were pretty terrible and, as already mentioned, many firms migrated into the safer territory of the management buy-out.

It is no coincidence that venture returns are often expressed by vintage year (Chapter 2). The economic climate of the years in which a fund is invested can be more important in determining the outcome than the quality of the venture firm. For instance, 'top decile' (the top 10 per cent) performance of the 1999–2000 vintage is likely to mean return of investors' capital without any profit (although this will not be clear for a number of years); the rest are likely not even to manage to return the original cash.

The best returns are achieved by investors who get in early and pay favourable prices, while those drawn in by the early successes are the ones who overpay. Bad vintage years follow good vintage years with a certain inevitability. Figure 3.1 shows the striking correlation between fund raising and returns (illustrated by US venture capital statistics, because of the considerably longer track record).

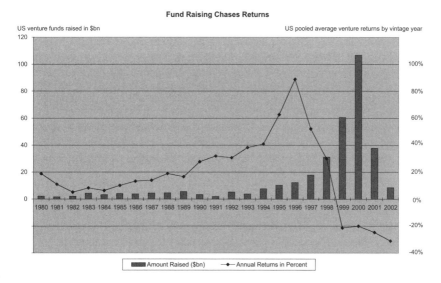

Figure 3.1 ◆ Correlation between fund raising and returns
Source: Venture Economics

Herds

Most categories of investors move in packs, but venture capitalists' herding instincts are particularly finely developed – and those herding instincts amplify the cycle. As the old joke goes: What do you get when you breed sheep with lemmings? A bunch of venture capitalists. Like other herding species, the pack has its leaders. As the backlash to the late 1990s excesses gathered pace, John Doerr of Kleiner Perkins Caufield & Byers, who had memorably dubbed the internet 'the greatest legal creation of wealth on the planet', began to attract brickbats. As the pain of the slump gathered, one angry venture capitalist complained: 'John Doerr was the high priest of the dotcom religion. He led us like sheep, and like lemmings we followed him over the cliff' (Veverka 2002).

So why do venture capitalists behave like this? Lack of information is one reason. Academic economists talk about herd theory – as it relates to anything from fashion, to broad social customs, to manias and panics. At its most basic, it describes how individuals copy each other, and do so regardless of what their own information is telling them. Thanks to Daniel Sgroi, Department of Applied Economics, Cambridge University, UK for the explanation and following example:

> *Imagine two restaurants, A and B, more or less adjacent to each other. A sequence of four potential customers walk down the road, each with 'private information' about A or B – a review, perhaps, or a recommendation from a friend. The first person's recommendation favours A, so he walks in, as does the second person, who has also been told to try A. The third person, according to herding theory, will go in even if his friend told him B was better. Why? Because he assumes the other two both have private information favouring A, which outweighs his single piece of information. The same will be true of the fourth, and every subsequent customer. All will herd into A on the basis of two pieces of information – and the two pieces of information may of course be wrong.*

It is not hard to see how this applies in the world of venture capital, an area where there is anyway exceptionally little information. No one really knows which start-up will succeed – hence the temptation to play follow-my-leader. Each believes the other person knows more. This is exacerbated when venture firms are new kids on the block, lacking networks through which they can originate proprietary deals and, often, not well versed in the areas in which they are investing. So they observe others, thinking these people must know something they do not.

Hence the first question most venture capitalists will ask when discussing a deal among themselves: Who else is in? Weaker VCs are constantly looking for the validation of others. The early days of the internet in Europe saw far too many local venture capitalists knocking off cookie-cutter copies of existing US companies. Investors get buffeted by the winds of fashion and become simply collectors of the latest fad – be it optical networking, nanotechnology, Wifi, or medical devices. As Thomas Hoegh of Arts Alliance, who also invests family money in other venture funds, says:

"I've been an investor in funds that were raised as software funds; before they had even deployed any capital, they moved to internet consumer, to business-to-business to ASPs (application service providers) to optical (networking) to biotech – with more or less the same team. Now they are doing nanotechnology – which is an area I am not quite sure really exists.

No VC will admit to following another's lead but the majority do."

Even Hoegh, who prides himself on his eclectic approach to the subject, admits harkening to the call of the venture elite – in what he now says is the dumbest deal he ever did. It was Kibu, a site for teenagers, supposedly representing the confluence of entertainment, community and product (teenagers trying new lipsticks, that sort of thing). The start-up was backed by Kleiner Perkins and Netscape co-founder Jim Barksdale was involved. Hoegh was invited in because he had invested in Spinner, the first streaming music site (sold to AOL): 'They were sort of heroes. I thought, Jim Barksdale and Kleiner can't be wrong, they are really smart people.' The teenagers thought otherwise and multimillions of dollars later Kibu was folded.

Venture capital is, peculiarly, one of the few industries where people *like* to have competition. They feel validated and reassured when scores of other people are going after the same opportunity. This behaviour is most pronounced at the top of a cycle, but also applies in a downturn. Even in permafrost conditions, VCs tend to show interest in the business plans everyone else is getting excited about. The pressure to conform is another aspect of herd behaviour. Anyone who expressed remote scepticism at any point during the internet bubble will remember the withering rejoinder: 'You just don't get it.' David Giampaolo, an entrepreneur and angel investor, illustrates both the tendency to ignore one's own gut feelings – and the conformist pressures:

"I am so much my own man, I am one of the least herd, consensus driven personalities. Yet I made some investments that went horribly wrong. Without a single exception, something didn't feel right, whether it was valuation, business plan, ramp-up rate. But, I thought, if Goldman are doing it, 3i, Bain, surely they are smarter than me. Even at this valuation, I should thank my lucky stars I am invited to the party."

He likens it to experimenting with drugs as a youngster:

"Everyone was doing it. I didn't like it and I knew it wasn't right, healthy or legal, but at that moment in time, if you didn't do it, you felt totally, totally out of it."

It's the fashion business, stupid

Misquoting Bill Clinton in the 1992 US election campaign, the herd are, in an important sense, fashion victims – during the bubble, in a literal sense. Everything about the internet was 'cool' and entrepreneurship was suddenly dangerously fashionable. At the epicentre of cool were the venture financiers. The cult of the celebrity was in full flood, even if European VCs did not achieve quite the rock-star status accorded their peers in the USA.

When Max Burger-Calderon took over as chairman of the European Private Equity and Venture Capital Association in June 2002, he told me part of his mission was to prove that private equity was not the fashion business. But the image, and indeed, psychology, may be hard to shift. Down to the very language it uses, venture capital is about fashion. Even in a downturn, certain sectors and deals are 'hot'. A German venture capitalist, in the teeth of the gloom following the collapse of the Neuer Markt, was telling me how the answer was to use deep scientific knowledge to find hot sectors. Ignoring for a moment the dubious logic of whether clever scientists will be any good at finding hot sectors, what does hot actually mean? Doesn't the fact that it is hot mean that by definition it is already overvalued? Don't VCs want to find areas *before* they are hot?

Sectors are mostly hot because another VC has got there first. The pack leaders determine how the others dress. If Kleiner Perkins is making money out of optics, then every self-respecting VC needs an optical company in their portfolio. During the bubble there were not just hot deals but hot VCs – in Europe often newly formed groups, many of which disappeared equally quickly. The hip internet crowd had barely heard of old-timers like 3i – and those that had, did not view them favourably. 'I heard they were the brown-shoe VCs,' as one US entrepreneur newly arrived in London put it.

But there is no safety in numbers – quite the reverse. Herd behaviour leads to massive overfunding in individual sectors, and it was happening long before the internet. The Harvard Business School study detailing the Winchester disk drive industry (high speed data storage for computers), shows how venture firms invested $400m in 43 companies between 1977 and 1984 (most of it at the end of the period, with $270m flowing into 51 financing rounds in 1983 and 1984). In 1983, 12 public companies had a combined market capitalization of more than $5bn. But it was an instance of what the authors call capital market myopia: 'Viewed in isolation, each decision seems to make sense. When taken together, however, they are a prescription for disaster' (Sahlman and Stevenson 1987).

As always, successful IPOs were an important catalyst. Seagate had gone public in September 1981, making lots of money for its backers, when its first product had been introduced in July 1980. But by 1983 over 70 companies were competing, pushing prices rapidly down, as rates of growth in computer sales were also slowing (and nowhere near matching optimistic projections of previous years). Yet 'as late as the fall of 1983, venture capitalists and stock market investors continued to pour money into the disk drive industry'. By the end of 1983, the capital markets, public and private, were going into reverse, and funding dried up not just for the disk drive manufacturers but for their suppliers and customers too. The carnage was such that by late 1984 'some of the public disk drive companies were trading at prices below net working capital per share'.

Capital market myopia reached its apogee during the internet boom, when some 8000 venture backed start-ups were created in three years – which, as Michael Klein of Citigroup points out, represented about 50 years' worth of IPOs.

An essential quality of the pack animal is of course amnesia, the ability to distance oneself rapidly from the latest stampede. VCs are masters at revisionism – as in 'we never invested in the internet'. The website will have been 'cleaned up' to remove all trace of the follies, though occasionally some entertainment can be had from an overlooked ancient press release. In the late 1990s, one leading US VC turned down one of today's more exciting 'deep technology' companies, e-mailing the entrepreneur that 'we only do internet ventures now'. When the dotcom bubble burst, the firm was boasting to me how it had invested in virtually no internet businesses.

Bubble trouble?

Alan Greenspan's famous bubble warning about 'irrational exuberance' – back in 1996 when the internet boom had actually barely got going – is in a sense misleading. Yes, the internet and all other venture capital fuelled investment spurts have a lot in common with all bubbles, such as tulip mania:

> *At first, as in all these gambling mania, confidence was at its height and everybody gained. Everyone imagined that the passion for tulips would last for ever and that the wealthy from every part of the world would send to Holland and pay whatever prices were asked for them.*

> (Mackay 1841)

But, as Sir Ronald Cohen of Apax Partners rightly argues, there is a difference between tulip mania and the frenzy surrounding the internet – or the personal computer boom, or early investment waves accompanying the invention of the railway or the motor car. These are instances of rational overexuberance, rather than irrational exuberance. The tulip bubble left behind nothing (except tulip bulbs), whereas whichever way you look at it, the internet will be an enduring powerful force for change.

'Investors correctly perceive that there is big change,' says Cohen, talking about the internet in the context of other investment rushes fuelled by spurts of innovation. 'But they value each opportunity on the basis that it is going to be the ultimate winner. Seagate was the ultimate winner from umpteen disk drive companies, Compaq and Dell from the PC revolution. There will be other bubbles – the next one leaving behind genetic medicine.' (This is presumably not to say there is not a string of seriously misguided investments along the way too, such as dog food online, wedding portals and teenage lipstick sites.) 'Bubbles are not to be avoided,' he goes on, 'but should be used [by venture capitalists] to generate superior returns.'

That means investing early. In the world of herds, the front of the pack is the best place to be. 'If I'm reading it in the *FT* I've missed the wave. I want to be reading it in Nerd World,' says Charles Irving of Pond Ventures. Some venture capitalists invested early enough in disk drives and were able to sell out while the euphoria lasted, just as the Kleiner Perkins and Sequoias and Benchmarks and others made huge wins from early internet investments such as Amazon, Yahoo and eBay. As the disk drive study says: 'Early birds are not always winners . . . [For instance, the technology may be *too* early to attract customers.] But late comers are almost always losers [because the venture capitalists overpay, the companies face massive competition and the capital markets go against everyone].'

In Europe, the lead animals had different problems. Atlas Venture, an international firm, was an early investor in the internet in Europe, using its experience from the USA. But the trapdoor – in the shape of the collapse of Nasdaq in March and April 2000 – fell shut on everybody's fingers on either side of the Atlantic at the same time. Being early in that instance did not help Atlas because the window was too short, even on concertinaed internet time scales, to exit those investments.

Bubble behaviour

VCs behave quite differently at different stages of the cycle. The top of the last cycle cum bubble was simply an extreme version of what has occurred before, and will happen again. Gold rush metaphors went into overdrive: we will build it and customers will come; capital is free; land grab is what counts. As Ernst Malmsten, co-founder of Boo.com, the category defining European internet excess story, describes: the team was outraged when JP Morgan asked if they had done any research for their global fashionwear retailer. 'Market research? That was something Colgate did before it launched a new toothpaste. The internet was something you had to feel in your fingertips. There were only a few questions worth asking. Is the market big enough? Can it work on the internet? Is anyone doing it already?'

One characteristic of a bubble is the seemingly unlimited belief that the new venture can only go up. Many venture capitalists now claim that they never fell prey to anything so foolish; they knew valuations were out of kilter, but they thought they would somehow sell out in time (and a few did). So what *were* they thinking? Perceptions of risk certainly alter across the board. As the joke goes, in a boom all the bankers want to become VCs and VCs to become entrepreneurs (and in a downturn the reverse). The psychology of the lottery takes over. As Martin Gagen, head of 3i in the USA, told me in late 1999: 'Investors are placing multiple bets because they know those that are successful will be hugely so.' Everyone (not just bankers) wants to be a VC. Corporations, investment banks, incubators, angels, leveraged buy-out houses, all are scrambling to be in the business of early stage investing, not least because they erroneously perceive it as a low-risk endeavour. Those supposedly in the know begin to talk about 'dumb' versus 'smart' money.

Venture capitalists meanwhile fund *real* start-ups as opposed to revenue producing companies, (see Figure 3.2 which again uses US statistics).

However much they intellectualize it, though – and they do – VCs, along with everyone else, are in the game of momentum investing. Company building goes out of the window and start-ups are backed not according to the strength of the business model but on the probability of them making it to IPO. For the companies, financial success – the amount of money you raise –

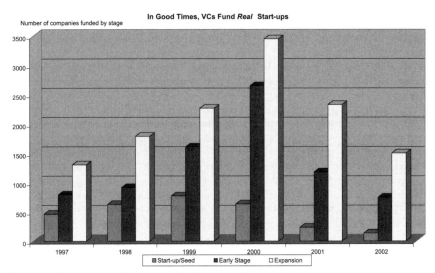

Figure 3.2 ♦ In good times, VCs fund *real* start-ups

Source: Venture Economics

becomes the chief yardstick of business success. The VCs sense perhaps that valuations are ludicrous, but they are convinced they will get out before any collapse.

Success breeds excess

Success goes to the head. Rolf Dienst is experienced enough to allow himself a wry chuckle at how this happened at Wellington Partners, the Munich-based venture capital firm he founded. 'We all thought we were heroes,' he says after the success of a couple of portfolio companies. One was Alando. The three Samwer brothers and three best friends, all barely out of college, got funding from Wellington for the sketchiest of business plans within 48 hours. A German version of eBay, it had the website up and running in two weeks, and four months later was sold to eBay for $50m. Other venture firms were enumerating the number of 'billion dollar companies' in their portfolio. Every venture capital firm thought they were well on the way to building 'the Kleiner Perkins of Europe'. Those that pile in late invariably lose, but first movers also run the danger of becoming so enamoured of their initial success that they stay in the market too long.

Meanwhile the high returns draw in capital. In the first quarter of 2000, US VCs raised $28.8bn, according to Venture Economics roughly the same sum that was raised in the six years between 1990 and 1995. In 2000 for the first time since the leveraged buy-out market got going in the mid-1980s, more money was invested by institutions in US venture capital than in buy-outs. More than 25 funds in excess of $1bn were raised in the USA.

At this stage of the cycle, the general partners appear to hog the power vis-à-vis the limited partners. They can raise ever bigger funds and they can demand yet higher fees. The LPs are left scrambling for access to the best funds.

Greed versus fear

But the general partners are subject to their own pressures, which exacerbate the cycle. The ups and downs of all financial markets are often characterized by the polar emotions of greed and fear: greed (or, less harshly, the profit motive) seizing investors on the way up and fear on the way down. Yet there was plenty of 'fear' – or at least pressure – during the boom. Says Adrian Beecroft of Apax Partners: 'There is real pressure. If you miss the wave you are going to look very silly compared to your competitors.' Interestingly some venture firms held out for a long while against the internet – before capitulating and rushing in when it was too late.

One Apax executive remembers PaperX as 'the ultimate temptation'. Apax had just lost two promising executives to Internet Capital Group (ICG), the internet holding group worth (on paper) multibillions. Here was an 'e-business solutions offering' for the paper and pulp industry. Apax led the first round funding of $15.5m: 'People were talking billions of dollars for individual exchanges. We said to ourselves, the return potential is so high, the fundamentals start not to matter.'

All investors are judged by reference to their peers, so being right is not enough. Tony Dye, chief investment officer of public fund manager Phillips & Drew, was dubbed Dr Doom for his predictions of a stock market crash years before it occurred. Dye, following years of underperformance because of his bearish stance, was forced out just before March 2000.

Another aspect of the fear is that everyone is dead scared they are missing out, which further drives the frenzy. As one entrepreneur puts it: 'You constantly saw someone else getting a higher valuation [in a private funding round] or yet another person who had just gone public for $2bn.'

VCs meanwhile are bombarded with business plans – and not many have the courage to adopt the filing method beloved of one individual, which involved dividing plans into two arbitrary piles and dumping one straight in the bin. Most are too paranoid that they might be missing the next big thing. This is one reason why due diligence is another casualty – there just isn't time. They are being pressured by someone else, always someone else, to do the deal; like Pixelon, the video streaming company which raised around $20m and spent $12m of it on a launch party in Las Vegas, entertained by The Who and others. The VCs later discovered the CEO had been convicted of fraud and embezzlement ten years previously.

With money 'a commodity', it is in some ways an ideal time to be an entrepreneur. Just as LPs are falling over themselves to throw money at venture firms, so VCs are scrambling to get into deals. The real power rests with the entrepreneur. Start-ups are receiving ten or more term sheets at a time and can raise crazy sums at even crazier valuations. Yet precisely because capital is so cheap, scores of companies are getting funded in the same area. Competition is fierce, and it is hard to rise above the noise. Moreover, having too much money can be bad for start-ups: 'Companies are like human beings; hardscrabble beginnings beget hardminded men' (James Surowiecki 2001, *New Yorker*).

An excess of capital pollutes the venture business in other ways. Managing a billion dollar fund is a very different business from managing a fund one-tenth of that size. The firm either has to make a lot more investments or bigger investments; either changes the nature of the game. Some firms hire new people, others do not; most partners end up sitting on far too many boards. Fewer deals are syndicated, individual companies get more cash – and the incentives get out of whack because the management fees, directly correlated to the size of the funds, have grown out of all proportion to the extra expenses of the business.

Downturn dynamics

Sometimes it seems as if there is only one switch at a venture capitalist's disposal – either full on or full off. 'A year ago VCs were lining up to give money to internet dog food companies; this year they wouldn't back an inventor with a working Star Trek transporter,' was one engineer's view in 2001 (Tredennick and Shimamoto, 2001). The bursting of the technology and telecoms bubble left venture capitalists holding by far the largest funds in history. They were awash with cash, but it was herd behaviour again, only in reverse. The tap was turned off. It became somewhere between extremely hard and impossible for entrepreneurs to raise money.

Venture capitalists will tell anyone who will listen how the bottom of a cycle is such a great time to invest – space is cheaper and available, there are great people to be hired, valuations are more realistic, competition from other VC-backed companies in the same space is dramatically reduced, everyone else has problems but their portfolio is in 'really good shape' – while not investing. The behaviour is not wholly irrational. Like plenty of firms Kennet Capital did not make a single new investment in 2001. That was in part because for a long while European private company valuations were stuck at levels twice as high as those in the USA, argues Michael Elias, managing partner. Private markets anyway take six months or so to adjust to a collapse in valuations in the public markets. Europe, which had not seen anything like the US excesses, also took longer to mark prices back down. Some of the worst investment decisions were made in late 2000 on either side of the Atlantic, when venture capitalists thought IPOs would be back within six months, so valuations for private companies remained extremely high.

Raw psychology also of course plays a huge part in investment behaviour. Whatever they may say, VCs are beset with problems in their portfolio. They can see their funds are never going to pay out carried interest, and they have exceptionally unhappy limited partners to deal with. The clichés about 'back to basics' abound, but in fact they haven't a clue which way to turn, and give a passable impression of deer in the headlights. Logically, what matters is where Nasdaq is in five to seven years, yet during the latter half of 2000 and through 2001, many VCs seemed to be glued to the index's day-to-day movements (before abandoning hope during 2002). One Silicon Valley denizen, visiting London in September 2001 and weighing up whether to sneak in a trip to the Frankfurt Motor Show, said on the eve of his departure that he would go 'if Nasdaq had a good close'. The ego becomes tied to personal net worth, which is in turn clamped to Nasdaq.

Mood swings seem to go with the territory. Just as venture capitalists are euphoric immediately after making an investment, thinking it will be the greatest deal ever, their egos make them uncomfortable with failure at the best of times, even though it is an integral part of the job. And of course failure after the bubble was on an embarrassingly grand scale. Readjustment was enormous for everyone – from twenty something entrepreneurs who thought they would retire wealthy within five years onwards. But even more so for the VCs, who, particularly in the USA, appeared for a while to walk on water. Suddenly personal reputations are reassessed as once charmed investments dive in value on the public markets. Joining those leaving the industry, both those who got rich and those who provided rank failures, were the bull market investors who could not make the adjustment to tough times.

In a downturn, the perception of risk swings by 180 degrees. (Following the dotcom collapse, B2C and B2B came to denote Back to Consulting and Back to Banking.) For the few deals that get done, venture capitalists take many months over decisions. They engage in 'proper' due diligence, consisting of endless attempts to 'derisk' a business through exhaustive financial analysis, with plenty of time built in for prevarication. Then they introduce all sorts of draconian terms into investment agreements in further efforts at 'belt and braces' risk protection. Most move away from funding pre-revenue companies altogether.

A large proportion of time is spent fixing the portfolio; deciding which companies survive and which do not, cutting costs, shipping out the Aeron chairs, changing CEOs. The risk reward picture suddenly looks rather different. Instead of 30 promising companies, the spreadsheets suggest there are suddenly only five with any real chance of success – and the less experienced VCs transmit their paranoia to the entrepreneurs they have backed. Firefighting is miserable work, and there is none of the euphoria of closing new deals. Indeed, the atmosphere itself saps the enthusiasm and optimism necessary for making new investments. One associate in a venture firm who had joined 12 months previously described to me his frustrations that no one anywhere in the firm had made a new investment since his arrival. A further destabilizing factor is that the glue which holds a venture firm together – the promise of future carried interest – is not there if the portfolio is in bad shape.

Meanwhile, many of the existing team's skills may be wholly inappropriate to the task. In Europe, and to an extent in the USA, the bubble drew inexperienced bankers and consultants into the business, who had neither seen a downturn before nor possessed any of the necessary qualifications for dealing with struggling start-ups. Verena Mohaupt, a co-founder of online consumer reviews company Ciao, commented at the end of 2000 how venture capitalists and entrepreneurs were all on the same learning curve. Many were contemporaries from the same business schools, investment banks and consultancy stables, she pointed out, making the whole system vulnerable to 'group think'.

Venture firm hiring had been excessively short-termist – as had indeed already been apparent well before the bubble burst. Carlyle Internet Partners was an example of a European fund that shipped out its e-commerce people, changed its name, and hired in various kinds of technologists as dotcom mania evaporated. Following the tech and telecoms collapse, some firms then rushed into biotechnology and healthcare to salve their wounds, suddenly hiring partners from large biotech companies and stuffing the advisory board with the appropriate sort of professor.

Investor relations is a topic that moves rapidly up the priority list in such conditions. General partners start to worry about how and when they will raise their next fund, not whether they can charge 'premium fees'. Many had made far-fetched promises concerning returns when they raised their funds during the late 1990s, and therefore had more than a little explaining to do to investors as the sea of red ink engulfed their portfolios.

Worries about fund raising exacerbate investment caution. Firms are not achieving exits – because in a downturn the IPO market is closed and mergers and acquisitions activity much reduced. Without exits it becomes much harder to persuade limited partners to invest so some firms are stretching out their investment period as far as they can.

Firms with a track record that only encompasses the late 1990s have struggled to raise new cash, so there is a dramatic winnowing among all but the most established. Even small outfits which made good investments tended to run out of cash and got painfully diluted in follow-on rounds. By some estimates, the number of early stage venture capitalists in Europe rose to 400 or more during the bubble. Only a small proportion of those will survive.

The only possibly creative part of the destruction that came courtesy of the latest bubble is the layer of venture capital infrastructure that has been laid in Europe, and the experience gained in what was and is still a maturing market.

The venture capitalists who survive should be better at their job, which they have now been reminded consists of spending five to seven years building profitable companies, not sprucing up concepts for the consumption of Nasdaq or the (late) Neuer Markt in 12 to 18 months. But the overexuberance has led to a very hard landing indeed and, with the wider collapse of confidence, has destroyed many otherwise viable young companies, and even more fledgling start-ups have never got off the ground. Nor is it all clear as to how much has really been learned by the more arrogant members of the community. All too many are blaming the market, pure and simple, without deeper reflection.

The best venture capitalists have to be those who keep the faith and who do learn; who make independent judgements that allow them to invest even through prolonged downturns, rather than casting around for the next wave and jumping on it when it is just about to break. But bear market investors, with the necessary schizophrenia that allows them to spend part of the day killing companies and the rest summoning up enthusiasm to back new ones, are a fairly rare commodity. As Sir Ronald Cohen puts it, 'You have got to be good at taking advantage of these ups and downs – it's like a yachtsman taking advantage of bad weather to get ahead.'

References

Kindleberger, C. P. (1978, 1989, 1996, 2000) *Manias, Panics and Crashes: A History of Financial Crises*, (4th edn.). John Wiley & Sons, USA.

Mackay, C. (originally published 1841) *Extraordinary Popular Delusions and the Madness of Crowds*, (1995 edn.) Wordsworth Editions Ltd, Hertfordshire.

Malmsten, E., Portanger, E. and Drazin, C. (2001) *boohoo: a dot.com story from concept to catastrophe*, Random House Business Books, London.

Sahlman, W. A. and Stevenson, H. H. (1987) 'Capital market myopia', the President and Fellows of Harvard College, Harvard Business School teaching note. This teaching note was prepared by Associate Professor William A. Sahlman and Professor Howard H. Stevenson. Reprinted by permission of Harvard Business School.

Tredennik, N. and Shimamoto, B. (2001) 'An engineer's view of venture capitalists', Spectrum Online IEEE (Institute of Electrical and Electronics Engineers).

Veverka, M. (2002) 'Pied Piper of the 'net: How John Doerr sparked the internet boom and brought home big profits', *Barron's*, 10 June.

An eclectic's history of venture capital in Europe

The reasonable man adapts himself to the world: the unreasonable one persists
in trying to adapt the world to himself. Therefore all progress depends on the
unreasonable man.
(George Bernard Shaw, *Man and Superman*, 1903)

FOR MUCH OF THE past two or three decades, being a venture capitalist in
Europe required almost missionary zeal. The pioneers of the industry were
themselves entrepreneurs. You had to be a true believer or faintly mad. It was
not until the late 1990s that one could legitimately talk about a venture
industry that supported young companies. The conditions that venture capitalists need to thrive and make money simply did not exist. Not least, there
was a dearth of backable propositions. During the 1980s, becoming an
entrepreneur was something strictly for the otherwise unemployable, recalls
Peter Englander, who joined Alan Patricof Associates (APA, now Apax) as it
was raising its first fund in 1981: 'In the 1980s, people who were attracted
to new ventures were, on the whole, oddballs. They tended to be people who
couldn't find a regular job. They were certainly not seasoned managers.'

It may have been the dawn of the Thatcher era in the UK, which championed the 'enterprise economy', fostered initiatives such as the Business
Enterprise Scheme and promoted the notion that making money was acceptable, yet entrepreneurship was still viewed as essentially an American phenomenon. It was almost unheard of for senior executives to leave the
corporate fold for a start-up. Such venture funds as existed were tiny and

companies could only secure investment of perhaps £2m over several rounds of financing, which severely hampered their prospects and more or less precluded establishing a US presence – the all-important destination for most technology companies. Few people really understood and bought into the uphill struggle involved in building young companies; certainly not the wife of an entrepreneur backed by one private equity firm in the late 1980s who went on hunger strike in protest at the disruption the business was causing to family life.

Today's seasoned operators wince when they look back on some of the distinctly dubious ventures they backed, such as MotoMop, a company building a giant motorized sponge to suck water off soggy cricket pitches and golf courses, backed by one Ronald Cohen (now Sir Ronald, industry doyen) of APA in 1982. Hands-on help in those days included the dispatch from APA of a Christmas hamper to the managing director. This individual had been introduced to the company by the venture firm to bring some much needed marketing expertise, but was struggling financially having been asked – as was customary in those days – to put £40,000 of his own money into the business. The sponge was 'very well engineered', but at £5000 apiece local cricket and golf clubs were not exactly queuing up. The investment lesson? The burning problem – venture capitalist like businesses that solve burning problems – was there, namely dismal British weather. But there wasn't a market at the price it cost to manufacture the mops.

Those few investments that made money did not do so for the most obvious reasons. National Telecommunications was another APA investment, this one by Adrian Beecroft, who had joined APA in 1984 from Boston Consulting Group. A PBX (private access branch exchange) manufacturer, exploiting the relaxing of British Telecommunications' monopoly, it had gone public, made some US acquisitions which had not worked, and it was burning cash. The basic business was solid, says Beecroft, but the bankers got alarmed, decided they wanted their £7m back and were poised to appoint a receiver. But Beecroft, who was running the business, having fired the chief executive, knew he had a trump card. The bank had neglected to get its paperwork in order. 'We said that's all very interesting, we agreed to give you a charge but you didn't take it. [The banker] went white, came back half an hour later, and agreed we were right.' Reversing its position in a matter of hours, the bank agreed to lend a further £2m. Six weeks later the business was sold to Alcatel for £40m – Beecroft's 'great escape', as he calls it.

Venture capital was, at the time, an obscure minority sport almost entirely unknown in the wider business world. Vicky Mudford, the first employee of the British Venture Capital Association, established in 1983, recalls punters calling up and asking for 'some of that adventure capital please'. A select few, though, knew about the mini boom in venture capital in America. Beecroft had been at Harvard (class of 1976) with John Doerr, partner at Kleiner Perkins and later America's best known venture capitalist in the internet era. 'By 1983 I had observed [Doerr] was living in a very big house on the top of a hill in San Francisco,' Beecroft recalls. The personal computer boom was in full swing. Apple had gone public in December 1980 and biotechnology company Genentech also obtained a listing in the same year.

The other significant problem for venture investors was the paucity of 'exit' routes through which they could realize cash. The Unlisted Securities Market, launched in 1981 offering companies less complicated listing require- ments than the London Stock Exchange, did show early promise. Acorn Computers, the home computer company co-founded by Hermann Hauser and Chris Currie, was among the 1983 crop of IPOs (bringing Hauser, briefly, paper wealth of £100m before it crashed with other PC companies and fell into the arms of Olivetti of Italy). But liquidity was extremely poor, making it nearly impossible for investors to cash out. In a pre-echo of the Neuer Markt, it flared and died without having created real substance (to be relaunched eventually as AIM, the Alternative Investment Market, in 1995). There was nothing in Europe to rival Nasdaq, the US market for growth com- panies, which itself only constituted a feasible destination for businesses that had built a significant presence in the USA. That in turn was impossible with the tiny amount of money provided by their venture capital backers. It was not until 1994, for instance, that Business Objects became the first European software company to make it to Nasdaq.

No wonder the investors of the day saw themselves as entrepreneurs. As an early Apax (then MMG Patricof) brochure proclaimed: 'We are entrepre- neurs . . . We have grown because we understand the entrepreneurial spirit and culture.' They were mould breakers in the way that today's generation of venture capitalists are largely not, which almost certainly led to a considerable degree of empathy between the backers and the backed. A number had immi- grant roots, often viewed as one of the catalysts to entrepreneurial drive. Sir Ronald, for example, arrived in England with his family in 1956 from Egypt to escape the Suez crisis, speaking barely a word of English. Some nine years later he was president of the Oxford Union.

Even 3i, which is generally assumed to have been a huge bureaucracy from birth, had not been at all that way in the early days. John Kinross, chief con- troller back in the 1950s, observed:

> *Both Bill [Piercy, the first chairman of ICFC, as the organization was then called] and I enjoyed playing (business) poker with people who were not*

trustworthy. It was our form of sport . . . one had to know when to call it a day and one had to be absolutely ruthless at times. If Bill and I had not been pretty opportunistic characters I doubt whether ICFC would have lasted more than five or seven years at most. Later we could afford to raise our standards and did so.

(Coopey and Clarke 1995)

At the same time, attempts at funding young companies had much earlier antecedents. While the roots of the venture industry in Europe are normally traced to 1945 and the establishment of ICFC by the Bank of England and the high street clearing banks, Britain's oldest venture firm is in fact Charterhouse, founded in entrepreneurial fashion by one individual, who was initially 'unsupported by either the interest or the confidence of the financial community' (Dennett 1979). In 1925 Hubert Nutcombe Home, an entrepreneurially minded type from the day he was forced to leave the army because of lack of cash, sat with a couple of friends in the City of London musing about 'what would happen if we asked the public for a certain amount of money to play ducks and drakes with'. That was the cue for the creation of Charterhouse Investment Trust. Itself a tiny trust, it established a subsidiary in 1934 called the Charterhouse Industrial Development Company (CIDC) in response to a (later famous) 1931 parliamentary committee chaired by H.P. Macmillan, a Scottish barrister, which had identified what became known as the Macmillan gap.

Still perplexing policymakers (not to mention entrepreneurs) today, the Macmillan gap describes how difficult it is for small and medium-sized enterprises to raise long-term capital. The committee argued that the links between banks and industry, including small innovative enterprises, functioned much better in Germany, France and the USA than in Britain, and that something should be done about it. CIDC – today's Charterhouse Development Capital, which like so many of its peers long ago moved up the food chain to focus on leveraged buy-outs – backed plenty of small businesses in its time, even if, as folklore has it, the owner-manager in receipt of CIDC's first cheque banked it and absconded, leaving no forwarding address.

It was not until after the war in 1945 that the first official response to the Macmillan committee emerged, with the creation of the Industrial and Commercial Finance Corporation (ICFC). Not that 3i – as is often assumed even today – was ever a government agency. While much of the impetus did indeed come from the government, the Bank of England prevailed in arguing for a private sector institution using the capital of the big five clearing banks and specifically 'keeping the government at bay'. But the banks didn't fall into line easily. They were eager to return to business as usual after the war and suspicious of a scheme that required them to do business with, as they saw it, 'the incompetent, the thriftless and the indolent, to say nothing of the unbusinesslike inventor, who are sadly apt to lose other people's money as well as their own' (Coopey and Clarke 1995).

For decades the bulk of ICFC's activities were broadly in the manufacturing sector (with an interest in service sector companies developing in the 1970s), but the first of many flirtations – or more protracted love affairs – with technology occurred in the 1960s, coincident with Prime Minister Harold Wilson's false prophecy of the new Britain that was going to be 'forged in the white heat of this [technological] revolution'. An initiative called Technical Development Capital to finance innovation was set up in the early 1960s and absorbed into ICFC in 1966. Questions were being asked as to why Britain was failing to commercialize its science, and (as still happens today) a batch of executives was optimistically dispatched to the Massachusetts Institute of Technology to find out how to do things better. There was the odd success, notably Oxford Instruments, a maker of high power magnets; ICFC first backed founder Sir Martin Wood in the late 1960s, a decade after he began the business in his garden shed. But while TDC's 'failures were less than expected', returns were in general 'not spectacular', and it was recognized that most customers had 'a long haul ahead of them' (Coopey and Clarke 1995: 86). Welcome to the financing of technology start-ups.

It was at the beginning of the 1970s, an unremitting decade in so many regards, that one of Europe's private equity visionaries first set up shop. In 1971, a year before the founding of Kleiner Perkins, Ronald Cohen and three partners established a corporate finance outfit called Multinational Management Group (MMG, later nicknamed Make Money Grow). Sir Ronald had graduated with an MBA from Harvard in 1969 and returned to Europe convinced that the internationalization of the concept of entrepreneurship was going to be 'the next big thing'. After two years at McKinsey, he decided he would build 'a major professional firm in this area of entrepreneurship'.

The French government was also getting interested in the technology companies growing up around Route 128 outside Boston and commissioned a report. Peter Brooke, founder of TA Associates, a prominent east coast venture firm, contributed a section on the importance of venture capital in the creation of technology companies (Gupta 2000). As a result, a number of tax incentives were put in place in France to encourage individuals and institutions to invest. In 1973 Sofinnova, one of today's prominent French firms, was created, with TA Associates among its investors. But Brooke was certainly under no illusions about the difficulty of doing business in Europe at the time. 'I must say it was tough sledding because of the socialist environment. Economic growth was stagnant. There was no initiative.'

MMG was also finding the climate pretty inimical. In 1976 the four partners, all Harvard graduates, wrote a paper on their analysis of the future. Two were extremely negative, but the other pair, Cohen and Maurice Tschénio, who today runs Apax in Paris, remained optimists. 'I wrote something about there being a relationship between perseverance and so-called luck,' says Sir Ronald. The following year, he teamed up with Alan Patricof, a hard-bitten New Yorker with a sharp tongue and a puckish sense of humour, to form MMG Patricof Group. At the end of 1980, he set out to raise the first fund from institutional investors for a vehicle called APA Ventures. It took ten months to raise £10m (Apax's latest fund is €4.4bn), with half the cash sourced in the USA. UK investors included the West Midlands Pension Fund, still an Apax investor today, which viewed the investment as one way to address its concerns about rebuilding Britain's manufacturing base.

The early 1980s saw a wave of new venture firms established, ranging from the bank 'captives' such as County NatWest Ventures, investing off their own balance sheet, to the likes of US style groups such as Advent Venture Partners, established by Sir David Cooksey in 1981, as the first foreign affiliate of TA Associates. ICFC (which changed its brand to Investors in Industry, and then to 3i in the early 1980s) with its almost monopolistic position, did not take kindly to the new arrivals and 'US style practices' – including providing equity (rather than debt, which was what ICFC largely supplied) and 'hands-on' support for investee companies. Sir David Cooksey recalls: 'We were an annoyance. Why were we providing equity to companies that "didn't need it"? But they were far too big and arrogant actually to consider us a threat.' A principal annoyance proved to be the magnetic pull that the newly developing industry exercised on ICFC staff. Well trained at what became known as 'the university of venture capital', they were easy prey since they lacked the industry standard compensation arrangements. Staff turnover in the early 1980s climbed to over 30 per cent.

Continental Europe

At the same time, a handful of firms was being founded in mainland Europe, but it was not an exercise for the faint-hearted. Suspicions of the business were particularly acute in Germany. Dr Jochen Mackenrodt, then vice president at Siemens in charge of venture capital, told the *Financial Times* in 1987: 'It was considered as a disease, not something to be copied . . . No one wanted US practices here.'

Take Techno Venture Management (TVM), the oldest surviving German venture firm and another TA Associates affiliate founded in 1984 together with Siemens, Matuschka, and Sir David Cooksey. Sir David recalls the only possible way to raise funds for the endeavour in Germany was via 'the back door into industry'. Mackenrodt, he says, did a superb job of arm twisting in the boardrooms of Daimler-Benz, Mannesmann and Deutsche Bank to 'do their bit' for the German economy. But the German approach to venture capital was distinctive to say the least. After three years TVM considered it a badge of honour that, while it had invested in over 30 firms in Germany and the USA, none of its investments had gone bust. In 1987 Peter Kaleschke, a managing director at TVM, told the *Financial Times*: 'In the UK people say it's too good not to have lost an investment, meaning you don't lose if you don't dare. Here in Germany we have a certain responsibility to show that venture capital does not mean just losing money and spending on risky things, but investing after thorough investigation.'

Thoroughness? Well, not invariably. Sir David remembers a spin-off from Siemens that TVM was backing. He had wanted to write into the investment agreement certain controls on capital expenditure but Mackenrodt told him firmly: 'You may need them in Britain. But in Germany we have much better disciplines and they are not necessary.'

Soon after the investment was completed, Mackenrodt was on the phone. 'David,' he said cautiously, 'I went to visit them. You are right. Outside the door are four brand new Porsches.' As Cooksey says, the only surprise was that Mackenrodt let on about what he had discovered.

It was also the period of a number of grand, but ill-starred pan-European schemes – such as Euroventures, set up in 1984 following an idea hatched by the Round Table of European Industrialists. One of various European schemes to bolster European competitiveness in technology, the industrial backers included Saint Gobain, Bosch, Fiat, Pirelli, Philips, Volvo and Olivetti. A grandiose concept, aiming both to foster links between big and small business, as well as to break down national barriers in Europe, it did not have the people to deliver and was filled with executives learning to be venture capitalists. One of its more prominent investments was Super Club, a Belgian video rental company which was rescued by Philips in 1991 after racking up losses of several billion Belgian francs the previous year.

A year later saw the creation of the largest venture backed start-up of its day. European Silicon Structures (ES2) was a prototype custom chip business set up in 1985 that drew in a roster of senior industry figures in an era when it was highly unusual for such individuals to leave secure highly paid jobs. Co-chairmen were Robb Wilmot, former chief executive of ICL and previously a Texas Instruments veteran, and Robert Heikes, a senior Motorola executive formerly with National Semiconductor, and the first CEO was Jean-Luc Grand-Clement, also of Motorola. The aim was to build a pan-European company from scratch at a time when governments were set on promoting national champions and, it was felt, hindering the creation of a strong competitor to the Japanese and the Americans. It was highly ambitious in every way, including its pan-European distributed business structure, with only a nominal legal headquarters; even the accounts were denominated in ECUs from the outset. David Cooksey of Advent injected the first $500,000 in seed capital (and produced space in Advent's offices in the early days) and the company, which built its own chip fabrication plant, eventually raised close to $100m by way of venture capital, corporate investment and grants. The first VC round contained a roster of firms from various corners of Europe (familiar names today such as TVM, Schroder Ventures and Alpha in Paris; and others long gone such as Four Seasons in Stockholm and Beaver Investment in The Hague). Rod Attwooll, a former senior TI executive who was running the UK (and who hired Robin Saxby, now Sir Robin, founder of chip design company ARM, as a sales manager), recalls how the principal difficulties were, as ever, explaining to investors what the company proposed to do; and getting the first one to commit. 'They all separately said they would invest if X would – and promised to talk to X. While weeks and months passed. In the end, we got them all into a room in a hotel in Brussels and told them to get down to talking to each other.' With hindsight, silicon fabrication on venture capital money was a tall order. ES2 was sold a decade after its founding to Atmel, a Californian company in search of a European manufacturing base (for an undisclosed but presumably nominal, sum).

During this period, venture capital was by no means synonymous with technology. My Kinda Town, for instance, was one of Sir Ronald's first deals, in 1982 when it had only one restaurant. 'From my American experience I understood [American family food],' he says. Another example was Waterstones, the book chain, started with ICFC money in the early 1980s, with later backing from APA, and sold to WH Smith in 1989. The approach to technology itself, meanwhile, was distinctly amateurish. Investors would be doing a biotechnology deal one day and looking at a disk drive company the next. Beecroft, who had a first-class degree in physics and had spent a spell at ICL before joining BCG, cheerfully admits that he was doing biotechnology as well as information technology investments: 'The only satisfactory thing I did was to hire Hamish Hale [who, at GD Searle, had set up the largest genetic engineering research group in Europe]. Being a physicist I didn't understand a word about biotechnology.' Now Apax has a team of around ten people in biotechnology, each specialized in their own niche.

A certain lack of confidence, as well as the restricted size of the funds, meant that deals were often syndicated around five or so firms. This made it very difficult to work out individual firms' track records because everyone claimed to have led the good deals, while there was a marked reluctance to own up to the (much more frequent) bad deals. It certainly tended to be thoroughly unsatisfactory from the entrepreneur's point of view, because, with no very obviously clear lead investor, each venture firm figured someone else would do the work of actually looking after the company. A lot of firms lost money and either closed their doors or opted for an easier life concentrating on management buy-outs, which were less risky and offered the prospect of quicker and more certain returns.

While Silicon Valley had already seen several mini venture capital investment cycles, the first real downturn in Europe (after a dip following the 1987 stock market crash) came with the recession at the beginning of the 1990s, after a peak in fund raising in 1989. Captives withdrew from the market and a number of independent funds folded. Apax had just finished investing its third fund – £75m raised in 1987. For a long time, the partners wondered if it would even return investors' capital. Between 1990 and 1994 in the UK there were virtually no exits – other than via the undertaker. Beecroft says Apax invested very slowly during that period. While he had learnt all about cycles from his days at BCG advising the paper industry, he says he knew he ought to be investing, but there was 'nervousness about whether it was going to get worse. It's so much easier to run other people's businesses'.

Anne Glover, who invested in (when she was at Apax) and later joined Virtuality, a virtual reality entertainments company, describes just how difficult it was for a technology company to get funded – conditions that sound eerily familiar today: 'You had to forecast the course of the entire investment and its return. There were no second stage investors [who would come in with further financing] and no loss-making public companies. You had to get to profitability on the capital invested. Very few met the criteria, this one happened to.' (The company was floated on the London Stock Exchange, and Apax made money, although it later went bust.)

Cash for young companies came from unlikely sources. While venture capitalists are today crawling over potential university spin-outs, the early days of Cambridge Display Technology, a company based on light-emitting polymer technology, were very different. The company, co-founded by Professor Richard Friend in 1990, had initially survived on (some fairly distinguished) business angel money from the likes of Hermann Hauser (who had taken his physics PhD at the same time as Friend), Esther Dyson, the US technology guru, and John Sculley, former CEO of Apple. But in 1993, after what Prof. Friend describes as an 'almost complete make-believe piece' in a Sunday newspaper about CDT being able to produce technology for 'a TV screen large enough to hang on a wall' attracted £400,000 from Phil Collins and other members of pop group Genesis, who 'did a bit of tech investing', the sum was matched by Cambridge University and some of the colleges, the first time the university had invested in such a venture. Prof. Friend claims that the Genesis manager 'knew more about start-ups than so-called VC funds. He understood there was a huge amount of distance to travel before being in product, that investors needed to be patient and put in several rounds of funding – which is of course hardly rocket science now. VCs would get stuck on some risky little issue that was not relevant. These guys turned up and got it.' Having invested, they were 'polite at board meetings, turned up at photo opportunities and eventually sold out and made a lot of money, not that they needed it'.

Early children of the recovery

In 1993, Michael Jackson, who had built Sage, the accounting software business, during the 1980s, made his initial investment in Select Software Tools. His venture firm Elderstreet was then arranged as a syndicate of business angels and Select Software was the first deal; Micromuse followed a year later. 'These [Stuart Frost of Select Software and Chris Dawes of Micromuse, who killed himself in his McLaren F1 in 1999, the year after the company's highly successful Nasdaq IPO] were deeply impressive entrepreneurs of a totally different calibre and vision from those I had encountered previously,' he says. 'They drew inspiration from US markets, both had read Geoffrey Moore [*Crossing the Chasm*] and were talking a quite different business model – namely cash burn. They weren't making money, and had no intention to make money in the sense that they were growing sales as fast as possible. They took it as read that you had to scale and go global.'

It was Sir Clive Sinclair, the boffin with a talent for inventing things but rather less interest in commercializing them, who was the household name in Britain; but away from the headlines a number of UK technology entrepreneurs were beginning to build companies. In Cambridge, 3i had invested in Peter Dawe, founder of Unipalm, whose Pipex subsidiary produced the UK's first internet access software. Jim Martin, then running 3i's office in Cambridge, recalls how when Dawe approached him in 1991 no one had heard of the internet. Unipalm floated on the London Stock Exchange in 1994, the first internet service provider in the world to launch an initial public offering, and was sold the following year to UUNET of the USA for £97m. Another notable success for the venture capitalists was Cliff Stanford, founder of

Demon Internet, backed in 1995 by Apax, which was sold to Scottish Telecom in 1998 for £30m.

Dr Chris Evans, the UK's best known serial biotechnology entrepreneur, was also attracting the attention of the VCs. A scientist who had to go to British Sugar to finance his first start-up Enzymatix in 1987, he took drug research company Chiroscience (later merged with Celltech) to the stock market in early 1994 after securing backing from 3i.

In a wider context, European successes were still paltry. It was not until 1998 that the first venture backed start-up broke the much talked about £1bn barrier when Computacenter came to the London Stock Exchange with a market capitalization of £1.1bn – an investment Apax had had to wait 13 years (it first invested in 1985) to see come through.

One of the crucial changes in the mid-1990s was the emergence in Europe of stock markets specifically designed for growth stocks. Some European companies were beginning to make it to Nasdaq, such as Business Objects in 1994, which itself constituted an important stimulus for the French venture capital community. At the same time there was a real sense that Europe was losing out. In the summer of 1996, Qiagen, a biotechnology company backed by TVM, became the first German company to list on Nasdaq – occasioning a lament from the head of its supervisory board, Carsten Claussen, who termed it a 'sad experience' that Qiagen had to go 'across the big pond'. 'Where there is lots of light there is also plenty of shadow.' (*Financial Times* 1996).

The Alternative Investment Market in London had been launched the previous year, replacing the USM, while Easdaq, a pan-European initiative, came into being at the end of 1996, with Apax-backed Dr Solomon's, the UK developer of anti-virus software, the first company to list. The Neuer Markt, the Deutsche Börse's market for growth companies, followed hot on its heels, opening in March 1997. Perhaps one of the most astonishing aspects of the boom in Europe was the way in which the Germans passed from the merest stirrings of an equity culture with the privatization of Deutsche Telekom the previous year to embrace the Neuer Markt in a frenzy – only to witness the exchange's collapse amid fraud, scandal and recriminations less than half a decade later.

Another important stimulus, the European Commission and a number of European governments were turning increasingly positive towards venture capital, recognizing its importance in creating jobs and hence fostering economic growth. The European Investment Fund in Luxembourg, which invests in venture firms rather than individual companies, has today contributed more than €1.8bn to some 140 VC firms. In the UK, successive

Conservative governments had produced various initiatives, such as Venture Capital Trusts (listed vehicles which provide tax shelters for individuals investing in portfolios of unquoted companies) and the Enterprise Investment Scheme (tax relief for cash into individual unquoted companies). But it was, ironically, the Labour government, in power since 1997, which ushered in a raft of measures including a capital gains tax regime now more favourable than that of the USA – quite a change from the late 1970s when the top marginal rate of income tax in Britain was 98 per cent. As one senior UK regulator says, the venture industry now seems to punch above its weight in Whitehall policymaking: 'It feels as if the industry has plants in the DTI and Treasury. A reference to venture capital pops up in every bit of legislation.'

While the German authorities have created plenty of difficulties for the industry with their volatile tax policies, its generous subsidy programmes (including TBG and KfW) have created a huge stimulus for venture capital in the late 1990s (as well as undoubtedly producing too many unsustainable companies in certain sectors, notably biotechnology). For every €1m invested by a venture capitalist, companies could attract another €1m from federal programmes, and a possible further €1m from regional sources, while the venture capitalists also secured government guarantees for half their investment. Canny operators of the system included Falk Strascheg and Gerd Köhler of Technologieholding, a Munich-based VC later sold to 3i, who produced some of the best venture returns in Europe in the mid to late 1990s.

At the same time, while the internet gold rush had swept the USA following the IPO of Netscape in 1995, Europe was very slow to wake up to the scale of what was happening across the Atlantic. Michael Jackson of Elderstreet tells of how, at the beginning of 1999, he flew to the West Coast to look for a large investor to kick-start a new fund. The scales fell from his eyes: 'There I was thinking Sage was a success – it had a market cap then of £1bn, maybe £2bn. They looked at me as if they were slightly sorry for me. The whole scale of it and the business dynamics, we just didn't start to understand it.'

In the bubble

One of the more striking aspects of the internet frenzy in Europe was its brevity. The 'dotcom summer' of 1999, ushered in with the flotation of loss-making start-up Freeserve on the London Stock Exchange, was a full three years after Alan Greenspan's warnings about irrational exuberance. Yet not much more than six months later came the Nasdaq crash which signalled the bursting of the dotcom bubble on both sides of the Atlantic – although nearly another year then elapsed before the much more extensive technology and telecommunications investment balloon deflated. This meant that venture firms, unlike some of their US counterparts, had much less chance to make strings of crass investments – but also only the briefest of windows to cash out from the public markets on some of those investments.

The earliest internet investors in Europe were not by and large the well-known venture firms. Pioneers included two former McKinsey consultants in Italy who in 1997 set up Net Partners in Milan, Italy, still today one of Europe's least developed venture capital markets. It took them nine months to raise €5m. Fausto Boni, co-founder, recalls attempting to explain to friends at dinner parties what they were doing: 'I'm sure when we left everyone was saying those two are mad.' But Net Partners made money by being early – with investments including Selftrade and QXL.

Meanwhile Thomas Hoegh, scion of the Norwegian shipping family with an arts and media background who had fallen into investing in the internet while studying at Harvard, set up transatlantic firm Arts Alliance. Early investments included Firefly in the USA and Lastminute of the UK: 'For a while we were heroes of the planet because we caught the B2C wave early.' Before long his activities came to the attention of some of the more prominent firms in Europe. At one point, five partners from one shop pitched up in his offices for a meeting. 'We must do something together,' they said, which he says he interpreted as meaning: 'We will learn everything from you so that we can crush you.'

Sweden meanwhile had as a region been early to the game, largely because of high internet penetration in a technologically literate population. Cell Ventures, one of Europe's first incubators, began investing in mid-1997. With almost no previous venture capital infrastructure, apart from a few angel groupings, Stockholm was suddenly overflowing with venture firms barely older than the start-ups they were backing. During 1999 and 2000 the Swedish Venture Capital Association added one new member a week, and at one point had at least 150 members.

In the UK internet investing did not get properly under way until early 1999. In France it was still later – the summer of 1999, with the IPO of art market portal Artprice, backed by Bernard Arnault, the prominent French businessman behind LVMH and Groupe Arnault, who was assembling his €500m Europatweb internet vehicle. 'Because the French basically respect big companies, the fact that Arnault was doing it caught people's attention,' one French venture capitalist remarks.

During the brief window before the market collapsed, a series of mini bubbles played themselves out in comically quick succession. Business-to-consumer (B2C) plays gave way within weeks to business-to-business (B2B) models which in turn were eclipsed by application service providers (ASPs). With the art of revisionism at which venture capitalists excel, investors would explain the compelling logic of a B2B model by highlighting the fatal flaws of the kind of B2C business they had cheerfully backed just a few weeks previously.

Capital was not only more or less free to companies, but also available in seemingly limitless supply to would-be venture capitalists. The hitherto tiny industry sucked in 'talent' from all directions – principally, but not exclusively from investment banks and management consultancy firms. Jean-Bernard Tellio, a Frenchman long on charm who later became the first (short-lived) managing partner of a €730m European internet fund set up by Carlyle, the Washington DC based firm, secured his entrée into the world of venture capital because he was buying art for Bernard Arnault, who then put him in charge of the group's internet investments on either side of the Atlantic. Those viewed as possessing even a little relevant experience were feted; like Simon Murdoch (who had sold his internet start-up Bookpages to Amazon) and Richard Tahta (a self-styled serial entrepreneur) who had called in to Chase Capital Partners, one the largest global private equity firms and an arm of the giant US bank, to ask for money. On the strength of their internet experience, the pair were able to curtail their fund raising when Chase agreed to set up a joint venture using €100m of its own cash. The venture was named Chase Episode 1, after the *Star Wars* film in which Tahta had appeared as an extra in a crowd scene.

VCs were not just cash rich; they had become instant celebrities. Vic Morris formerly of Atlas, and, during the bubble, an entrepreneur brand new to venture capital, recalls: 'You went to First Tuesday [the networking event that had started as a friends' cocktail party in a Soho bar in late 1998] and it was like being a film star. Looking back you wonder why we were all so caught up in it.' But 'we' were. Buy-out firms suddenly threw trusted investment principles to the wind and plunged in. Investment banks, unseated from their pedestals as masters of the universe by the dotcom millionaires, were also desperate to be involved. As one venture capitalist said to me at the time: 'It drives them batty that there is now another superior race – people who were maybe their inferiors at Harvard – who don't wear ties who appear to be having fun and who are making a ton more money than them.' (*Financial Times* 2000) In mid-2000, Goldman Sachs was expecting to invest around $600m in technology companies in Europe during the year, which would have made it one of the most active early stage investors. (It subsequently grew very shy about its numbers, so it is not clear how near it got towards its target.)

The pioneer venture capitalists saw it as their moment in the sun. Like his partners, Gerry Montanus at Atlas simply 'lived' in the office during 1999 and 2000. 'But I had waited 16 years for this [since joining Atlas in the Netherlands in the mid-1980s]. It was a sudden change in the energy in Europe.' The transatlantic firm saw business models that were 'proven' in the USA – in hindsight proven only by the financial markets' appetite for their IPOs – and 'jumped in'. Indeed Atlas gained an unfortunate reputation for being one of the most gung-ho internet investors. The firm, which started as a unit inside a Dutch bank in 1980, had expanded elsewhere in Europe but had been late in opening an office in London. It was anxious to promote itself aggressively – which it did very loudly with the funding of health products e-tailer Clickmango in eight days in the autumn of 1999. 'The perception that we did a lot of e-commerce was totally wrong,' says Montanus. 'Our visibility was dominated by that and, to be honest, we encouraged that visibility. It harmed us. We were not very smart at profiling our success stories' [which included the sale of Element 14, the Cambridge chip company spun off from Acorn, to Broadcom of the USA for $594m].

It was a seller's market, and entrepreneurs could pretty much dictate their terms. At the end of a first meeting people were asking you for a term sheet [letter of intent],' says Pierre Morin of GRP. 'They were telling us they had already received two or three from well-known venture capitalists and wanted to close within the week.' When socialites Trinny Woodall and Susannah Constantine funded shopping advice portal Ready2 – at that stage 'a business plan and two pretty girls', as Trinny's brother Mark recalls – the deadline for the close was Trinny's wedding. Within a year the process between first meeting and closing had stretched to six months – and the timing of completion was less amenable to the pressures of the social calendar.

Valuations were spiralling out of control, though that did not mean everyone was satisfied. Andrew Hawkins, a sophisticated banker then at West LB, had met up with Anne Winblad of Silicon Valley venture capitalist Hummer Winblad at a conference in San Francisco. Pets.com, one of the firm's portfolio investments, was going great guns. '"Why don't I build Pets.com in the UK and sell it to you, and we can all make a lot of money," I said to her, almost joking.' She liked the idea, Hawkins returned to the UK and, with school friend Nick Barnard, built the business – or rather the website called Petspark. Six months later he flew back. 'Right, I've done it. Will you buy it?' Much to his disappointment, she suggested he meet with Pets.com, with the idea they inject further cash into the pets portal. Distinctly reluctantly, he set off for their offices. Yes, they would invest $5m plus another $3m in kind in the form of database technology to forge a 'global partnership'. The only problem was the valuation. They were sticking at $22m for the business [pre-money, namely the value before the new cash]. He rang Barnard. 'Nick, I'm so sorry, this is the best I could do.' Hawkins was, he admits, 'really upset and angry'. The pair had invested £30,000 nine months earlier and now it was only worth a paltry $22m, for 'a functioning website, first mover advantage in the UK, and, of course, unlimited upside potential'.

Business plans were being valued at 50 or 100 times next year's sales – but if venture investors stopped to query, they found the first round had closed. Indeed, they would do more or less anything to get into what they perceived to be a 'hot' deal. Mark Suster was raising money for his B2B construction site BuildOnline. One of the prospective investors had an investment in a Formula One team. Eddie Jordan was duly roped in to ring BuildOnline's founder to suggest various ways BuildOnline might be promoted at events. As it happened, neither he nor Suster, a gritty southern Californian with a serious interest in current affairs, gave a damn about the sport anyway. If they had got 'Henry Kissinger or somebody' on the other end of the telephone, Suster says he might conceivably have been a tiny bit impressed. A German financial institution, desperate to be included in the deal at the eleventh hour, was less subtle and simply offered Suster and the founder of the business $1m in cash each to allow them into the deal – an offer the pair had no hesitation in declining.

Zum Himmel jauchzend, zu Tode getrübt
Exulting to the heavens, cast into deepest gloom.

(Goethe)

One of the more remarkable aspects of the frenzy was the energy with which Europe's largest, but hitherto largely equity averse, economy embraced venture capital. The supposedly inflexible and risk-averse Germans seemingly cast aside all lingering suspicions about equities, entrepreneurs and money making, and rushed headlong to indulge what a short while ago had been dubbed unnatural Anglo-Saxon practices. Pivotal was the – briefly – galvanizing effect of the Neuer Markt, which saw more than 350 companies floated in less than four years. At one point there were said to be 120 venture capitalists in Munich alone, and the imbalance between VCs and entrepreneurs was reaching ridiculous proportions. 'You have a huge [though desperately inexperienced] venture capital community and few entrepreneurs. It is supposed to be the other way round,' said one business angel at the time, noting that Germany had produced more than the European average of 'boy band

copy and paste start-ups', namely internet companies started by youthful business school graduates mirroring existing US counterparts. Everyone was
stumbling around in the dark, management teams learning on VCs' money,
VCs on investors' money (not that all were around long enough to do much
learning).

By far the best investment deal of the period was pulled off by the two
founders of Technologieholding. Spotting the eagerness of Anglo-Saxon
investors to secure a foothold in the red-hot market, they peddled their company to 3i in February 2000 a month before the Nasdaq crash with a price tag
of DM333m (£103m). Just 18 months later, 3i, weighed down by its ailing
technology portfolio, shed 17 per cent of its staff, including a large proportion of the Technologieholding executives.

Incubators

If it were possible, the people behind the rash of 'incubators' across Europe
were yet more incompetent than the venture capitalists – who incidentally
they soon claimed they would be putting out of business. In the UK alone,
about 100 such vehicles were created in the second half of 1999 – offering
dotcoms a variety of services, mostly of distinctly dubious quality, often in
exchange for a very large chunk of equity. Many raised money on the public
markets, helped by the eye-watering valuations being achieved by the likes of
CMGI and Internet Capital Group in the USA. Later dubbed incinerators for
the speed with which they burnt through cash, incubators were primarily successful at parting the public from their cash. Antfactory, which in fact raised
money from private sources, stood out not just because of its ludicrous name,
but as the fund-raising machine par excellence. Packed with investment
bankers slumming it on salaries of 'only' £100,000, it changed its business
model innumerable times (later denying it had ever been an internet incubator) while raising about $190m, much of it from other venture capitalists.
Every time I talked to chief executive Harpal Randhawa, he seemed hazy on
the details of the portfolio but razor sharp on the state of the next round of
fund raising.

Other fund-raising successes included iworld, a wireless incubator in the
unlikely location of Malta. Deutsche Bank, Hikari Sushin and others paid
$37m for just over 10 per cent of the company in July 2000. The idea of incu-
bators was itself not so stupid – that start-ups needed help in an environment
where everything was a race to market and the venture capitalists, up to their
ears in new deals, were in no position to help their portfolio companies. But

the model, which was asset and people intensive and dependent on fast exits to pay the vast overheads, was fundamentally flawed.

Of course very few of the dotcom types were passionate entrepreneurs. They set up garden sites knowing nothing about gardening, and online drug stores without knowing the basics of the regulatory environment that would render their operations illegal. More importantly still, they knew nothing about the persistence and doggedness necessary to be an entrepreneur; the main aim seemed to be to 'get the money thing sorted' before they turned 30 so that they could figure out what they really wanted to do with their lives.

By the spring of 2000, 'dotcom' had become a word of abuse, but everyone fondly hoped the March and April Nasdaq 'correction' was just that. And the sense endured that the stock markets would still fund 'real technology companies'. Telecoms were roaring ahead following the $203bn hostile takeover by Vodafone Airtouch of Germany's Mannesmann at the end of 1999. Young venture-backed companies such as Bookham Technology, TeleCity and Orchestream were still managing to list, while the UK chancellor, Gordon Brown, was calling in the services of an academic economist specializing in game theory to help him flog third-generation licences to telecoms operators in the UK for £22bn that April. (More than €100bn was spent across Europe for the 3G tickets, which less than two years later looked to be more or less worthless.)

Sentiment in the venture capital and the wider entrepreneurial community remained misguidedly buoyant. Take Barcelona May 2000: the Industry Standard, a technology magazine group founded in San Francisco in 1998, was on the march. It was staging its first European conference and everyone was there. True, there was a frisson of nerves – after all Boo had just collapsed, taking with it $135m of investors' money, and Net Imperative, another prominent start-up, bellied up during the bash. But the party was essentially still in full swing and its star guests were Benchmark, the full complement of partners from Silicon Valley installed in duplex suites at the top of the Hotel Arts as they prepared to announce they had put together $750m to invest in European companies. Moving in a phalanx, these preternaturally tall men in shades reminded one conference participant as 'something out of *Reservoir Dogs*'. Their first investment was in online betting service Flutter.com, which was just closing a second round of financing, raising $33m to value the company, which had barely launched its website, at $170m.

Elsewhere, the 'new economy' was very much alive and well. Indeed the next generation of venture capital company was being formed – or so it was claimed at the time. The top names in venture capital, leveraged buy-outs, management consultancy (and one investment bank) took their dancing partners to attack the next big thing after the pure-play start-up – the integration of online and offline business. Accel teamed up with buy-out legend KKR to form Accel-KKR; Boston Consulting Group, General Atlantic Partners and Goldman Sachs set up iFormation; and eVolution was formed by Kleiner Perkins, Bain and Texas Pacific Group.

The big idea was to create carve-outs using the assets of big established global companies, together with the venture creation savvy of the VCs, the financial engineering skills of the buy-out whizzes and the strategic input of the consultants. The creation of eVolution, for one, was symptomatic of the time. One strand of the story concerned two Bain consultants, Stan Miranda and Fritz Seikowsky, who wanted – with pure bull market chutzpah – to build the 'Kleiner Perkins of Europe', namely a pre-eminent venture capital fund. They were consultants with rather more buy-out than venture experience, but, hey, who cared. It did not make sense that there was no Kleiner Perkins in Europe and they had been involved with Bainlab, the Bain incubator which 'seemed to be working'. 'Looking back on it,' says Miranda now, 'you see that it would take years to build a venture firm. Today you would seek to attach yourself to a firm that was nearly there.'

So the two went on an initial fund-raising exercise and secured $50m from one large European private equity firm. But the chief executive of Bain was anxious to check how the firm's biggest private equity clients felt about the project and talked, among others, to David Bonderman at Texas Pacific Group. Bonderman had just invested in Internet Capital Group, so was gung-ho about everything net-related. Forget Europe, he apparently said, let's make it global. 'But we needed a VC,' says Miranda, 'so we did a beauty contest. Kleiner was not really even in the beauty contest. They were the most reticent. But we made little matrices – as consultants do – ranking four different options. Kleiner came out way on top.'

A meeting was held at Kleiner Perkins' offices on Sand Hill Road – John Doerr and the whole Kleiner team on one side of the imposing board table, the proposers, including CEO of Bain, and David Bonderman, on the other: 'No one knew what they are thinking. Suddenly Doerr says "it's a cool big idea".' But it was no longer Miranda's and Seikowsky's business – 'it was completely out of control'. eVolution went into hibernation a little over a year later, after just three investments, having concluded that creating e-business spin-offs from large corporations was neither that cool or that big any more.

One of the first players to withdraw from the scene was Arnault, who pulled the IPO of Europatweb in June 2000. Boo, in which Arnault had invested $10m, had collapsed the previous month and the markets were leery of incubation, a model with which the group was still closely associated.

Europatweb, one of the biggest pots of internet cash around, had been Arnault's baby, to which he devoted huge amounts of time in the early days – much to the disgust of senior figures at LVMH who were missing his attentions. He had faithfully attended Europatweb's Friday weekly meetings, which often included the whole team from around the increasingly far-flung global empire. He would take an interest in minute details of the portfolio and investment prospects, down to the colour of the advertising campaign of Zebank, an ambitious retail financial portal. And he was always available. 'Any of us could call him and he would answer the phone right away,' says one former executive. But one Friday that September Arnault was not present. 'It was abundantly clear you would never see him again,' says another former Europatweb employee. The Arnault empire was not like a long-term private equity fund. It needed cash back from its investments and with the IPO window shut, the model did not work. Arnault, once so immersed in the business, had made one of those hard unsentimental decisions for which he is known and pulled back.

Burst bubble

And it had all seemed such a sure-fire bet. 'In a low inflationary environment with high technological change which is more risky, a technology or a non-technology portfolio?' was chief executive Brian Larcombe's rhetorical question at the end of 1999 (*Financial Times*, 2 December). Less than two years later, 3i sacked 17 per cent of its staff – the first lay-offs at the group in more than a decade – following massive losses on its technology portfolio.

Retreat of the rock stars

Some venture capitalists stopped investing when Nasdaq first cracked. Elderstreet, having shovelled out far too much cash between October 1999 and March 2000, called a halt that April and did not make another investment until well into 2001. Says Michael Jackson: 'We looked at our portfolio and said to ourselves: Oh my God what have we done?' Later that year, the canny Jackson pulled off a deal with Dresdner Kleinwort Benson, selling the management company (owned by three individuals) for over £10m. But for most the unreality persisted and 2000 was indeed the peak year for investment across Europe, fuelled by mobile internet frenzy and investments in supposed 'real' technology such as optical networking. Even towards the end of 2000, valuation logic was still deep in cloud cuckoo territory. Says one observer: 'Investment bankers were arguing for reducing the price of an IPO "because there is a real feeling that 10 times next year's sales represents real value but 15 times doesn't". When the valuation is 50 times this year's sales, you had to think: On what basis are you coming to this conclusion?'

As Nasdaq continued to slip, the pile of dotcom casualties mounted and the era of the down round (financings at a lower valuation than the previous round, causing painful dilution to the management team and early investors) was ushered in. With cash no longer free, bloated start-ups began cutting costs and laying off staff and venture capitalists, borrowing a term previously largely unknown outside the emergency rooms of US hospitals, went into 'triage' mode, sifting through their portfolio companies deciding which should live and which should die. At the end of 2000, the IPO game was over and prospective flotation candidates such as Mediasurface, the content management software company, saw their offerings pulled, sending the companies into punishing 'cram-down' rounds to secure cash from their venture backers to limp on.

The 100-year flood

For a long while though, the downturn remained a financial market rather than an economic phenomenon. John Chambers, chief executive of network equipment giant Cisco Systems, put that right in the spring of 2001 when he talked in apocalyptic terms of the precipitous fall in IT spending. It showed, he said, how a 'once in a 100 year flood can happen in your lifetime'. The bursting of the dotcom bubble was still on everybody's lips, but the contraction in IT spending and the telecoms collapse were to have an infinitely greater impact on the real economy and financial market confidence. In 18 months from March 2000, the stock market value of telecoms operators and manufacturers fell by $3,800bn from a peak of $6,300bn – which compares with Asian stock market losses during the financial crisis of the late 1990s of just $813bn (*Financial Times* 2001).

The venture capitalists went steadily further into hiding, some drawing the portcullis down on new investments with a ferocity that mirrored the intensity of their over commitments. Europe had not seen anything like the excesses of the USA, but then the industry had shallower roots and many operators were far more inexperienced. It actually took far longer to dawn in Europe that the party was really over, and those investments that were made in the first two-thirds of 2001 tended to be at still unrealistic valuations.

VCs may have claimed the main reason they were not investing was that entrepreneurs had not 'adjusted' their valuation expectations, but the truth was many were shell-shocked and preoccupied with tending their portfolios. The spin machines went into overdrive as every shop claimed to have spent only a 'tiny percentage' of the portfolio on dotcoms. With all the energy they could muster, they told anybody that would listen that things were 'back to normal' – in other words to the sanity of the period before collective bubble mania set in. If anyone truly believed it before, they could scarcely continue to do so following the tragic events of 11 September 2001. The erosion of confidence had come in waves – first the collapse in public market valuations, then the realization of the extent of the collapse in IT spending, the telecoms implosion, 11 September – immediately followed by the series of accounting, fraud and corporate greed scandals kicked off by Enron which unleashed the wider collapse of confidence in corporate America.

The shakeout of venture firms is a much more long drawn-out and gruesome business than the fall-out in the companies they back. Even though vast swathes of portfolios are under water, having lost large amounts of investors' capital, private venture firms can continue to eke out an existence on the management fees of the current fund for a long time before they are forced to confront reality and face up to the fact that institutional investors will never entrust them with their money again. For a public venture capital company, the end comes much more swiftly, as the incubators and some of the few quoted VCs such as 2M in Denmark discovered. Many of the US firms which rushed into Europe, preaching their superiority to Europeans in matters venture capital, have withdrawn equally fast – including Whitney, Bowman, Geocapital and Draper Fisher Jurvetson (DFJ).

The DFJ story illustrates how internationalization strategies appear often to have been less than meticulously planned. The firm is a famous Valley outfit that has taken literally the fact that venture capital is a franchise business. Built on the strength of the firm's brand, DFJ had lent its name to a host of franchise funds across the USA. When it was approached by two individuals who ran an obscure operation in Switzerland called ePlanet, it signed up to a joint venture to extend the exercise internationally. So DFJ ePlanet was launched, allegedly with a fund of $690m to invest around the globe.

Not long afterwards John Fisher, a DFJ founder, arrived in London to help build the operation. But his sojourn was relatively brief and he had returned to Redwood City, Silicon Valley by the end of 2001. A DFJ spokesman later described Fisher's stay as 'really a sabbatical' and explained that Fisher and his family had been travelling a lot: 'You know, it's been kinda tough in the Valley in the last couple of years, draining for a lot of people.

John saw the opportunity to go over there. It was not meant to be for a long period of time.' Meanwhile the two individuals from ePlanet were in charge and their interest in DFJ appeared largely confined to its name. They upset the team they had hired and in early 2002 the operation blew apart after two partners left (following earlier departures by two others) – leaving the ePlanet duo desperately spinning something about a change of strategy.

What is left?

During the bubble I recall one of the *Financial Times*'s foreign correspondents (in a country yet to suffer dotcom mania) complaining about the amount of space devoted to the subject: 'It's become the Venture Capital Times,' he grumbled. Venture capital and entrepreneurship is no longer the height of cool. Governments are no longer quite so interested either. Verena Mohaupt, a young glamorous face of dotcom Germany as a co-founder of Ciao.com (a consumer choice site so far surviving) and a shrewd observer of the scene, was during the bubble, invited regularly to Berlin to be consulted by the Germany chancellor on barriers to high-tech entrepreneurship. The government still wants her advice, but now the subject is 'family issues'. Banks and corporations have been steadily pulling out of the private equity business, including venture, having bloodied their noses. Perhaps the sourest taste left behind by the bubble has been in Germany, where the Neuer Markt fell 94 per cent between March 2000 and September 2001. During 2000 it attracted 133 IPOs, as German and non-German companies alike were attracted by the wild valuations on offer. With its lack of regulation, it had been the wild west – with violations ranging from entire companies' revenues generated almost entirely from fictitious customers, to widespread disregard of basic rules such as the lock-up period (during which shareholders are proscribed from selling shares). One entrepreneur told me the maximum fine for breaking the lock-up was about $100,000, so it was viewed as 'essentially just a transaction cost'. In 2003, the Neuer Markt was closed and the surviving companies transferred to a section of the Deutsche Börse.

And yet. Europe has gone through a huge learning exercise courtesy of investors' money. There is a much higher level of awareness about entrepreneurship; most European universities now teach entrepreneurship courses, for instance. The infrastructure necessary to build young companies is growing, in terms of more experienced service providers such as lawyers and accountants. There is a real effort in certain centres, particularly around university hubs such as Imperial College London, Cambridge and Oxford Universities and Munich – through the Munich Network – to keep the momentum going. But it once again requires stamina and a good dose of both the grit and imagination shown by the early pioneers of the 1970s and 1980s will certainly be needed before Europe has a properly mature and sophisticated venture capital industry.

References

Campbell, K. (1999) 'Technology fever starts a gold rush', *Financial Times*, 2 December.

Campbell, K. (2000) 'Hatching under a new wing', *Financial Times*, 18 May.

Coopey, R. and Clarke, D. (1995) *3i: Fifty Years Investing in Industry*, Oxford University Press, Inc., New York.

Dennett, L. (1979) *The Charterhouse Group 1925–1979: A History*, Gentry Books, London.

Fisher, A. (1997) 'Cautiously prodding at a mentality', *Financial Times*, 6 January.

Fisher, A. (1996) 'A venture across the pond', *Financial Times*, 24 July.

Gupta, U. (ed.) (2000) *Done Deals*, Harvard Business School Press, Boston MA.

Roberts, D. (2001) 'Glorious hopes on a trillion dollar scrapheap', *Financial Times*, 5 September.

5

Silicon Valley compared

If I have seen further, it is because I have stood on the shoulders of giants.
(Sir Isaac Newton 1676)

At particular times a great deal of stupid people have a great deal of stupid money and there is speculation and there is panic.
(Walter Bagehot)

TOM PERKINS, co-founder of Kleiner Perkins Caufield & Byers (variously known as KP or Kleiner) and one of the legends of Silicon Valley venture capital, was making a rare appearance in London. It was the launch of Favonius Ventures, a European venture firm which had landed Perkins on its advisory board. The venture capital bear market notwithstanding, the event drew most of the members of the local London venture community eager to hear the great man. Perkins is not an impressive public speaker, fiddling constantly with his glasses and the microphone, yet the audience hung on his every word. Afterwards an eager young Asian entrepreneur rushed up. The guy's business had four different product lines, how should he allocate his time? Focus on one of them, Perkins advised. 'That's brilliant,' said Mr Sycophant. 'No it isn't,' said Perkins, faintly irritably, when he'd gone, 'it's just common sense.' Probably sounding a bit unctuous myself, I asked him what Europeans have got to learn from the USA in venture capital. 'Everything,' he said bluntly.

Legends like Perkins still hold their fascination. Yet Europeans have also grown heartily sick of hearing US VCs suggesting for years that they alone had the answers in the business of venture capital. Hence there is not a little *Schadenfreude* at the decimation in the US venture community following its bubble binge, which saw $161bn invested in just two years (1999 and 2000), according to Venture Economics. Yes, this may be the system that created the Suns, Oracles, Dells and Ciscos, but cynical Europeans question whether the whole edifice has not been finally exposed for what it is – an environment honed with great sophistication for the peddling of vapourware and pure hype.

So what exactly do US venture capitalists remain so superior about (apart from the extraordinary pile of cash they have amassed personally – the best well north of a billion, at least on paper; with even the really incompetent putting away $50m or so). It comes in Perkins's answer to my second question: 'At what point did KP became a legend?' 'We broke the mould from the beginning,' he says firmly. 'We were operational people and we created companies.' He cites Genentech and Tandem, two of KP's earliest investments. That was the beginning of the 1970s, the dawn of the industry, when there was frankly not much of a mould to break. But Perkins goes on to explain that his main competition was Arthur Rock, 'and he was a Wall Street [financial] analyst'.

The veneration of the 'operational' versus the financial background has been central to the Valley's view of itself. Company building is what they do – or say they do. Perkins, who cut his teeth at Hewlett-Packard, the original Silicon Valley garage start-up, where he was the first MBA recruit, established and developed its computer division during the 1960s. The late David Packard was his mentor, and he clearly still worships him.

The fact that Rock was from Wall Street, of course, is also significant – highlighting cultural differences between the West and East Coast, and the fact that the 'US model' was not always homogeneous. In the past, at least, the Bay Area VCs of northern California would look down their noses at their peers in the second centre of US venture capital around Route 128, outside Boston, regarding them as clubby, stuffy, risk-averse, old-money types, preoccupied with financial engineering (halfway to Europeans, one might almost suggest). The denizens of the East Coast, for their part, harboured slight suspicions about the gung-ho, free-wheeling, brash informality and pioneer spirit of the investors out west – and would point out that their supposed native caution stood them in good stead when it came to resisting the wilder excesses of the boom. (While the gap today has narrowed substantially, not least because a number of venture firms have offices on both coasts, differences persist – down to the nuts and bolts of slightly varying styles of term sheet.)

It is also of course misleading to suggest that US venture capital activity is confined to these two centres. Other important clusters have emerged around top universities, research centres and large corporations, including in San Diego, Boulder, Seattle, Austin, and around Washington DC. But the Valley constitutes the heart of the US industry, and has represented the 'US model' in its purest form, which is the excuse for making it the focus of this chapter. And a curious place it is too, full of puzzling contradictions. In this crucible of great ideas and creativity, it is at the most dreary and unremarkable provincial diners that entrepreneurs and VCs pull out their Palm Pilots over breakfast to talk deals. First-time European visitors, who cannot help but associate great wealth with culture and sophistication, are invariably fazed by the pedestrian nature of the hangouts, like the famous Bucks in Woodside or Late for the Train in Menlo Park. They are in for a further surprise when, along Sand Hill Road, the six-lane highway connecting the cream of the US venture community, there is barely a cell phone signal. The Valley, which is not a geographic valley but a sprawling suburban mess, lacks any cosmopolitan pretensions whatsoever. Even at the height of the bubble, the society columnist from a San Francisco paper based in Palo Alto regularly bemoaned the lack of suitable material.

While in the business of churning out world-class companies, much of the Valley ethos is insular in the extreme; for years venture capitalists would pride themselves on the fact that they never invested in a company more than 45 minutes' drive away. Self-preoccupation reached considerable heights. Ruthann Quindlen (2000) explains how 'the road [Sand Hill] has taken on a persona of its own . . . You will hear people say Sand Hill thinks like this . . . Sand Hill didn't go for that idea.' She tells a tale against herself of a speech she gave in Pebble Beach to the National Association of Broadcasters, 100 miles down the coast entitled 'A View from Sand Hill'. Only slowly did it dawn on her that nobody knew what she was talking about because they had never heard of Sand Hill.

Not that anyone was allowed to voice such heresies in the go-go years. In the latest downturn, by contrast, the most severe technology recession in its history, Valley knocking is very much in fashion, as scores of disenchanted dreamers have left the place in disgust, whether of necessity or their own volition. And a large section of the remaining community sank into gloom. As Guy Kawasaki, chief executive of Garage Technology Ventures, suggests, the Valley has always been a bipolar sort of place: 'Things are never as good – or as bad – as they seem in the Valley.'

And yet that is why it is easy to forget that, when it is buzzing, the Valley is one of the most vibrant places on the planet. With its world-class universities of Stanford and Berkeley and research institutes such as PARC (Palo Alto Research Center), the Bay Area breathes technology. Even the waiters in Il Fornaio [in Palo Alto] know more about web services, one feels, than half the European venture community. Rod Attwooll, a chip industry veteran who has worked in both Europe and the USA, describes the difficulty he has had in explaining to European investors the technology at various start-ups in which he has worked: 'We would desperately practice on as many friends as possible to see if *they* got it. In the Valley, though, there was always a VC who had a friend who had just done a PhD in the subject you were trying to explain.'

The romance of the place lies in stories like that of internet networking giant Cisco Systems, founded in 1984 by two Stanford students, Sandy Lerner from the business school and the nerdish Len Bosack from the department of computer science (later husband and wife, and later still divorced). The company (Cisco, as in San Fran) got started in the traditional fashion – credit card finance – before seeking venture capital three years later. Some 70 VCs turned down the pair but Don Valentine, founder of Sequoia, took a different view and agreed to inject $2.5m for around 30 per cent of the company – which was worth $10bn the day Cisco went public (Bunnell 2000). Less than 15 years later, Cisco briefly overtook Microsoft as the largest company in the world.

Europeans have always struggled to understand the sheer scale of the venture endeavour (including the period of grotesque excess). One UK venture capitalist moving to the USA in mid-1999 recalls looking at a company's balance sheet showing negative retained earning of $47m. Someone must have made a mistake, he thought. Surely this did not mean the company had $47m in VC funding? That was not very much, it was explained to him. Another European investor, in the glory days, referring wistfully to Kleiner Perkins, observed how the firm was simply in a different league: 'They are looking for industry changing opportunities which make them 30 or 100 times their money. We think we are doing well when we make ten times our money.' KP partner Vinod Khosla, whose companies included Juniper Networks and Cerent, is credited with having more or less put the (now heavily challenged) optical fibre industry on the map. In its first three decades, KP likes to boast, it has invested in companies that have created more than 250,000 new jobs and over $100bn in new revenues (and over $650bn in market capitalization, though the latter slippery figure must be up for revision).

The well-oiled machine was sputtering rather than purring following the bursting of the bubble. But before considering the changes afoot in the industry, it is worth stressing the depth of the infrastructure, built on years of experience, that remains. In this tight community, everyone just *knows* how the venture process works – whether because they are Stanford engineering graduates who attended a venture course at the entrepreneurship centre taught by Tom Byers (brother of Brook, one of the founders of KP), or because their friends have been involved in a start-up backed by a Sand Hill Road firm. While most European founders would be unlikely to know anything about the performance of individual venture firms, young Valley entrepreneurs gossip about the personal IRRs of each partner of a firm that they are contemplating approaching. The network effect is pervasive. Everyone along the chain – start-up entrepreneur, venture backer, corporate customer, investment banking adviser – knows each other. Again, they were at Stanford, in a prior start-up, or at Hewlett-Packard together. The professional support services of lawyers, accountants, headhunters, are steeped in the venture business. Many have built their very practice around the industry – like Wilson Sonsini Goodrich & Rosati, the leading law firm (which has gone through a corresponding painful shrinkage through the venture downturn). The area even has its own specialist bank, Silicon Valley Bank, attuned to the needs of entrepreneurial companies. Large corporations, meanwhile, are, even in tough times, still far more open to doing business with young companies, not least because many were once venture-backed start-ups themselves. (In Europe by contrast, the backing of the best possible VC would cut little ice because chances are the finance director of a large corporation would not have heard of the firm.) Nor has the burst bubble quashed the celebration of entrepreneurship in US society at large, and the Valley in particular. The failed dotcomers attract mirth or scorn, but not genuine company founders. And, even in the teeth of a technology recession, every VC will invest in the real stars, no matter what the idea.

Again, the whole system for academic spin-outs is well honed compared with Europe (where the subject is, however, commanding considerably more attention today). Professor Richard Friend, a distinguished Cambridge professor who has co-founded two technology companies, says: 'I recognize I have a small fraction of the skills needed to run a company, but I marvel at how my peers in US academia don't have to lift a finger [in the company formation process].' Venture capitalists spend months or years courting academics, take the idea and plug in the management team: 'They [academics] are under more peer pressure *not* to [get diverted], at least in my area. The pressure to be top in research is of a totally different order. They rank themselves all the time. If you start a company it would mean taking your eye off the ball, they wouldn't do it. So there is this tremendous support structure.'

As for the venture capital community, one of its most distinctive characteristics – a function of the maturity of the ecosystem – is its 'class'-based system (a hierarchy that is only just beginning to develop in Europe). There is a very well defined top tier of venture firms in the USA, and nor is it simply the 'top tier' and the rest; the ranking extends, or at least has done in the past, down to 'third tier' venture capital firms as the pyramid widens. In the rarefied air at the top of the top tier, one sees mostly clearly how venture capital is a franchise business. As already discussed (Chapter 2), the two biggest determinants of success for any venture fund are vintage year – the year it was raised, hence determining the period in which it was invested – and the strength of the franchise. The franchise power of a Kleiner Perkins or a Sequoia brings with it, first, a monopoly on the best entrepreneurs. When Jim Clark wanted to start Healtheon (later merged with and renamed WebMD), his third billion dollar company after Silicon Graphics and Netscape Communications, he went back to KP (investors in Netscape) for funding. He was clearly not in search of cash. The pull of a brand name may also allow such firms to cut the better deal. The chief executive of one Sequoia portfolio company describes the process at what he views as one of the Valley's more ruthless firms: 'There is no emotion. It's all business. They will elbow out other firms to get a higher stake. It is called being Sequoiaed.'

The fact that the top tier firms attract the best entrepreneurs is one reason why they invest at the beginning of each technology wave, and reap the corresponding rewards for being early. Amazon (Kleiner-backed) was funded long before the business to consumer frenzy got going; Ariba (Benchmark) was early to the 'business-to-business' game; Cerent (Kleiner again) more or less created the photonics wave.

It operates at every level. The best headhunters want to work with top tier names, which helps their companies attract the best teams. The best law firms will be involved. Portfolio companies become 'hot' quicker because they are almost guaranteed press attention. (While the top tier display trappist tendencies with regard to speaking to the press about developments at their own firm, they are experts at using the media to promote their investments.)

Customers and suppliers are easier to find if you have top tier backing than if you are funded by some middle ranking, also-ran venture shop. Steve Katz at Powermarket describes how the brand has helped him: 'KP helps in getting the initial meetings – there is always a KP partner who can get you in through the door.' Then, for large corporations nervous of buying from a start-up that they fear might not be around to service its software, the KP name is again helpful: 'If the guy with the pen in his hand is hesitating, a phone call from John Doerr or Ray Lane [former number two at Oracle, now at KP] will do wonders to reduce nervousness.'

Meanwhile the much-vaunted KP *keiretsu* – the networking effect between its portfolio companies – functions not through formal relationships, but because there is a 'strong obligation' for companies to buy from one another. It was particularly effectively during the bubble, when boosting revenues (rather than profits) was the name of the game. Having a set of marquee name customers was also helpful when it came to the initial public offering.

Brand is hugely powerful, too, in that IPO process. If five companies with five different backers are all scrambling to go public at the same time, it is likely to be the one backed by the top tier VC that will attract the best investment bank. Even in the public markets, the identity of the venture backer of a company makes a big difference; a bit like which university or college you went to, says one non-top-tier VC wearily. During the bubble the top tier VCs milked that franchise to the hilt – so hard, indeed, that they are now in some quarters nicknamed the FTTs (the former top tiers). The franchise got overstretched at every level.

Here is one way the wheeze worked. 'Strategic' investors (corporations) got roped into providing 'dumb money' into highly priced pre-IPO rounds and buying some of the company's products or services at the same time. The venture firm would approach the chief financial officer, rather than the IT department, proposing a $20m investment: 'This is going to be a $10bn IPO, we can get you in at $1bn, you will make 10 x,' the promise ran. 'And by the way, with your $20m investment, will you buy $20m of software?' Apparently a win–win situation for either side: the company could show extra revenues and had plenty of money, the two things it most needed to go public (in addition to the backing of a well reputed venture fund). The only problem was that, at the tail end of the bubble, the start-ups never made it out onto the market and the CFO was left with $20m of software which the IT department told him was useless – particularly so nine months later when the start-up itself went bankrupt.

Relationships with limited partners also got stretched. It is a huge privilege as a limited partner to be admitted into one of the top tier funds. For years, allocations would routinely be cut back by large amounts even for those admitted into the hallowed circle, so the game became an effort of gaining favours to reduce the size of the cutbacks. So, in the early part of the downturn, some firms seduced their investors, particularly the smaller, less powerful ones, into investing directly into later stage follow-on rounds, when valuations were still high but funding from other venture firms was becoming tough to obtain. 'We are just missing $5m, this will help us get things done fast,' the investors were told. Hints would be dropped that they would be looked on favourably when it came to assessing allocations for the next fund.

The post-bubble shake-out across the industry will be prolonged – with between a third and a half of all US venture firms possibly disappearing. The carnage will be worst in the firms which had only raised one or two funds. With nothing but a dismal, end-of-bubble era performance record, they will be unable to return to investors for more cash. Perhaps the more interesting question is what happens to the top tier. The vast proportion will probably survive. Existing investors who have made handsome returns over many years will forgive them one or two duff funds (and access will possibly remain just as difficult). At the same time, the damage to the franchise value should not be estimated, and will have to be quietly rebuilt over years. The KP *keiretsu* after all is seen by some as having, in its way, contributed to the bubble by inflating revenues of participating companies.

The issue of succession will loom particularly large. Individuals who have made vast sums of money may well lack the motivation to carry on through testing times. Those firms with inequitable distribution of carried interest – with too much still going to retired partners as well as to the senior incumbents – may well have done a bad job of building the next generation and so may not endure in their current form. Some individuals will spin out into new firms, just as Benchmark was created in the mid-1990s from former partners of Merrill Pickard and Technology Venture Investors. Each cycle opens up the way for new groups to rise to the top, and this outsized cycle will be no different.

So what is right and what is wrong about US venture from the company's point of view? Do American venture capitalists help their companies more than European VCs? Are they really company builders? In the early days of the Valley – and of US venture capital more widely – success was built on a strong feeling of partnership with the entrepreneur, and often that came because investors had operating backgrounds. Don Valentine, founder of Sequoia Capital, who likes to quip he went to Fairchild Semiconductor Business School (he had joined that company in 1959, two years after it was started, in a sales and marketing role), talks about building Sequoia: 'We all had operating backgrounds, having been in small companies, and so were very empathetic with the entrepreneur in the start-up world.' Elsewhere, he says: 'We were going to build companies. We were going to build an industry once in a while but we were not going to do anything that required a lot of financial cleverness, because we didn't have any and we didn't need any . . . We were company builders' (Gupta 2000).

In the late 1990s, by stark contrast, when venture fund sizes exploded and firms raised money not because they needed it but because they could, any pretence at company building was jettisoned (although you would not have known it from the rhetoric). Falling over each other to do deals, some partners sat on as many as 16 different boards – and barely made board meetings by phone. While Europeans have been (rightly) criticized for drip-feeding their companies for years, the US problem has been the reverse – producing an entire failed generation of start-ups, force fed on a glut of capital, and with correspondingly twisted DNA. Close to the head of the procession of massively overfunded deals was online grocer Webvan, which raised a total of $1.2bn in venture funding (valuing it at the pre-IPO round at an estimated $4.3bn) before going bust 18 months after it went public. Just as Benchmark was crossing the Atlantic and boasting it would teach Europeans the art of company building (*Red Herring*, May 2000), this was the very moment when almost every US VC was simply priming for the public markets start-ups that were nothing more than concepts.

The billion dollar funds had arrived and no one had time to reflect that 20 years ago the average fund was about $20m, with two or three general partners each managing three to five investments. Europe did not have the monopoly on inexperienced VCs. One lesser known investor describes his elation at luring a top tier US VC into one of his portfolio companies – as an investor and board member – only to find the individual concerned was 'a very bright, very articulate ex-investment banker who had no industry experience and didn't bring a thing to the table'.

Today the picture is a good deal more complex. The best VCs can do powerful things for their companies, as in the instance of the founder of a Sequoia-backed company needing to make a difficult sales call. The right colleagues to support her were not around. So she rang Don Valentine, who was not the Sequoia partner on her board. Valentine came to the meeting and the company got the business. Another Sequoia example, Jerry Rudisin, founder and chief executive at Nightfire Software, describes how Sequoia partner Mike Moritz interviewed every new executive who would be directly reporting to him (Rudisin): 'It's my decision, obviously, but Sequoia are sticklers for high calibre people. It is better to live with a vacancy than a weak candidate, was their line.' This was during the bubble, when hiring was excruciatingly difficult. While other start-ups were content simply to rope in bodies, Moritz told Rudisin it was worth waiting for the right (senior) people, even if it took a year.

At the same time, one should be aware of some of the myths. The importance of an operational background – often cited as one of the big differences between US VCs commonly perceived to have it and European investors who do not – can be exaggerated. Plenty of the best known US VCs do not have operational experience; Moritz, for instance, was a journalist. There is also a school of thought that says too much involvement by former entrepreneurs, too much company building in other words, can suffocate a start-up: 'Since they are operating guys themselves, they have very strong opinions on how it should be done. They tend to smother the management team, they can't leave them alone, they are looking over their shoulder constantly,' says one former venture capitalist. As one US VC (without an operating background) puts it: 'No one would think of putting Hollywood agents in movies or vice versa.'

The fact is that the alchemy of venture capital is a peculiar and precarious balance for which there is no one single template. The foundations of the industry were, to a large degree, built by entrepreneurially minded types, often but by no means always with operational backgrounds: 'The great contribution of Arthur Rock, the Wall Street analyst, was in his shrewd judgments of people' (Valentine in Gupta 2000). Their successes delivered the great franchises in the industry, whose successes in turn became self-fulfilling. The bubble has certainly jeopardized that balance.

Venture capitalists forgot how to do their job properly – including how to search for deals. Well into the downturn a friend of mine ran into a VC from one of the smaller firms at PARC. 'You must tell me where to go [to find new deals],' he said to her. In the old days, he explained, 'we used to go tinkering for deals', but then he like others got fat and lazy as entrepreneurs flooded into the office and booted up the PowerPoint presentation. The VCs did not have to lift a finger. The spirit of partnership between entrepreneur and venture capitalist has also been compromised as risk-averse VCs have put ever more harsh terms into their agreements (see Chapter 13), pitting the two sides against each other in what is no longer a common endeavour.

Most significantly, the large funds have made it more or less impossible for themselves to do small deals. Some have even resorted to putting large chunks of money into private investments in public securities (PIPEs). Most have certainly moved later stage – they can finance C rounds (third rounds of financing) at A round prices, which means they can pay $20m pre-money valuations for companies with $20m in revenues. This allows them to check off a number of risk elements immediately. It also means that, as and when an exit window does open up, they can be quickly out of the gate – and all firms are desperate for exits so that they can return some capital to their investors, which in time will allow them to go fund raising again. The problem is that investments of two or three million dollars into early product development of a promising technology have dwindled alarmingly and the innovation machine is sputtering. Perhaps the biggest lesson of the Valley's recent bust is that venture capital does not 'scale'. The billion dollar funds took the business dangerously far from its roots.

At the end of each cycle, the Valley questions its future – and the gloom is deeper than ever this time. But memories are also very short, and extremely selective in the venture business. The balance will be restored, the infrastructure is still in place. Even initial public offerings will eventually recover – and a couple of decent IPOs are probably all it takes to kick start the machine again. European venture capitalists and entrepreneurs need to understand the power as well as the limits of the Valley model as they think about the way forward for venture in their own region.

References

Bunnell, D. (2000) *Making the Cisco Connection: The Story behind the Real Internet Superpower*, John Wiley & Sons Inc., New York.

Gupta, U. (ed.) (2000) *Done Deals*, Harvard Business School Press, Boston MA.

Quindlen, R. (2000) *Confessions of a Venture Capitalist*, Warner Books Inc., New York.

6

Other species:
angels and corporate venture capitalists

Angels

All the angels we know anything about are men.

(John Oliver Hobbes)

Whenever I attend a gathering of business angels, the occasion almost invariably seems to degenerate into a really good grouse about venture capitalists. Sometimes it can seem as if there is open warfare between the two classes of investor, when they are in fact two vital constituents of the same food chain. Venture capitalists tend to turn up their noses at most angels, regarding them as distinctly unprofessional and, well, slightly 'below the salt'. Angels either pay too much for young companies, they believe, setting up 'false expectations' in the mind of the entrepreneur, or are 'greedy bastards' who play on ignorance and take enormous stakes for very little money (and even less expertise).

Angels, unsurprisingly, heartily resent such attitudes. Says David Beer, who runs Beer & Partners, one of the UK's larger angel networks: 'Lots of VCs wouldn't hold a candle to our investors.' Jack Lang, former chief technologist at NTL and a prominent Cambridge business angel, adds: 'The

problem is – and I'm sure there are exceptions – that venture capitalists are neither venture nor capitalists. They try to take very safe and rather slow decisions, which are not very good nor entirely rational. And they don't have as
much money as they claim.' Lucius Cary, who has made more than 70 investments in very early stage businesses in the UK, claims he hardly knows a
single entrepreneur who has a good word to say about venture capitalists:
'But publicly there is an awful lot of biting of tongues because VCs do have
money.'

Of course, venture capitalists view angels as rivals, getting to invest in
companies before the venture capitalist does. Yet angels, often lacking the
resources to put more money into an investment, fail to capture those very
high returns. Hence the heavy dilution they face becomes a source of real tension. 'Venture capitalists screw you (as an angel) to the ground and I speak as
a venture capitalist,' says a senior figure in the Cambridge community.

David Giampaolo, who has merged three angel networks (VCR, PiCapital and iGabriel) to form a single entity that is both well connected and professionally run, argues that there is 'animosity on a deal by deal basis. But you
can't say all VCs are the devil. Just as they can't say all high net worth individuals are stupid so let's crush [by heavy dilution] them'.

Business angels are wealthy individuals who use their own cash – and often
their entrepreneurial and business skills – to back early stage companies. They
are to be distinguished, in terms of their net worth and probably business
acumen, from the alternative source of very early stage funding, namely the
three Fs – friends, family and fools. The monicker derives from the rich financiers of Broadway theatre productions and is intensely misleading. Whereas
the Broadway financiers were genuinely engaged in acts of philanthropy,
business angels are, or should be, hard-nosed businessmen involved in a commercial relationship, and not always necessarily behaving very angelically. The
wider catch-all term 'private investors' is probably more appropriate, but the
angel term remains common parlance (and so will be used here).

The angel community in Europe remains unsophisticated and disorgan-
ized compared with the USA. (Statistics on the angel market are even sketch-
ier than with venture capital. It is a little known fact that, according to some
experts, the cash supplied by US angels actually exceeds by some way that provided by venture capitalists. That applied even in 2000 at the height of the
bubble when $100bn was invested by so-called professional venture capital-
ists.) The silver lining is that, while American angels have been heavily
exposed to the internet craze and consequently badly burned, European
investors were newer to the game and the fall-out has been less severe. In the
UK, many had the good fortune to be forcibly excluded from the market by

the rash of newly created incubators which mopped up a good proportion of the crazier dotcom propositions.

The sources of wealth are also very different. In the USA, at least until recently, much of the cash has been earned in the technology sector – and by middle and senior ranking Cisco, Microsoft or Oracle executives as well as by successful entrepreneurs. In Europe, by contrast, much of the wealth is still old money, old *economy* money, or money earned from property or financial services. A few of the most prominent technology entrepreneurs such as Dr Mike Lynch of Autonomy and Sir Robin Saxby of ARM are investors in their own right. But, surprisingly, the Great Eastern Investment Forum, an active angel network in Cambridge, counts not a single technology millionaire among its members – despite the ample number created by companies such as ARM. Nigel Brown, founder of NW Brown, the financial services group which established GEIF, says: 'The few people who have made money from technology businesses [in the UK] tend to be risk averse. Maybe that is because they are smart and realize how hard it is to make money out of tech and acknowledge the role that luck plays in success.'

Private investors tend to invest in the industries in which they have made money, and which they feel they know and understand, so the origins of angel wealth impose a significant extra barrier to young technology companies in Europe, while also affording more of a chance to certain non-technology businesses. One of the first deals completed by the newly merged VCR/PiCapital was for Bodas, an upmarket lingerie company.

Angels and venture capitalists inhabit the same ecosystem. All too often, this crucial fact gets lost. Times are tough and animosities flare as angels see their stakes crushed in heavily dilutive later financing rounds. Yet this is precisely when it is all the more imperative that the two parties work together symbiotically. When the bulk of venture capitalists are moving to larger, later stage investments, credible angels are needed more than ever to step in at the outset. Otherwise venture firms will, in time, be very stuck for deal flow. A logical response might be for venture capitalists to cultivate dedicated networks of the more sophisticated angels, but remarkably few European firms seem to be trying to do that. In a funding bear market, some angels will say they intend to finance a company to profitability without planning to involve venture financiers at all. 'The very term follow-on financing makes me shiver,' says one scarred angel.

Decide early in the fund-raising process if angel financing is the right tactic. An easy mistake to make is wasting time with venture capitalists when the timing, size of the investment, or its nature is wrong for that market. Britart, an online contemporary art site, successfully raised angel funding, but not without losing time talking to a lot of venture capitalists first. Giles Howard, managing director of Britart, was doing the rounds in search of £1.5m – his first institutional round after angel seed finance – at the beginning of 2001: 'All the smaller VCs are staffed with people with not a lot of experience. They were very badly burned [after the bubble]. Nobody seemed to be investing. It was pretty clear they had lost the ability to judge anything; they were too shell shocked.' The timing was wrong, the amount was certainly too small for most venture capitalists – and being an e-commerce company a year after the dotcom bust was social death in the faddish world of venture capital. In the end he went back to angels and raised £700,000, less than he had planned, but enough to take him to profitability on a slightly scaled down plan.

When raising angel money, it is crucial to understand how it differs from venture capital, and the strings with which it comes. This in turn will help you avoid the sort of deal structures that put off venture capitalists at a later date. The basic difference is simple enough. Angels invest their own money, while venture capitalists invest on behalf of others, mostly institutional investors. This means, among other things, that angels can often move a lot more speedily.

Alain Falys, chief executive of Open Business Exchange, who seems to have corralled half the *Sunday Times* Rich List as backers, was on the Eurostar in early April 2000 and just about to enter the tunnel when an important telephone call came through. Falys was still working at Visa International at the time, but hard at work for his idea of an electronic invoice delivery service. The caller was John Hunt, a serial entrepreneur and one of the founders of First Tuesday. 'Would $100,000 help?' Hunt enquired. Later in the fundraising Falys went to see Peter Ogden, co-founder of Computacenter. Falys had worked at a company in Paris that had been a joint venture with Computacenter, so he went to see Ogden – for advice, not money. 'Can I put some money in?' Ogden asked. Falys said yes, how much did he want to put in? 'How much do you need?' Ogden invested $500,000. These were the heady days of 2000, clearly, but Falys's angels were also serious backers, who reinvested in subsequent rounds after the market turned. At any stage of the cycle, active angels will tend to react much more quickly than a professional venture capitalist. They are working on their own, they may know the industry well, and they do not have an investment committee to convince.

A venture capitalist will want detailed market research, which he may well try and charge the company to carry out. Angels, on the other hand, will tend to ask themselves: 'Does this look like a big market?' Even those that do carry out very detailed research will generally be faster. To the extent they are businessmen rather than financial investors, they may ask very different questions. Falys again:

"Because they are business people they were more concerned if the client would take on the service. There were more practical questions on customers and implementation. The VCs were more about when we would reach cash break-even, and what our multiples at exit might be. I have never had an angel putting conditions on exits or even forcing me to venture an opinion on exits."

At the same time, angels come in many hues and, just as with venture capital, care is required in choosing the right sort of investor. The dotcom bubble brought in a lot of 'newbies' to the game, most of whom have disappeared (at least for now). During the bubble, if people heard the word technology, they pulled out their cheque book; just like the trader in Haarlem, during tulip-mania in the seventeenth century who 'was known to pay one half of his fortune for a single root, not with the design of selling it again at a profit, but to keep in his own conservatory for the admiration of his acquaintance' (Mackay 1841: 89). Many of these managed to be both ignorant and interfering. A software engineer recalls the breed:

"They weren't experienced angels. They just had a lot of dough. They wouldn't leave the companies alone. What they really wanted to do was show off, tell the world they knew how to do it."

There is a lot of confusion as to the extent to which angels wish to roll up their sleeves and get involved in the companies they back. Doug Richard, founder of Cambridge Angels, an exclusive network that deliberates over dinner at high table at a different Cambridge University college each meeting, is convinced that involvement in the company is more or less a defining quality: 'People become business angels because they want to participate in – rather than just put money into – a new venture.' A serial entrepreneur himself, he explains: 'I live for this stuff. I love starting companies.' Giampaolo, by contrast, says a large proportion of the members of his network *don't* get involved, although he believes that is down at least as much to time constraints as to a matter of preference. Be sure whether you are getting financial investors or entrepreneurial angels (a mixture may work well).

So entrepreneurs need to be clear what sort of relationship the individual angel, or group of angels, envisages. Obviously one of the biggest potential benefits of angel money can be the association with a businessman with real operational skills – the area in which venture capitalists are so often deemed to be lacking. As Giampaolo puts it: 'It is not that venture firms don't contain a lot of bright people. But the support, advice and wisdom you get may be greater. I'm not saying they are smarter but [those you get involved] may have a bit more time and a bit more passion.'

Cary adds: 'When angels ask what can they do to help they generally seem to mean it. With VCs you feel less that they are trying to help and more that they are simply out to make as much money for themselves as they can.' But like venture capitalists, they do not always deliver. Lennart Ramberg of Altitun in Sweden got angel funding from one of Sweden's most prominent angels (who, as sometimes happens, formalized his investments and became a venture capitalist): 'He spent ages telling us what an intimate relationship he had with his companies. We have talked on the phone maybe twice since.'

A significant downside to consider is that you are dealing with an individual, not a professional firm. The venture capital process can be something of a lottery in terms of the characters involved, but with a business angel investor you may be yet more exposed to an individual's idiosyncrasies. Beware of the type, for instance, who is convinced that the way he did things the 'last time' is the blueprint for all future success. Talk to other companies this individual has helped fund. Do they possess a string of awkward preconceptions? What were the (inevitable) disputes about? How did they behave when things started to go wrong? Angels do not have the deep pockets a venture capitalist has (or may have) and, of course, it is their own money. Will they panic and suddenly seek to withdraw money? If a €2m investment is going wrong for a venture capitalist sitting on a €100m fund, that is one thing; for an inexperienced angel with €750,000 on the line – possibly a substantial chunk of his investable fortune – it is another. The wrong sort of angel, without the mandatory nerves of steel, can amplify the problem considerably. 'If it's most of your fortune and it's in trouble you will be there 24 hours a day, and you will make the trouble seem bigger', says one angel who has learnt the hard way.

One category of angel to avoid is the virgin angel – someone who has never done it. There are a surprising number of people who like to imagine they are angels. The idea of backing high-risk companies appeals, but when it comes to signing a cheque they become afflicted by sudden seizure of the wrist as it dawns on them they may never see the cash again. They can clearly be quite considerable time-wasters.

Hunting down good angel investors can seem daunting to all but the exceptionally well-connected entrepreneur. There are basically two routes – trawling to the outer reaches of your professional and social circle, or finding an established angel network. The former may not be as hard as you think, with a little imagination. If you choose the latter route, you need to do your homework because all networks are very much *not* equal. The most developed angel market in Europe, the UK, has no shortage of networks, though of a distinctly uneven quality. In other countries, organizations are developing. Peter Jungen, a German entrepreneur who knows his way around the upper echelons of the German government, adopted the top-down approach to creating local organizations. Within three years, the number of angel networks climbed from zero to 48: 'The idea is to attract people who have money and operational skills, but who don't know how to engage. People don't become business angels naturally.' Unfortunately, the appetite for risk investing took a huge knock in Germany after the bubble burst, and the nascent angel activity was almost entirely choked off.

But while networks in the USA are on the whole very professionally run, too many of those in Europe are not. They are subscale, with too few members and hence a poor quality of deal flow, and providing a fraction of the services they claim to offer. One well-known regional UK forum is described by one of its detractors as 'infested with bankers, lawyers and accountants trying to sell their services'. Many also charge high fees – sometimes imposed on the company raising funds, sometimes on the investor. Not that the fees have proved high enough to cover their costs. A lot had a flawed business model in the first place, insofar as they were too dependent on successful realizations to meet often unrealistically high overheads, which of course failed to materialize in the downturn. PiCapital, for instance, established at the end of 1997 with the backing of such luminaries as veteran venture capitalist Michael Stoddart had, after more than four years, yet to secure a complete exit, but had high overheads, including offices in Mayfair.

Giampaolo's new group, which screens companies to present at regular meetings to investor, aims to address those problems – attaining scale and furnishing a professionally run service. One important element of that is recommending to members that they reserve funds for follow-on investments, as all too few did during the bubble period only to see their stakes crushingly diluted. It is also clearly in the company's interests to know it has angels for whom the involvement is not just a single throw of the dice. Soon after the merger, Giampaolo was able to point to a successful exit for one of the PiCapital portfolio companies too.

When structuring an angel deal, entrepreneurs need to think about future funders, including the venture capitalist. Venture investors say they will be put off by fragmented, complicated structures (as if their own, incidentally, were something other than hideously complex). Nigel Brown, partner of the Cambridge Gateway Fund, says 'off-putting body language' includes situations where an angel has grabbed 80 per cent of the equity, or 'festooned the capital structure with different classes of shares and too many pre-emption rights'. Having too many private investors dotted around the world – which makes a production of basic things such as collecting signatures – is also cause for concern.

The beauty of angel money is that it should actually come with simple documentation. Lucius Cary made his first 40 investments with a two-page letter which everybody signed. It cost nothing and no lawyers were involved. The first investment he did with 3i caused some consternation. A 3i executive asked to see the legal agreement – and he produced the letter. 'No, the *legal* agreement', he said. When the executive got over his astonishment, the letter was duly dispatched and deemed to be perfectly legal. (Cary now invests through a public company vehicle and things have to be more formal.) Often angels will invest in ordinary shares – forgoing the multiple rights that attach to preference shares, the VC instrument of choice. One may legitimately question why angels do not protect themselves with preference shares, but tax can be one reason. The generous tax schemes that now apply in some European countries, such as Enterprise Investment Scheme relief in the UK, generally stipulate that the investment is made in ordinary not preference shares (although private investors operating through trusts are not concerned by such matters). The investment agreement will certainly be much simpler.

Unlike a venture capitalist, the angel is most unlikely to insist you install a new chief executive. Investing their own, not other people's money, they are much more inclined to take a pragmatic view. 'Warranties', says Lang, 'are probably not worth the paper they are written on.' It is impossible to generalize about how much equity to cede at this stage. Says Richard: 'In the myopia of optimism, many angels don't take enough equity at the start. The road is longer and demands more money in more rounds than anyone ever expects.' Others get away with being fantastically greedy. A large minority stake is probably the maximum you should consider giving up.

One instrument to consider seriously if you are planning to bring in VCs at the next round is a convertible loan, which gives the angels shares at a discount (perhaps 15 or 20 per cent) to the price of the new round. This addresses the problem that angels are often judged by the VC to have paid the wrong price (sometimes too much, sometimes too little). Interestingly, angels appear to have adjusted their return expectations in a downturn far more quickly than venture capitalists, meaning that they are theoretically at least a source of considerably cheaper money. When many VCs apparently still had their heads in the clouds, cheerfully talking about '10x' returns – a multiple of ten times their money – angels were already conceding that their expectations have been lowered dramatically. Many say they are looking for multiples of between two and five times.

The angel community is a crucial source of early stage finance and, while immature in Europe, it is developing despite the downturn. This form of investing arguably has a particular appeal at a time of falling public markets insofar as private investors enjoy added control over an angel investment. At the very worst, they can tell themselves, they are losing money at their own instigation, rather than paying the investment professionals to do it for them. Individual angels say they have become more discriminating investors as a result of the money lost in recent years. Lang admits to being 'much more sceptical as to whether an idea has got legs. In the old days, people would say: The internet is immense, we will do it on the internet therefore we will be immense. Today you have to argue to me much more why you will get a proportion of that market.'

Adds Giampaolo: 'You can be young and clever, but you can't be young and wise. For me it's been so humbling, I didn't bet the farm, but I put a meaningful amount of post-tax earnings into [investments in the bubble period].' The subsequent fall-out brought him back to his roots: 'I won't invest in people I don't know. You have to get enough soundings from people who have already invested in [these entrepreneurs]. And I don't want to hear how someone has floated nine companies. I'd rather hear a story about how they handled a rough patch.'

Links

European Business Angel Network   www.eban.org
(umbrella organization and gateway
to (a not yet very comprehensive) list
of national networks)

National Business Angel Networks   www.nationalbusangels.co.uk
(the UK government-backed national
angel network)

UK private investor network   www.picapital.co.uk

Great Eastern Investment Forum   www.geif.co.uk
Cambridge, UK

Munich angels   www.munichnetwork.com
(for German business angels, there is
an excellent set of links via the TBG
site)   www.tbgbonn.de

British Venture Capital Association www.bvca.co.uk

French networks   www.leonardofinance.fr
                                         www.croissanceplus.com
                                         www.franceangels.org

Angels and Venture Capitalists compared

Angels

Positives

◆ Invests in earlier stage businesses

◆ May well possess operational experience, industry knowledge

◆ Exhibits passion and commitment

◆ May (or may not, see below) be better at supporting management through bad times

◆ Not as focused on exit, may have longer time horizons

◆ Moves quickly

◆ May be less influenced by the fashionable 'space' of the moment

Drawbacks

◆ Limited resources

◆ May panic when net worth goes south

◆ May be an interfering idiot in search of a job

Venture capitalists

Positives

◆ Credibility for the company as a result of backing from a big name venture capital firm

◆ Deeper pockets

◆ Extensive network (true at least of the better VCs)

◆ As a professional investor may (or may not) be less prone to panic when things go wrong

Drawbacks

◆ Less ready to commit to very early stage businesses

◆ Focused on exit and financial return to the firm's investors

◆ May lack operational experience

◆ Investment process is laborious

Corporate venture capitalists

A corporation cannot blush.
(attributed to Howel Walsh)

Corporate venture capital funds work on the Lifo (accounting) principle, one senior European venture capitalist likes to quip: Last in, first out. This refers to the tendency of corporations to plunge into the venture business at precisely the wrong moment in any cycle. Hence their reputation for being suppliers of 'dumb money' and the certain disdain in which they are generally held by 'professional' venture capitalists.

Corporate venturing is a loose term that can signify a host of different activities, and at its broadest simply denotes a minority investment by one company in another. For entrepreneurs in search of cash, the most relevant form is the in-house venture fund or division, set up by a large corporation to invest in promising external start-ups. Such corporates may have a number of motives for getting into the business, ranging from the lure of financial gains in buoyant markets, to strategic objectives such as gaining a 'window' on new technologies. They can be a useful source of capital for young companies and may also provide anything from the endorsement of a brand name corporation to useful customer, supplier or distribution relationships. But the limitations of this source of capital need to be well understood alongside the potential benefits.

Corporate venture funds certainly chased the new economy of the late 1990s in their hordes. Arriving late in the day, attracted by the lucrative returns financial investors were seen to be achieving, they got caught up in the fashion of the moment, and overpaid for bad companies in an overheated marketplace. In the bubble, losses were further exaggerated because many corporate funds invested relatively large amounts of cash in later funding rounds – where valuations were particularly excessive and the collapse consequently the more brutal. The bulk of the new entrants then inevitably rushed out again in short order as they found they were not making easy money. Losses had mounted and shareholders had gone from viewing a listed company's venture fund as a natty accessory whose very existence enhanced the share price, to regarding it as a drag on resources and earnings and a distraction from the core business.

In the USA, a third of the corporate venturing community active in September 2000 had stopped backing start-ups a year later and overall investment levels had collapsed 80 per cent, according to Venture Economics, the US private equity research house. The very fact that venturing is not one of the core activities induces extra angst. For a venture capitalist, making losses is, at least in theory, seen to be part of the game; for a corporate, venture losses take a good deal more explaining. 'Most corporates' core competence is not investment, so they fail', says Mike Volpi, a senior Cisco executive and former chief strategy officer, bluntly.

Young companies seeking corporate venture capital need to think about some of the basic differences between this source of financing and traditional venture money. First, as has been seen, it is a good deal more capricious. The limited partners of a venture fund commit for ten or more years, whereas the corporate limited partner can often effectively turn off the tap at an instant's notice. Those with a longer track record such as Intel Capital, SAP and Siemens are likely to be safer bets. But brand names do not of themselves furnish any sort of guarantee as regards longevity. Dell Ventures, the corporate venturing arm of Dell Computer, was a well-structured group, but the volatility of its earnings – enormous profits in the good times almost immediately followed by gaping losses when the markets reversed – created pressures which, along with tensions surrounding the remuneration structure, caused the outfit to blow apart.

When corporations decide to fold their venturing units, this robs portfolio companies not just of a future source of cash but may bestow on them an entirely new owner – and hence destroy the non-financial aspects of the relationship. A number of companies have offloaded their technology portfolios to a breed of specialist private equity player called secondaries funds which specialize in buying unwanted private equity holdings from institutions.

Further, while the goals of a venture firm are pretty clear – achieving strong capital gains within a defined period of time – the motives and drivers for a corporation are considerably more complex. Is it engaging in the activity primarily to make money, to learn about new potentially disruptive technologies, to boost sales, or because everyone else is doing it and it thinks it cannot afford to miss out? Many will have a mix of 'financial' and 'strategic' goals. But what exactly does 'strategic' mean, and how do the two differing objectives mesh? Not infrequently, these are issues about which the corporation itself is pretty muddled.

Broadly, strategic corporate venturers are in the game for the direct benefit they believe the investment will bring to the growth of their business. Corporate venturing was among the remits of Nick Earle, that rare breed of an Englishman with marketing talent, who ran Hewlett-Packard's internet business and strategy in the late 1990s. In between throwing 'the best party ever' in Silicon Valley – the location was a mansion in Atherton with sharpshooters to protect the 25 Picassos flown in from Europe – he was also overseeing the building of a then fashionable *keiretsu* of e-commerce businesses within the venture unit. 'I wasn't measured according to gain on equity,' he says, 'I was measured on orders. It was all about a catch-up play for HP on the internet.' The unit – whose investments included $10m into EasyEverything, the chain of internet cafés, because Earle 'just liked' Greek entrepreneur Stelios Haji Ioannou and 'believed he could do it' – brought $500m of new business to HP in 12 months, Earle claims.

At the same time, 'strategic benefits' can be pretty loosely defined. Intel Capital, which has invested since the early 1990s around the world, from Santa Clara, California to China, would, at least for many years, invest in anything that enhanced the use of the personal computer, and inevitably became tagged as following the 'spray and pray' approach.

During a downturn, those entities investing purely for financial motives pretty much evaporate – as the markets go against them and they discover that the business of making investments is rather harder than they anticipated. Those that are purely strategic, while apparently more durable, do need to have a parent that is able to understand, and stomach, large losses. The most effective units are probably those which combine a team that has proper venture capital skills – able to negotiate term sheets and so on – with a strong idea of the kind of strategic value the investment can bring to the wider group, and the ability to follow it through.

It is important, again, to understand the structure of the operation. There are many different models, which can range from a look-alike venture capital fund in a discreet unit with a dedicated team and pool of money, to much looser arrangements where there is simply a sum of money allocated by the board (the fruit of a decision that could be just as quickly rescinded) and a bunch of people who are only devoting part of their time to the endeavour.

Various hybrid structures have also emerged in Europe. One of the most ambitious has been b-business partners, set up in March 2000 by Investor, ABB and others, mostly prominent Swedish companies with connections to the Wallenberg empire. Originally a €1bn pan-European e-commerce investment vehicle (later moving into 'real' technology), it was structured as a company (not a fund). In tune with the times, it was initially going to float within three years, and it sat somewhere between a pure venture capitalist and a corporate venturer. The advantages of the corporate connection included supposedly superior technical due diligence resources – and, of course, a hinterland of powerful customers. Each deal would be sponsored by one of the shareholders. It was a neat idea but extremely hard to execute. Did the sponsor have any real clout with those in the organization making the buying decisions, for instance? The fact that it was not dependent on the purse strings of a single corporate also looked superficially attractive, but in practice there were already delicate negotiations when ABB hit its own troubles in early 2002 and needed to return to its core business and pay down debt, leading it to sell most of its shareholding to Investor.

Another important factor is where the unit sits in the organization and the level of seniority of the individual to whom the venture guys report. If it is the chief executive of the overall company, that is clearly telling. Groups which have the full, long-term support of the board are rather more likely to be successful. These board members need to understand the venture capital process – that losses materialize long before profits are forthcoming – and to have ways of measuring the strategic as well as financial benefits. Meanwhile, decision-making processes may be a lot more bureaucratic and slow moving than in a small venture partnership. In some large US corporations, European start-ups can find themselves receiving approval at regional level, only to experience a delay of many more weeks as a separate set of US bosses have to sign off on the deal.

An additional conundrum for corporate venturing outfits relates to the remuneration and the calibre of the staff. During the bubble, corporate VCs with hastily assembled teams were some of the most inexperienced operators around. One was heard referring, apparently in all innocence, to a colleague, describing his qualifications to be a venture capitalist: 'He was at Insead at the same time as Julie Meyer [a founder of First Tuesday] you know.' Somewhat ironically, corporate venturing units were set up in the internet boom partly as a mechanism to retain 'talent' by giving people the opportunity to work in a more entrepreneurial environment, with the potential for greater rewards. Outside such frenzied periods, the opposite problem is often cited; namely that the best people want to work in the mainstream part of the business, not in an apparent outpost. In terms of competing for experienced venture capitalists, meanwhile, there is an additional problem in that the carry system (see Chapter 2) is almost impossible to reconcile with most corporate hierarchies. If things are going well, employees within the venture division, on carry-type rewards, could in time be earning more than the chief executive, creating a clearly unacceptable imbalance. Another difficulty is knowing how to reward those around the organization who may be contributing considerably to any successes.

This can lead to unexpected problems. Lennart Ramberg of Altitun, a Swedish optical start-up, recalls a sudden hitch with Telia, the Swedish telecoms operator, which had invested in the company in January 2000. Altitun was poised to close its sale to ADC Telecommunications for $832m – making history in Swedish terms. But was there anyone around from Telia to come to the signing? 'It was extremely disorganized. It was impossible to get anyone to come to the final closing. [The Telia executive] said: "I'm probably not as enthusiastic about this deal as you are. I'm about to go to bed".' Ramberg's observation was that there was 'something horribly wrong in the incentive structure – if there is one'. That is not to say that there are not good people within corporate venture capital, but those that are effective will need extra skills – not least the political nous and clout to get things done in a big organization.

How to make it work

When picking a corporate venture backer, try and ascertain what their goals are

Do their goals seem to make sense? One newly formed corporate venturer observed in some astonishment: 'We spent an intensive two weeks getting to know the company – and they must have spent all of 20 minutes asking questions about how we work. It is amazing.' Clarity at this stage will help the relationship later. If the thinking seems woolly, it probably is, which could spell trouble down the road.

Understand your own objectives

Do you essentially want the name? Or a hard-to-get early reference customer? Or access to distribution channels? Even more than with venture capitalists, the exercise should be about more than just securing an infusion of cash.

Plenty of young companies take corporate money for window-dressing purposes, which can be a perfectly sensible motive. Even the most promising start-up will itself have next to no visibility in the wider world, and in Europe the brands of good venture firms are not necessarily that widely known either. Being backed by a well-known multinational technology corporation, on the other hand, can send a powerful message – to customers, suppliers, future employees and investors. But young companies looking for a deeper relationship with their backer have to bear in mind that an investment from the venture arm does not confer the right to walk straight into the group chief executive's office.

Some corporate VCs will fund the investment and then make introductions on the business side later, using the promises of future relationships almost as a bargaining chip to secure a better financial deal; others will show their hand earlier. 'We almost decouple the two. We certainly like to add value even if we do not invest,' says Diana Noble, chief executive of Reed Elsevier Ventures, the venture arm of the Anglo-Dutch media group.

Find out about the experiences of other companies in the corporate's portfolio

Are initial promises fulfilled? Having the corporate as a customer, or as a distribution channel, can obviously be very valuable – particularly in a downturn when start-ups face a raft of extra hurdles selling to big corporations, whose energies are focused elsewhere and who question the longevity of any small company. Marc Zuegel at Allianz Venture Partners says that a small company can spend 12 to 18 months selling into a large organization. He claims AVP can cut the process down to three to six months.

Access to established international distribution channels could, for instance, be immensely valuable to a start-up in the early stages of globalizing its activities. But you need to know how you will achieve that. Remember that the corporate VC deal makers are not the decision makers on operational matters, even if they are probably the first point of contact.

Don't underestimate, either, the difficulty of actually making it happen. Accenture, the global consultancy group, announced a $1bn commitment to venture capital in 2000 and two years later took a $212m charge, closed the operation and sold the bulk of the portfolio to CIBC. The idea had been that not only would the brand assure plenty of deal flow but that Accenture consultants would provide a valuable distribution channel for small software companies. Getting it to work was obviously another matter. Nor does global expertise in enterprise resource planning within big companies necessarily bring with it the skills to deal with small entrepreneurial businesses.

Understand the dynamics of the structure

Try and find out about the decision-making process. It is likely to be much more cumbersome than that of a venture capitalist. John Taysom, whose first corporate venture investment on behalf of Reuters – Yahoo – later proved to be a bit of a winner recalls having to secure more than 30 signatures to authorize the deal. A common complaint is the difficulty of getting a final commitment. Just when you think you have got there, up pops someone else with a view – and possibly a veto. Who takes the final decision? Is it the group that manages the fund, or are there additional layers of executives involved? What exactly are they looking for? Some corporate venturers will invest in a business with a product that colleagues say they themselves would never use; others use the results of in-house technical due diligence as the basis of their decision making.

Try and ensure useful input from the corporate VC to your board

Corporate venture capitalists often opt for observer status because of concerns about director liability. But the right individual can offer a valuable perspective on wider markets and trends. One entrepreneur backed by Intel Capital recalls the board observer was a line manager rather than an investor from Intel Capital. 'His title changed every three months, so it was impossible to tell what he actually did. But he seemed to have a senior European job and what was important is that he was very helpful in terms of his views on marketing,' says the entrepreneur. Think through concerns about confidentiality, though. There may be meetings from which the observer should be excluded, particularly if you are considering selling your company to the corporate.

Aim for the right mix

Young companies will often want a complementary mix of traditional venture capitalists and a corporate VC. As Mike Volpi of Cisco Systems says: 'A smart entrepreneur will bring in VCs and corporates in the right mix.' Many corporate VCs will not lead a financing round, instead taking part in a venture syndicate and relying on a credible VC. But they will ask similar questions and will generally pride themselves, rightly or wrongly, on applying 'normal VC criteria'.

Research by the London Business School (Maula and Murray, 2002) found that venture backed IT companies which launched IPOs during 1998 and 1999 and which had backing from more than one corporation received higher valuations when they listed than those with either a single corporate venturer or those with just venture backing. One reason, they argue, is that multiple investors mean reduced potential for conflicts of interest. Not that the two types of investor will always get on. Some venture capitalists may have deeply held prejudices about corporate VCs who labour under unwieldy decision-making processes and fail to deliver on time (not to mention possessing an uncertain commitment to the whole area).

Think through possible sources of conflict

Will the choice of one or other corporate VC limit your future customer base because of competitive issues? Will the two companies become direct competitors – like streaming media company Real Networks, which took a chunky investment from Microsoft only to fall out badly when the latter brought out its own competing software.

Will exit routes be limited because you are prevented from selling to a rival? Look at the term sheet carefully. If you have other venture capitalist investors, they should be allies in fighting unreasonable demands because they will not want their own position jeopardized.

Are there other awkward competitive issues? One company complained that, some while after its IPO, when its stock was languishing in the '90 per cent' club (the less than exclusive group of stocks that had lost more than 90 per cent of their value since their peak), its corporate investor sold its position, halving the already fragile price, because it had not switched from a rival provider of servers to the company's own servers.

Sometimes the deal can hamper your style more generally. Corporates can for instance be oversensitive to branding issues. When it launched a promotion for furry handcuffs on its website, Lastminute.com apparently received a call from Intel, one of its early investors, saying that this sort of activity contravened the terms of the agreement (which part being not entirely clear). Lastminute sent Intel a pair of handcuffs, jollily pointing out the Santa Clara-based giant was 'handcuffed' to the small company.

The best corporate venturers, however, do have important things to offer an early stage company. For the relationship to work it has to be a clear two-way street. You need to be sure there are compelling reasons why the corporation can be useful to you, and be clear that the corporate sees strategic value in the relationship in its own quest for innovation as a source of future long-term growth. Too many start-ups have taken the corporate shilling without giving much thought to any of these issues – and come to regret it.

References

Mackay, C. (originally published 1841) *Extraordinary Popular Delusions and the Madness of Crowds*, (1995 edn.) Wordsworth Editions Ltd, Hertfordshire.

Marla, M. and Murray, G. C. (2002) Corporate Venture Capital And The Creation of US Public Companies: The Impact of Sources of Venture Capital on The Performance of Portfolio Companies. In Hitt, M. A., Amit, R., Lucien, C., Nixon, R. D., (eds) Creating Value: Winners in the New Business Environment, Oxford, Blackwell.

Links

Corporate VCs

www.evca.com
www.intel.com/capital
www.corporateventuringuk.org

PART TWO

The process

7

Fit for venture capital?

You have deeply ventured;
But all must do so who greatly win.
(Byron, *Marino Faliero*, 1821)

IN THE SUMMER OF 1999, Ernesto Schmitt, a twenty-something management consultant, raised venture capital valuing his proposal for an internet music site at $20m – and was five times oversubscribed. Peoplesound consisted of a business plan and a team of four individuals, two still in full-time employment elsewhere. The launch of the site was four months away when the funding round closed. Schmitt, who certainly did not lack for self-belief, told me a couple of months later that half the venture capitalists he saw said he had to be joking. The rest 'got over the pain threshold and were willing to pay for a good deal'.

For a period of about 18 months in Europe, from early 1999 to the summer of 2000, venture capital was virtually free as venture investors poured money into start-ups at dizzying valuations. John Bates, the former CEO of a string of venture-backed start-ups, who teaches entrepreneurship at the London Business School, gave a class on how to value a business plan in order to raise cash. When I ask him what he told his students, he laughs and says it is 'too embarrassing' to recall. Since the downturn, venture capital has returned to its more natural state of being expensive money that is hard to procure. As we have remarked, there is no lack of jaundiced entrepreneurs who vow they will never take venture capital again. A good proportion were naive about what the process entailed in the first place. Not unnaturally, they grabbed venture capital because it was so cheap – and only found out later about the many elements that could come back and bite them.

Others have a point. The bubble sucked in countless inexperienced investors who, out of ignorance or arrogance or both, did scandalously unprofessional jobs. Most established venture investors were also culpable of smothering start-ups in capital and cheering them on their trip to the moon one moment, and pulling back sharply in panic the next to insert egregious financing terms and thereby drive a serious wedge between them and the management with whom they were supposedly in partnership.

The questions to ask

As an entrepreneur, the trick is to go into the relationship with your eyes open, understanding the advantages – namely what are you getting in exchange for parting with a portion of your company's equity – and also having thought through the strings that are attached. The smarter venture capitalist realizes it is not in his interests to upset the management he has backed. 'Don't take our money if you want a quiet life,' says one investor, summing up the realities of venture life. 'But venture capital is the way to get maximum leverage to grow fast.'

Why should I even consider venture capital?

If your image of the venture capitalist is of a money-grabbing individual taking a large slice of your equity and interferring with your business while all the time pursuing a hidden agenda of trying to boot you out from your own company, venture capital is not for you. However, if you buy into the dream and believe you are going to create the next Cisco Systems or Genentech – or, let's face it, a much more modest but fast growth business – venture capital is more or less the only route.

At its best, venture capital is a partnership. Together you and your investor aim to build a bigger, faster growth business. The standard venture capitalist's line to persuade you to part with a piece of your precious equity is it is much better to own a small piece of a larger pie than a large piece of a small pie. As was noted earlier, while you ask your banker how much money he will lend you, you should ask a prospective venture partner how much money he will make you. The venture capitalist is not there to run the business for you. But, if he is doing his job properly, he offers sound advice based on experience, enabling him to spot and interpret patterns in your company and industry that perhaps you cannot see. He should be able to use his wide network to help with anything from sales leads to recruitment. He should provide rigour and focus, and generally help you make that bigger pie. But you need to be convinced of the value of the offering, as well as to pick a good investor. Too many venture capitalists get away with providing next to nothing – not least because entrepreneurs end up taking their money with far too little thought.

The acid test for a venture capitalist is when second- and third-time entrepreneurs who are independently wealthy come for backing – like Jim Clark, already mentioned, who called on Kleiner Perkins to build both his second (Netscape) and third (Healtheon, now Web MD) billion dollar company. He clearly felt he would be more successful with KP money than without.

At what stage will the venture capitalist invest in my business?

The funding life cycle of a young venture capital backed business looks something like this:

1 **Seed.** The beginning of a company's life cycle when it is developing a prototype product and the business plan.

   Who invests: friends and family, angels, specialist seed capital providers, venture capitalists (when the market is really hot).

2 **Start-up/early stage.** When the company is developing the product, manufacturing, testing with early customers, through to early customer sales.

   Who invests: venture capitalists, depending on the cycle. Also some angels.

3 **Growth.** The company is making sales (and in a bear funding market will have needed to demonstrate profitability), but needs more capital, for example, to develop further products, increase capacity, internationalize.

   Who invests: venture capitalists, and corporations and banks in bull markets.

4 **Pre-IPO or 'mezzanine'.** This form of funding occurs when the market is open for initial public offerings. During the bubble, pre-IPO constituted mid-stage, because companies could be floated when they had few customers and were heavily loss making.

   Who invests: venture capitalists, corporations, banks, crossover funds (which invest in both private and public equities). These late stage investors, who are hoping for a quick turn on their money from an IPO or sale of the business, contribute cash but comparatively little 'value add'.

5   **IPO.** Introduction to the public markets. When the markets are receptive to IPOs, these represent an 'exit' for the venture capitalist, in time, as well as an opportunity for the entrepreneur to sell some of his holding. (A sale of the company to a corporation – 'trade sale' – is a much more likely 'exit' route.)

Who invests: large public institutions and retail investors.

Mike Doonesbury, the US cartoon character, was explaining internet logic to his daughter. 'Profitability is for wimps,' he tells her. 'It means your business plan wasn't aggressive enough. It's OK to lose a lot of money as long as it's on purpose.' The stage at which a venture capitalist will invest depends heavily on the state of the cycle, as we have already seen. At the top, the exuberant herd moves to the earliest and riskiest stage of the business, splashing out multimillions on sometimes unproven technologies at valuations that are highly favourable to the entrepreneur. When the market turns, venture capitalists batten down the hatches, and making profits suddenly becomes *le dernier cri*.

To the extent they invest at all, the bar is raised dramatically. They seemingly want it all: a company with revenues, proven technology, a more or less complete – and star – management team, and profitability within sight. And for all this they will intend to pay a very modest valuation. 'Team, technology, traction [VC jargon for sales]' become the three watchwords; moving later stage and 'derisking' the name of the VC game. The collapse in valuations also means that investors can put money into more developed (and therefore theoretically less risky) companies at the sort of valuations they were paying previously for seed or start-up exposure.

Another crucial factor in the stage at which a venture firm will invest relates to the size of the fund it manages. Apax Partners, which raised €4.4bn in its last fund, cannot sensibly invest in chunks of €1m or €2m. The firm insists it still invests in early stage companies, but in order to make an impression on a fund that size it sets the bar almost impossibly high, namely those it thinks will make it a profit on its investment of €100m or so. To avoid wasting a lot of time, find out – from other chief executives, advisers including lawyers, and the like – what sort of deals venture capitalists are actually doing, and select investors who are appropriate to your stage of business.

How do I fund the business until I get to the point where I can try to secure venture capital?

Assuming the venture capital cycle is not in one of its overheated moods, your business will in its initial phases follow the traditional rite of passage for start-ups – bootstrapping. You get going anyway you can with the help of credit cards, bank loans, second mortgages. Many young technology companies earn consultancy income on the side. And of course, there is no substitute for funding from customer revenues. Start-ups often make the mistake of trying to perfect the product before launch. Don't. Go out and get customers. You can then fine tune the product as you learn more about their requirements.

If you sell any equity it will probably be to the three Fs – friends, family and fools. Angels are an important alternative source (Chapter 6). Incubators are another possibility. Heavily tarnished as a concept from the dotcom days, when such outfits were among the most profligate and incompetent investors around, incubation, if properly done, can have its merits. It is a separate subject, but some useful links are included below. The one-line piece of advice is: Be careful not to give away vast chunks of equity (most certainly not a majority stake), and be sure to understand precisely what services you will actually get in exchange.

The silver lining to the fact that venture capitalists have turned scrooges is that bootstrapping in the early days by and large creates healthier companies. As one (well-heeled) venture capitalist remarks: 'It's a bit like when your father gives you a BMW as your first car. You don't appreciate it as much as the beaten up old banger you might buy with your own early salary cheque.'

Marcus Lovell Smith, who has had venture capital multimillions in previous businesses – including Piping Hot Networks, a one-time hot start-up caught by the collapse of its customers, the alternative telecoms carriers – is bootstrapping his latest venture and senses 'more creativity and buzz with no loss of efficiency' when no one, from the team to the design consultant and patent lawyer, is getting paid.

What makes a venture capitalist invest?

The people, the market, and the technology: but in what order of importance? It is a bit like the argument among winemakers. Is a wine's primary quality down to *terroir* or is it due to the winemaker's art and technology? In either case, the debate is fierce and the answer ultimately unknowable.

Many venture capitalists will say they look for three elements when they invest – people, people, people. Consciously or unconsciously they would be harking back to General Georges Doriot, the French-born Harvard Business School professor who co-founded ARD after World War II, and who believed that picking the right individual was the name of the game. Benchmark, the Silicon Valley firm that backed eBay, would be an example of a firm that unashamedly sets out its stall as being completely people oriented.

Contrast Don Valentine of Sequoia, backer of, among others, Apple Computers, Atari, Oracle and Cisco. As an early employee of Fairchild Semiconductor he was one of the few in the Valley in the early days who understood technology: 'I would invest almost exclusively based on market size and momentum, and the nature of the problem being solved by the company. I always felt that trying to choose people was very difficult' (Gupta, 2000).

Interestingly, venture capitalists change their minds. Hermann Hauser, the Austrian-born entrepreneur turned venture capitalist, and the face of high-tech Cambridge, says he now puts the market first: 'Because unless it is big enough and important enough, the company is never going to make it. That's a big change for me because I always used to put technology first.' Number two is people, he says, and number three – 'sadly' for the PhD physicist and founder of Acorn – is technology. So why has he changed his mind? Possibly, says a colleague, because he has just had a failed investment where there was an outstanding team and really good technology, but the market simply did not develop fast enough.

There are regional differences across Europe, which go well beyond the obvious sector specializations such as mobile technology in the Nordic region or optoelectronics in Scotland or computer security businesses in Ireland. In France, for instance, with its cult of the brilliant engineer, there is a tendency for investors to be swayed by the pure beauty and elegance of the technology (at the expense of its commercial application). In Germany it is noticeable following the downturn how venture firms are reaching for the supposed safety of deep scientific knowledge in the partners hired, leading to a certain bias in the sort of businesses backed. Unsurprisingly, the differences become more pronounced the smaller and the more regionally based the fund. At the same time, venture capitalists across Europe should be looking for broadly similar things in the three categories of people, market, technology.

People

Investors look for a strong (but not necessarily complete) management team with the ability to execute: the entrepreneur as lone bloke in the garage is pretty much a myth. Their ideal will be a repeat entrepreneur, surrounded by others who have also done it before, who display leadership, can embrace risk, deal with ambiguity and uncertainty, and make an idea happen. Yes, they want it all. But they also have to recognize such individuals remain a rarity in Europe. Evidence of execution skills in past positions, of whatever kind, is certainly regarded as paramount (by contrast with the bunch of operational incompetents VCs managed to back during the bubble).

Market

Venture investors want a big opportunity – a market that is big, big and growing, or growing rapidly. Big and declining is much less attractive because it leaves much less margin for error. Since the internet disasters, most are wary of a market that does not yet exist. False market assumptions were the undoing not just of pet food online businesses but also of many of the so-called 'real' technology businesses. The wave of optical start-ups, for instance, were mostly not very innovative, me-too businesses, which were relying (wrongly) on an explosion of demand from the telecoms industry that could not be met by the incumbent suppliers. Plenty of VCs have not yet thought through the implications of the past few years and still talk far too vaguely about 'growth opportunities'.

For a large international venture capitalist, 'big' means a market of a billion or so dollars within a few years. For this reason, they will also look for a business that has the potential to grow internationally. Kevin Comolli, managing general partner in Europe of Accel Partners, a prominent Valley firm, says: 'For a while, the bar we were convinced was realistic was: Can this become a billion dollar company? [in market capitalization]. Now we don't believe that will come back, even in a recovered market.' At the same time, the firm still looks for large international winners. 'We passed on a good opportunity in Germany recently. I'm quite sure it will be a very sizeable regional business. But we are about building global companies.'

Smaller domestic and regional VCs will have completely different criteria, and may be content with a business that is regionally dominant. To illustrate the range, Springboard, a UK venture capital firm which specializes in backing proven management, seeks relatively modest companies that will be worth 'a minimum of £25m' within seven years (and 'cash flow neutral' in year two).

Technology (or product or service)

The best business, to a VC, is a simple solution to a big and pressing problem. It must have a strong and defensible position. Since the downturn, the mantra has been that it must constitute a 'must have' for customers rather than a 'nice to have'. A piece of enterprise software, for instance, must show a clear and fast payback to the customer for his outlay. Other considerations include whether there is a sensible route to market that is not too expensive. Is it realistic to do it with venture funding – or do you need 5000 people and the research and development capability of a multinational? Is it a company, or is it actually just a feature for someone else's company?

It is something of a myth that venture capitalists are looking for brilliant new ideas. Only a minority will invest in truly 'disruptive' technology. What they actually like best – and this comes back to the herd-driven mentality – is a management team with proven execution skills, operating in a 'hot' sector.

Do VCs ever fund non-technology businesses?

Selling pet food online was hardly a technology business. But yes, the glamour and excitement of the venture capital business derives mostly from its association with technology. That, the argument goes, is where the hyper growth (that drives exceptional capital gains which compensate for the risk of investing in early stage businesses) is mostly like to come from. Often forgotten is the passage of other fads, such as speciality retailing in the UK in the 1980s (Waterstones, My Kinda Town, The Covent Garden Soup Company).

While one could legitimately question whether, in an environment of lower returns, at least a proportion of VCs might sensibly cast their net wider, this is not something most will discuss. Top flight venture capitalists, certainly, concentrate on technology. But 'generalist' investors still exist – 3i, Europe's largest venture capital provider according to some measures, will still back a broad range of young businesses. Regional venture funds, including those backed by government, also tend to have more catholic tastes, as do the (remaining) captives of financial groups.

Almost more important than whether it is technology or not, is whether it is yesterday's fad – in which case, illogical as it may be, you will almost certainly be wasting your time. For months, even years, after the VCs had lost their dotcom millions, they were still getting dotcom plans flooding through the door – and straight into the wastepaper bin.

I've heard VCs talking about lifestyle businesses. Are they referring to yacht-building businesses in Antibes?

No. To a venture capitalist, a lifestyle company – his idea of a nightmare – is a small, low-growth business, funding a steady income to its founders, but with no prospect of an exit for the investor, so, from his point of view, going nowhere. If you have one of those, you should on no account be looking for venture capital. Misaligned objectives are one of the biggest causes of misery between VC and entrepreneur.

A twee early 1970s advertisement for ICFC (now 3i) pictures 'two men of business, Mr Tortoise and Mr Hare'. Mr Tortoise had spent years building a small firm that was 'very sure and very steady', but needed money for expansion. Mr Hare had a small business too, but 'fast and furious was its pace'. For him, it seemed, making a million overnight was slow progress. Mr Hare had lots of exciting ideas. 'You can't lose if your money's with me.' Rather extraordinarily, ICFC in the ad decides both have 'shown a good use for the money you need' and gives them both the cash. The ad does not relate what happened (Coopey and Clarke 1995). Mr Tortoise sounds like he has a lifestyle business and would not get funding these days. But then one rather hopes today's 3i would see through Mr Hare's bluff too.

So exactly how expensive is VC money?

Venture capitalists do not exactly go about advertising this, but for an early stage deal they have traditionally been looking to achieve an annual return of between 40 and 60 per cent a year. This will seem astonishingly high at first (and second) sight. Remember, though, the client – the institutional investor. A ten times return of capital over five years works out as a return of about 60 per cent per annum. That is without the hefty fees the venture firm levies. And of course this would be a very risky investment, meaning that only a very small proportion of the portfolio will hit the ball out of the park to produce the 5 or 10 times return. I have asked many firms whether, with returns from the public markets likely to be in the mid-single digits in coming years, they have adjusted their calculations. After all, most will these days·pitch to their investors a margin over stock market returns, rather than an absolute figure. Interestingly, at the buy-out end of the market, return expectations have indeed been adjusted downwards.

Adrian Beecroft at Apax, however, explains that early stage returns 'can't be pushed around nearly so precisely'. Emphasizing the risk element involved, he says that out of 150 venture capital deals, Apax has actually only achieved a ten times multiple on its money four or five times (even with the help of the bubble). 'Figuring out the price of start-ups is much less scientific [than buy-outs]. It is not susceptible to being done in a sharp pencil kind of way.'

An Apax study a few years back looked at the rate of return achieved versus expectations going into the investment. For buy-outs, it projected an average of 30 per cent and achieved 45 per cent. On start-ups it projected 60 per cent and achieved 45 per cent. So the firm was getting the same returns, based on very different expectations. Beecroft reckons this shows how his team were swayed on the one hand by the entrepreneur's natural optimism, and on the other by the mentality of big company types trained to manufacture conservative budgets. 'It's a useful thing to have twigged when deciding which deal to approve.'

Gerry Montanus at Atlas Venture adds that while public market returns may be down dramatically, the risk profile of venture investing has gone up because it has become correspondingly more difficult to exit businesses. 'Venture capitalists have to fund companies for longer.'

At the same time institutions vary enormously in their return criteria. Index Ventures, the Geneva-based, pan-European investor, for example, looks even in a downturn to back big winning companies that are capable of being taken public. 'We won't invest if from the get-go we know it is not an IPO candidate,' says partner Neil Rimer. 'In our profession you always want an IPO. Most exits are trade sales. *But* the best trade sales are if the IPO is there as an alternative or if the company is acquired shortly after.' And IPO's traditionally produce the biggest home runs.

But there are other sorts of venture capitalist. Stephen Ross, chief executive of Springboard, says: 'I consistently want to get £3m or £4m from an investment of £0.75m, over seven to ten years.' Captives of banks, which invest off the bank's balance sheet, tend to have lower return criteria as well.

How much equity do I give up?

Venture-backed funding structures are in flux. The US model, which had become increasingly common in Europe, was for a company to give away, say, a third of the business in its first institutional round of funding – series A funding in American parlance – in the expectation that it would do further rounds (series B and so on) at fairly frequent intervals, inviting in new backers prepared to pay steadily increasing valuations before going to the public markets.

In a downturn, procuring any kind of follow-on funding is extremely difficult, let alone at the same or stepped valuations. Companies have to accept much lower valuations (down rounds) if they can get funded at all. The renewed interest in building businesses that produce real profits also changed the game. Venture investors started to encourage companies to raise less money, but to make it last for much longer – giving them 18 months of 'runway' rather than five or six months. Many wanted the company to be able to get to a cash break-even position by that point. Syndication is back on the agenda, as venture firms team up with at least one other like-minded and well-funded peer, so that, if necessary, the two can fund the company to exit if they cannot attract new outside investors. Some VCs argue that, with two firms investing together in a very early stage (therefore very risky) company, they often need a combined stake of more than 50 per cent. When Benchmark and Accel backed Activiti, a software company started in 2002 by John Newton, founder of content management software company Documentum, each VC took 30 per cent (in a large funding round). Others still maintain that taking more than half is excessively demotivating to founders and management.

The combination of the low valuations on offer, the reluctance of some investors to take majority ownership, and the uncertainty regarding future funding rounds, has made it very difficult to finance businesses with large capital requirements. Nor is accepting venture capital purely about parting with equity. The terms of the agreement (Chapter 13) give the investor all sorts of powers despite their minority position. While the venture firm is not seeking to run your business for you, this is the way in which it exercises control in order to bring the rigour and focus that, in theory at least, builds the bigger pie.

The issue of control is an interesting one. In a sense, once you take a single euro of outside money you are giving up control, because of the elements in the investment agreement. Says one European venture capitalist based in the USA:

"Europeans tend to be more emotional about control. Americans are more money driven, but in Europe (particularly southern Europe) control comes up a lot. In Italy for instance it is so deeply ingrained, 51 per cent control is what people care about. In the US entrepreneurs are far more resigned to the fact that they may or may not control the company. For Americans, the issue is how much money will I make?"

As Guy Kawasaki of Garage puts it: 'It is a misconception that if you have 51 per cent, you control the company. Once you have taken a dollar of institutional money you are working for the institution.'

So what exactly is an exit?

Before signing up to venture capital, you need to be realistic about the investor's need for an exit, which is how the firm returns cash, hopefully with a nice capital gain, to its limited partners. Otherwise this imperative will come as a very nasty surprise indeed. Not all venture firms explain this process as well as they might. In hot markets the exit could be as soon as 18 months. A more realistic assumption is between five and seven years.

There are essentially two forms of (successful) exit – an initial public offering, or a sale to a large corporation. A flotation does not of course constitute an 'exit' for the company, but rather a transition to another form of funding, namely cash from institutional and retail buyers of public equities. Venture capitalists, though, will take some or all of their proceeds when they can by selling their shares on the public market (subject to so-called lock-up agreements which specify the timing of share sales). Some firms will hold on to a proportion of their shares in the hope of capturing further growth, and may remain on the board.

The stock market's receptivity to IPOs is highly unpredictable, however, and so in practice, most companies will be acquired. 'Trade sales', as they are known in the European VC lexicon, can be wild successes – such as the acquisition of Element 14 by Broadcom for $594m. Or they may be distress sales – sports internet company Sportal, subject of a £275m bid during the boom, was sold to a UK online gambling company for a nominal sum after the bubble had burst. Or anywhere in between.

Start-up companies are occasionally sold to another financial owner, such as Cambridge Display Technologies, whose backers included CRIL, a now defunct Cambridge seed fund, and Young Associates, which sold a majority stake to Kelso, a New York later stage investor, and Hillman Capital. The other kind of exit is via the undertaker – namely the liquidator.

What is this I hear about them removing the founder?

It is quite rare for the founder of a company to have the skills, the adaptability, the patience, the single mindedness and the stamina to take his creation from inception to an initial public offering and beyond, or even to the point at which the business is sold to a trade buyer. Bill Gates (Microsoft), Michael Dell (Dell Computers) and in Europe Mike Lynch (Autonomy Corporation) and Bernard Liataud (Business Objects) are the exceptions. You and the venture capitalist set out to make the best success of the company you can. If that means bringing in a new chief executive to manage growth or the transition to a public listing, the venture capitalist will do it. It is never easy. A good venture capitalist will not do it lightly (though many VCs are far too hasty to 'change management' at first sight of a serious problem). But it is part of the game. In many cases, founders recognize the need for a change and move successfully and happily to a new role, such as that of chief technology officer, or take on the chairmanship or a non-executive directorship. Provided it is managed properly, the founder will keep his stake and, or so the idea goes, everyone will make a lot of money. If you cannot contemplate this happening you should perhaps consider whether you are in fact running a lifestyle business.

Can I expect a VC to sign an NDA?

No US venture capitalist will sign a non-disclosure agreement (NDA), and it is becoming less usual in Europe. One in two entrepreneurs still ask for one though, says Pierre Morin of GRP, a US fund with a presence in Europe: 'We almost never agree to sign one.' The venture investor's argument is that ideas are a dime a dozen, and the value of the business is in the execution. 'Guys, your best NDA is yourselves, namely your execution skills,' says Morin.

A venture capitalist ought not to survive long if he gains a reputation for being unscrupulous. That said, there is clearly no shortage of disreputable outfits out there. You are obviously much safer if you go for an established firm with a track record. At the same time, entrepreneurs backed by well-known firms tell me business plans that come through the VCs' door regularly pitch up in the portfolio companies' e-mail as 'FYI'. If you have really confidential material which you still feel the VC should see, then show it to them in your offices at an on-site meeting.

Will they expect me to put up money?

A requirement for entrepreneurs to put up cash they did not have by, for instance, taking out a second mortgage was an integral part of the bad old days of pre-bubble European venture capital. Even in the so-called dotcom summer of 1999, Carol Dukes, founder of ThinkNatural, a beauty products site, met one investor that was very keen for her and her co-founder to put their life savings into the business 'to show commitment'. It was like bacon and egg, it was explained to her, the chicken being involved, but the pig committed. 'Yes I thought,' says Dukes, 'but the pig is dead. If you put in so much that you stand to lose everything if you fail, you become so risk averse you won't be able to move.'

VC attitudes have matured. One investor says: 'We appreciate it as an additional sign of confidence, but it is not a requirement. When we are comparing a company where the management has put up cash and one [where the individuals have similar means] where they have not, obviously we feel better about the first. Also, it is a question of proportion. If someone puts up $100,000 when he's made many millions, I'm not sure that is a good sign. I might almost prefer he put up nothing. It looks as if he is not serious.' On the other hand, one could see some VCs taking the line that, had the generation of late 1990s entrepreneurs felt the threat of financial pain, they might not have frittered away so much money.

Past failure is regarded as a badge of honour these days, right?

The lack of acceptance of failure in Europe has been much lamented and is commonly regarded as one of the reasons why the region falls well behind the USA in the entrepreneurialism stakes. Everyone is now trying so hard to redress the balance that it is becoming almost conventional wisdom that failure is good, which is clearly nonsense. An arrogant dotcommer with a flaky business model who burnt through millions of dollars of other people's money is not a more backable proposition the next time round. Most venture capitalists realize this. They will look at the causes of failure. If you were honest, worked hard and did not squander excessive quantities of cash on Aeron chairs, they will view you very differently from if you presided over an exploded dotcom.

Giuseppe Zocco at Index Ventures thinks European VCs might even be slightly more forgiving than in the USA: 'Because we have so few serial entrepreneurs, we are more inclined to forgive the first mistake.' One important question is whether you have come to terms with failure. If you are still saying it is someone else's fault, you have probably not. Equally important is the attitude to a past success. Venture capitalists are long on people acknowledging the importance of luck, of being in the right place at the right time and not being hubristic (an area in which the VCs set an excellent example themselves, you understand).

How long will it take?

This depends on the state of the cycle and on the stage of the business. Atlas famously agreed a term sheet for Clickmango in eight days in the heady days of late summer 1999. Charlie Muirhead (see below), a 26-year-old serial-entrepreneur, spent a year securing funding for Nexagent, his latest start-up. With a nascent business – and some of those deals do still get done – a venture firm may work with the embryonic start-up (sometimes even before a company is formed) for nine months or more exploring the opportunity, developing the business plan, recruiting, getting office space and the like. But be prepared for the fact that fund-raising is a very time-consuming exercise that cannot help but distract you from running the business.

Can I stand it?

The founder of Hotmail pitched fruitlessly to 20 VCs before getting funding from Draper Fisher Jurvetson of Sand Hill Road. And that was in the heady late 1990s. Persistence and a high tolerance of rejection are essential qualifying attributes. But then those are qualifying attributes of entrepreneurs too. VCs rarely say yes – but rarely say no either. 'Come back when you have five clients.' 'We really like you guys, but we have three concerns' (always three concerns). Most venture capitalists appear not to be able to say no, which is bad business practice when you think about it. Too often they are fence sitting to see if a big-name investor starts warming to the company.

Don't forget there is a multiplicity of possible reasons behind a no or a not yes: the venture capitalist is too busy with other new deals; he is plagued with portfolio problems; he is preoccupied by fund raising; he is out of cash (and not quite admitting to himself he won't raise another fund); he is too paranoid to invest because of past mistakes. Learn what you can from that particular dialogue and move on to the next prospect.

How much will it cost?

Raising venture capital is unfortunately an expensive exercise. Unexpected costs include the VCs' due diligence costs (which can easily amount to around 5% of the sum raised). Lawyers' fees – the company's and the VC's – can also run to another 5 per cent. (Perhaps counter-intuitively, the better the legal advisor, the simpler and clearer the documents should be, and hence the more reasonable the fee.) A few VC firms charge a deal fee – reflecting a banking mentality. A number also take a fee for sitting on the board (though that is more often in a 3i type structure, where 3i appoints a non-executive on its behalf).

A year on the funding trail

Charlie Muirhead has more than his fair share of entrepreneurial genes in a preternaturally entrepreneurial family. At 26, he had braved the teeth of a bear market to raise £10.4m in venture funding from big name venture capitalists for networking company Nexagent – his fourth start-up. His two siblings are no slouches. Older brother Richard is entrepreneur–in-residence at Accel, having previously worked at Orchestream, the data

▶

prioritization networking company, which Charlie founded after dropping out of a computer science course at Imperial College, London. William, the younger brother, meanwhile, is keeping up the family tradition, having started his first business straight out of Edinburgh University.

Armed with ample doses of self-belief, Charlie Muirhead appeared not to blench as fund raising for Nexagent dragged on for one long and uncertain year amidst the accumulating rubble from the telecommunications industry collapse. Former investment banker Andrea Bonafe, a warm-hearted and shrewd Brazilian woman who was chief financial officer of Nexagent for that period, recalls how, after a rare minor triumph in the midst of the endless setbacks, she would give Muirhead a peck on the cheek and remark, 'Wow that was a good day.'

'Babe,' he would say, 'I never have a bad day.' Bonafe was 'never in doubt we would raise the money – even though I knew the numbers [including the company's hefty burn rate]. That is simply what Charlie transmits'.

To Muirhead, whose Notting Hill cool amply hides any geek features, the worst crisis seems genuinely to count as a learning experience. He has made 'huge strides' he says, since Orchestream, his earlier start-up. But his story, which spans the pre-boom era to the telecoms collapse, contains lessons for all and underlines how selling a vision to venture capitalists is, even second time round, uphill work.

While many British entrepreneurs are accused of thinking small, that is not a Muirhead failing. Perhaps it is in the blood – from the parents, a pair of hippie Australian lawyers who emigrated to Britain in the 1960s and set up a law firm – where his mother (now divorced) still practises. His father, who then went into the music business managing the likes of Phil Collins, now specializes in new media.

It was the mid-1990s when Muirhead, then 20 and sporting a ponytail, first made his rounds of the few UK venture capitalists interested in funding very young businesses. 'People's knowledge of technology was very limited. And there was a lack of confidence that something significant could come out of the UK. We told them we were going to build something that could compete with Microsoft or Cisco. People would say: "I find that hard to believe."'

Orchestream was going to solve the problem of what Muirhead dubbed the World Wide Wait, by prioritizing data as it flowed around the network. But, repeating the oft-heard complaint that European venture capitalists spend too long poring over the numbers and pay too little attention to the idea, Muirhead recalls how investors would 'analyze our revenue model as if it *existed* when it was merely [a product of] speculation. The one thing you know in an early stage company is that the business model is *wrong*, that the way you say you are going to get to market is *wrong*'. Having rejigged Nexagent, moving away from addressing the telecoms industry to global corporations more generally shortly after he secured venture capital, he speaks from painful experience.

In 1998 Muirhead flew to the west coast to see if the US venture capital community was more receptive. The business was at 'early proof of concept stage'. He got in to see a roster of the top names, and there was 'some enthusiasm', but no one actually bit – and, in typically parochial Valley fashion, they would certainly all have required him to move the business to the USA: 'VCs don't tell you why they are not investing – because you are too young, your numbers are too big, who knows? Perhaps they should spell it out.' There had been two early exceptions of backers prepared to take a risk. Terry Matthews, the Welsh-born entrepreneur and founder of telecoms equipment maker Newbridge Networks in Canada, invested through his venture firm Celtic House. 'We hadn't even decided what we were doing at that point,' says Richard Muirhead. 'From one meeting to another the pitch would change.' But Matthews knew about networks and his gurus at Newbridge Networks performed the due diligence (research) on the embryonic business. The other believer was Simon Acland at Quester, a UK venture firm. 'Simon saw in me someone who had interesting ideas and a team, was keen to learn, could listen and take criticism,' says Muirhead. 'Essentially, he made a bet on me and the space we were in.' I asked Acland what was there to invest in. He laughs. 'There was some software and Charlie's great vision.'

By the summer of 1998, however, the markets in Europe were warming to technology and Orchestream hauled in a big dollop of cash in a round led by Atlas and Kennet Capital. Another Deutsche Bank-led financing followed in 1999 and the company went public the following June (with revenues of £411,000 in the first four months of 2000) – after the dotcom crash, but in the period when confidence in internet infrastructure companies was holding up. Aged 24, Muirhead entered the Sunday Times Rich List at an estimated (paper) net worth of £30m.

Orchestream, which briefly leapt to a valuation of nearly £900m, crashed back to earth, as most of its (fairly select band of) customers, the alternative carriers, fell by the wayside. The company also parted with Ashley Ward, the chief executive with grey hair who had taken over from Muirhead. Long since crashed out of the Rich List himself, Muirhead much later revealed that 'one of Cisco's major rivals' offered $30m in cash for the company in

March 1998, when he still owned more than 35 per cent of the business. Any regrets? 'No,' he shrugs, 'I can do it again.' Which is what he is doing with Nexagent, founded in 'stealth mode' in the summer of 2000 and financed in a seed round at the end of that year by iGabriel, the angel network Muirhead also started that summer, roping in top names including US IT guru Esther Dyson.

Nexagent was a yet grander vision, aiming to link data networks across multiple carriers around the world. 'Nexagent does for data services what you take for granted in making a telephone call – that you can call anywhere in the world, at reasonable cost, regardless of which carrier you are connected to,' Muirhead explains. This time he fielded an impressive coterie of senior managers from the outset; Chris Gare, previously director of advanced services at Cable & Wireless, as well as other senior telecoms and technology executives from C&W, Cisco and elsewhere.

At Dyson's PC Forum conference in early 2001, a gathering of the glitterati of the technology world in Scottsdale, Arizona, Muirhead was talking to financiers about raising £20m or £30m. This was before the decimation in the telecoms industry, and the general collapse in confidence post 11 September and corporate America's string of scandals. The cycle swung against him with brutal force and rapidity: 'We went from talking about doing £20m or £30m at some ridiculous valuation to worse than pre-boom conditions, not even being able to do £5m for [giving VCs] a third of the company.' While the business was making progress, investors were demanding ever higher hurdles in terms of revenue predictability – at plummeting valuations.

Muirhead had certainly understood the importance of creating competition between venture capitalists. In mid-2001, he says, the company had ten VCs seriously interested: 'The art in venture capital is to make everyone feel they are competing. A key driver for them is fear of losing the deal.' But he failed to capitalize on that interest. By the time he eventually got a term sheet (initial commitment letter) from Atlas – as late as November, a couple of months after the company, strapped for cash, had had to arrange a bridge loan with its existing investors – it was the only firm left in the game, 'though of course we never let on to them'. A big mistake, which Muirhead readily acknowledges, was not to take cash when it was there. 'We were going to do a "small" round, with £2m each from four Orchestream backers – Celtic House, Quester, Atlas and rvc [the former Reuters venture capital arm that is now independent].'

Atlas, a well-established transatlantic firm, said it wanted to do more. 'They wanted to lead [the financing]. But we wanted to save them for the next round [a further much larger financing round they planned to do later in the year]. It was an error when we had that interest. We put them off, and they got sour.' The team then focused on Quester. While Acland, who had spotted Charlie in the early Orchestream days, was all for it, his partners were less enthusiastic, arguing that the money would only last the company for six months, which was insufficient 'runway' in an exceptionally chilly market. By this time most venture capitalists, if they were investing at all – which most were not – were looking to fund companies for 18 months and expecting them to reach profitability by then.

Over the summer a term sheet arrived from another Orchestream backer, but again Muirhead did not proceed: 'They wanted us to [be a software company and] license the technology rather than being a services company, which meant we could do it on less money.' Throughout the process there was the familiar problem of getting investors to buy into the dream. Muirhead was that rare commodity in Europe, a serial entrepreneur, but that did not seem to be helping. 'He had raised money before, but in an up market,' says one observer of the process. 'He had not learnt that selling the vision was not enough'. It was a grand vision, a vision that no one could quite explain and something investors certainly could not pigeonhole. Meanwhile the market was going down, fast. Says one venture capitalist: 'Because of his enthusiasm, Charlie believes more information is better. He would lose the audience after 10 or 15 minutes. He'd say: "It's complex, I can't make it more simple." He tried to impress by being over-complicated, not focused.' Venture capitalists hate complexity. The business plan alone was rumoured to be 400 pages. One of the UK's smartest angels said he did not understand the proposition.

Muirhead also burnt bridges with investors who felt his valuation expectations were 'through the roof'. One recalls the valuation as being $50m or $60m pre-money that summer for a proposition that was essentially still in vision territory. Investors were also nervous about the burn rate. While they were initially impressed by the senior management he had pulled in, they soon began to complain about a 'top heavy' structure more suited to a company that was about to go public. Says Muirhead, 'People kept saying: "You are too 2000. It is a 1999/2000 take-over-the-world business plan."'

While Atlas had, understandably, gone away in a bit of a sulk after its rebuff earlier in the year, Muirhead refused to take no for an answer and he and Bonafe worked hard to revive interest. Bonafe, who had struck up a rapport with Jonathan Wolf, an exceedingly smart associate working with partner Gerry Montanus, kept feeding him with information about the company's progress. Wolf remained very loyal, says Bonafe. 'He kept saying: "I really think there's something there, but it is not well communicated."' Montanus himself, who had sat on Orchestream's board, says: 'I continued to follow him

– because Charlie is Charlie.' Eventually, Muirhead rang Montanus to try and start serious talks. By this time Nexagent had, like Orchestream, done the grand tour of US venture capitalists – an unfruitful trip in the sense of securing term sheets, but useful because some of their savvy questions about the business model had helped clarify thinking. Says Bonafe: 'We had made a quantum leap in our ability to explain what we were doing. We suddenly understood that selling the vision was not enough. Conversations with customers were getting more real. So we said to ourselves, let's meet Atlas again.'

Atlas talked to customers and eventually a term sheet was agreed in November. 'Gerry came to Reading [the company's headquarters] with the revised term sheet,' says Bonafe. 'He saw the demo, and the senior management went to lunch. After lunch the rest of us left. Charlie and Gerry eventually emerged with the thing signed.' Among the conditions was finding a credible co-lead investor. As the downturn bit, venture firms were increasingly looking to partner with each other, not purely to share risk, but also to bring more minds around the table. They also wanted deep-pocketed companions along the road ahead, given that attracting subsequent funding from other investors had become a nightmare.

Benchmark had been among the firms which turned down the company earlier in the year, but Muirhead had met Bruce Dunlevie, the US partner then living in London, and interest had been rekindled. Atlas was also talking to the firm, including to partner Barry Malone, a former Irish telecoms entrepreneur. 'Benchmark backs ideas and teams,' says Bonafe. 'The big hurdle was to prove to them we could do something no one else had managed to do. They didn't really think about – I'm being simplistic – the whole budget problem. They are real venture capitalists.' Muirhead was asked to write a 'white paper' answering specific complex technology questions posed by Andy Rachleff, a partner back in Palo Alto specializing in networking and communications.

As the company hung on, it was piling up debts and it was negotiating furiously with, among others, the Inland Revenue. In the constant search for cash, Bonafe filled out a 90-page report applying for a research and development credit, one of the UK government's measures to help cash-strapped young companies. Nexagent was granted £475,000, most of what it had requested, only to find its debts to the Inland Revenue had been deducted before it got the cheque.

It took until February 2002 to finally complete the deal – £10.4m (in two tranches) co-led by Atlas and Benchmark, with Quester coming in for a smaller amount, alongside one newcomer (Lago). 'I am still pinching myself

I got it done,' said Muirhead six months later. And he neglected to mention that, in addition to the tribulations of a dozen-plus months on the fund-raising trail while running and developing the business, he was also assailed by Orchestream's woes (with Goldman Sachs selling Orchestream shares pledged by Muirhead for a loan he had taken to fund Nexagent). Like most angel networks, iGabriel was also struggling (before merging with VCR/PiCapital six months later). But then: 'Babe, I never have a bad day'.

One of the prices for raising what counted, by now, as a very large sum, was that it came in tranches, with £4m of the £10.4m only payable when certain milestones had been achieved. While the nature of these hurdles was not disclosed, one is understood to have included signing up a certain number of telecommunications companies, in an effort to achieve commercial validation of the service. Because of the crisis in that industry, the model was changed a few months after the funding to target large multinationals more generally. 'Now we have got four VC firms we need to convince that we have got a real business, including one with partners a long way away in San Francisco who see a company not achieving what it said it would. Will we keep the same valuation? You have to be very careful the way you set milestones,' says Muirhead.

The other milestone, it transpires, is hiring a chief executive. Of course Muirhead had already gone through the transition (at Orchestream) that can be many a founder's nightmare. When asked what he feels about the prospect, he says, just slightly too tetchily: 'Anyone who knows me well will know I am much more interested in leadership, analysis, evangelizing.' But he also agrees that it is a balancing act. The venture capitalists want a 'seasoned' CEO, but attracting a high calibre CEO to a company that is not yet making revenues is a challenge. With Nexagent now his fourth company (including one started at Imperial College), Muirhead says the process becomes 'more and more intuitive'. He will 'inevitably' become a stronger and more compelling leader he says, and 'get more credible despite not being a natural manager'. He gives himself about a decade to be 'ripe to be CEO'.

References

Coopey, R. and Clarke, D. (1995) *3i: Fifty Years Investing in Industry*, Oxford University Press, Inc., New York.

Gupta, U. (ed.) (2000) *Done Deals*, Harvard Business School Press, Boston MA.

Links

US site loaded with information about entrepreneurial financing needs such as debt versus equity trade-off	www.capitalconnection.com

Miscellaneous sources of finance:

Incubators: UK government backed organization	www.ukbi.co.uk
French incubators with close links to research institutes	www.franceincubation.com
UK government loan scheme	www.sbs.gov.uk
Venture leasing: still much more common in the USA than Europe. One is European Venture Partners	www.evp.co.uk

Other:

Munich business plan competition via www.munichnetwork.com	
UK government SMART awards	www.businesslink.org
ShellLive Wire (start-up help for 16- to 30-year-olds in the UK)	www.shell-liveWIRE.org
Prince's Trust (Prince Charles's charity for disadvantaged people under 30, includes grants, loans and mentors for those starting a business)	www.princes-trust.org

8

Approach

I would never invest in somebody who couldn't figure out
how to get an introduction to me.
(US venture capitalist)

VENTURE CAPITALISTS NEED effective filter systems. One of the simplest and
one to which they adhere rigorously is to look only at investment prospects
referred by trusted sources. The way in which you approach investors tells
them, they believe, plenty about the way in which you will approach your
market. Relying largely on referrals happens to make their life a lot easier too.
At the same time, you might well think that having to resort to the power of
your personal rolodex is an alarmingly haphazard way of going about raising
venture capital. You would be right. That is one of the many less-than-ideal
features of this cottage industry.

Gerry Montanus at Atlas Venture, which was getting 40 or 50 plans a day
at the height of the bubble, most of them unsolicited, still gets plenty of e-
mails that kick off: 'Dear Atlas Venture executive'. That, he says, is 'so dumb,
it's a disqualifier right there. People have not even taken the trouble to find
which person within the firm is the right one to approach – which is easily
accessible information'.

It is one of the curiosities of the venture capital world that firms measure
themselves in the pecking order partly according to the number of unsolicited
plans they receive. Being able to say you see 5,000 a year supposedly means
you are a better venture capitalist than only seeing 1,500. It is a measure of
the power of the brand. Yet they grow suddenly rather coy when asked how
many unsolicited plans they fund. The more honest will generally admit that
it is 'almost none'. One wonders why they bother with the 'Submit Your

Business Plan Here' corner of the website. The first rule is to leave that field unclicked and to get a proper introduction.

It's clearly tough if you are a first-time entrepreneur, and you don't have much of a network. But begin by researching your venture capital prospects' websites. As you will quickly discover, VCs' websites are embarrassingly bad, which is odd when you consider their line of business. Many are clunky, hopelessly out of date (except for the failed investments, which disappear from view with great efficiency) and unimaginative. But they do contain basic information about the team, their names (!) and areas of specialization, and about portfolio companies. An introduction from the chief executive of a current or former portfolio investment is almost certainly the most powerful route through the door. Network like crazy to see if you can reach one of them. You might, for instance, have a customer in common. Other possibilities include business angels, trusted advisers such as lawyers (make sure you hire a well-connected lawyer, see below), and industry experts. Many venture capital firms have advisory boards; find out who sits on them, and consider if you have a route to any of those individuals. One entrepreneur I know suggests getting a friend to pose as a journalist to find out what the firm is really interested in at that moment and whether they are genuinely investing. A glance at the press release section of the website is a simpler way of gauging recent activity levels.

Identify which partner to approach and look at their background, their board seats. While you may well be passed to an associate initially, the aim is to start as high as you can. Associates can be extremely knowledgeable, but if you are unlucky you will chance on a zealous gatekeeper of the worst kind. Once you have secured your introduction, write a short e-mail and attach the executive summary (*not* the business plan, they don't want that at this stage, which again makes you wonder about that section of most websites). VCs themselves advise that, while it often annoys them, you should follow up with a call, asking if they have seen the mail, if they think it is interesting, if you can have a meeting. You do need to bug them. Some are very busy, many are very slow at turning plans around. The other approach is to engineer a 'casual' meeting with a VC.

Life's a pitch

Pitching is an integral part of business life. People pitch their companies to customers, suppliers, partners, and journalists, all the time. They do not always do it very well. As a writer for the *FT*, I certainly received my share of poor pitches. As in every line of business, the idea does not sell itself. You need to tailor it to your audience. Investors need to know why they should invest. Neither the idea nor the technology – particularly not the technology – is seductive in itself.

A well-prepared 'elevator pitch' is an essential constituent in the entrepreneur's armoury. A US concept, it refers to a chance encounter between entrepreneur and investor in an elevator; the former must enthuse the latter about his proposition before the doors roll open again a few floors on. Its precise origins are obscure, especially when you consider few buildings on Sand Hill Road are more than two storeys high. But having a honed elevator pitch is a prerequisite for the successful 'chance' meeting.

Perfect pitch

The first principle of a successful pitch is indeed to 'assume short buildings', according to Bill Joos of Garage Technology Ventures, a Valley-based outfit that specialized in grooming entrepreneurs for venture capital (Hoult 2000). Pare your message down to its essentials – any entrepreneur knows far, far too much about his own company – while giving free rein to your enthusiasm. Practise in front of colleagues and friends and give them permission to be ruthlessly critical. Capture your audience's attention. A reverse example from my *FT* days were the publicists who would ring up with the opening line 'I'm from a small PR company in Warrington'. Joos suggests word play to grab attention ('at Garage . . . we start up start-ups'). You can work with alliteration and rhythm too. Keep the pitch free of jargon and acronyms and don't claim to be a 'leading' anything. Articulate the burning problem that you are solving for your customers. Get the investor nodding in agreement. Get him intrigued and wanting to know more. In dating speak, says Katia Verresen, the former head of Garage in Europe, it is a question of 'wearing enough that he wants to take it off'. Finish the pitch by asking them if you can have a meeting.

The opportunity for the chance meeting is created, fairly obviously, by attending events that VCs attend such as conferences, trade shows, exhibitions, university functions. Remember you are 'always on'. Verresen tells of a French entrepreneur who had approached countless, but *sans issue*. She was out riding in the Bois de Boulogne one afternoon and fell into conversation with another rider, a serial entrepreneur, it transpired, on his second venture-backed company. He gave her a warm introduction to his VC and she secured a meeting.

Winning a competition is another route. Some, notably business plan competitions, will be directly linked to opportunities to present to VCs.

Others may be industry competitions whose award ceremonies are attended by VC investors. VCs' herd instincts can well be further stimulated in such environments.

Finally, is there any way to get VCs to call *you*? Apart from getting funded (entrepreneurs say the phone rings incessantly after a funding announcement), the only other way is to put it about that you are not interested in taking venture capital. A software entrepreneur I know stumbled on the last technique quite by accident.

Plan

The single most important ingredient in successful fund raising is time. Leave much longer than you think you will possibly need – six months or more – because as you start running out of time and a cash crunch looms, your ability to negotiate drops dramatically. As an entrepreneur, you are working to a completely different timetable from the VCs. In a downturn, investors will let the process drag on for months, even if they are not purposely stringing the company along. And plenty do the latter. Mark Suster of BuildOnline says: 'If they are leaning against the deal, they may not tell you for a month or more, simply because they don't want someone else to do it.' Referring to arguments he had with some of his early backers resisting dilution as second-round funding talks were progressing, he adds: 'I said to my investors, "You are sitting around waiting for me to be on my death bed. Then just as I'm about to die you will throw me a life line and that's how you screw me."'

Make sure you plan the process. Take the advice of Stuart Evans of Plastic Logic, a seasoned chief executive who has raised venture capital for two businesses, and 'ensure you know what is coming down the pike. When you write the business plan, assemble the extra stuff the VCs will need for due diligence later. If you have two or three lever arch files you can hand to the VCs, it makes it more efficient and will impress them'. Evans secured funding in April 2002, having spent two-thirds of every long working week since the previous September on the fund-raising trail.

Given the time commitment and the opacity of the market, you might well be tempted to hire an adviser to smooth the process. But beware. A large number are expensive incompetents. I managed to sneak a look at the list of prospects drawn up by one firm on behalf of a start-up looking to raise less than £1m. It included US internet group CMGI (about five months *after* it imploded), Bridgepoint, a mid-market buy-out house that invests between €15m and €100m in established businesses and a collection of the most obscure tiny VCs no one had ever heard of.

Most VCs heartily dislike advisers, whether it is the head of entrepreneurial services at a big five accountancy firm, or a partner at a corporate finance advisory boutique (the latter being assumed to be failed venture capitalists). For one thing, investors know by definition that the deal is the reverse of proprietary and will be being shopped around the market. Says one VC: 'It's just a big turn-off. You probably don't get a meeting if you have an agent, except during the bubble when investment bankers were touting deals all over the place.' He acknowledges that, in the less mature European marketplace, it is still fairly common practice. Not only do many advisers have patchy rolodexes that may be weaker than yours, but their interests are also poorly aligned. Their one aim is to match young company with VC – and they are not going to think terribly carefully about whether it is the right partner. Advisers are also generally paid on a percentage basis (perhaps 4 per cent, with some warrants), so it is in their interests, but very much not yours, to raise as much cash as possible.

Get an adviser if you really must and you think you have genuinely found a good one. Far more importantly, concentrate very early in the process on getting a good, commercially minded lawyer who knows the system. That means someone with sound business instincts who is a problem solver, not a term-sheet junky intent on maximizing problems and obstacles. You need someone who can explain how the VC will behave; what the implications of various clauses in the term sheet are; what is 'market' and what is not. While experience levels are improving in Europe, many lawyers are less than competent in this field and have only done a handful of deals (and hence have no real idea what are market terms, for instance). Also, lawyers tend to answer questions, rather than highlight problems.

One entrepreneur, going through a term sheet with his lawyer, reached the section on warranties, which looked pretty harsh to him. So he asked if these were standard. No, they are not standard, said the lawyer, who had however failed to volunteer any such intelligence himself. Remember, also, lawyers are one day negotiating for an entrepreneur, the next on behalf of a venture firm. One excellent lawyer with whom I was discussing term sheet structures, and who knew I was writing from the point of view of entrepreneur, would say: 'You would want to see this.' But 'you' was invariably the VC. Countless times I would chip in: 'And from the point of view of the company?'

How many VCs?

It is a bit like job applications as you prepare to leave university. Do you concentrate on five potential employers, in the belief you will be better prepared, or do you go for **30** prospects to maximize your chances? Evans thinks of fund raising like a sales campaign: 'Not snake oil or used cars, but professional relationship selling. And the more calls you make, the more sales you make too.'

Michael Ledzion of Polight in Cambridge reckons there is a limit, though: 'There is a tendency to want to talk to everyone. You do have to be realistic. A lot of people don't know what they want and use the process to find out. We talked to 50, exchanged business plans with 20, and got very serious with five. But don't waste time with investors who don't have a fundamental interest in your market space [his is data storage]. You don't want to be having to persuade them about the merits of the market as well as about you.'

Equally, be sure they are interested in your stage. As already noted, many VCs claim to invest in 'early stage' businesses when they do not. Ledzion says: 'Keep checking even as you get to know them. How many early stage deals have they done? What is the target for the portfolio? If they admit they are actually a bit overweight in early stage then that is a big red flag.' Remember, VCs rarely say yes – and rarely say no.

Reference

Hoult, J. (2000) 'Perfecting your pitch', *Fast Company*, October.

Link

Silicon Valley outfit with a lot of information on how to raise VC, including how to pitch

www.garage.com

9

Choosing a venture capitalist

Good judgement comes from experience.
But experience comes from bad judgement.
(Bruce Dunlevie, partner, Benchmark Capital)

John Cash arrived in London from the Bay Area four years ago with a personal mission to make Cambridge the 'Stanford of Europe'. The 35-year-old former consultant from McBain is on the Eurostar, returning from a weekend in Paris, and barking into his mobile phone: 'Doug could easily view it very, very negatively. The impression that is given is crucial,' he says to his interlocutor. Doug is chief executive of a Cambridge-based 3G wireless business, the first investment Cash made when he arrived in Europe. Those were the days when he was downing Dom Perignon with Doug as he sought to distinguish his term sheet from the 11 others sitting on Doug's desk.

Doug had been persuaded to let Cash's firm do the full $15m investment – not just because it was offering the highest valuation, $75m post-money, but also because he had talked articulately and persuasively about his venture firm's company building skills. Now times are tough, Doug's company is downsizing rapidly and, in his increasingly desperate attempts to drum up customer interest, Doug now takes Ryanair. The company still pays Cash's business class-fare, though it did almost consider querying his bill from the Hotel de Crillon last time he was visiting VCs in Paris in connection with the new funding round.

Doug, who does not yet know he is about to be fired, would say he never saw much of Cash and his supposed company-building skills in the

▶

early days. When he turned up to board meetings he mostly seemed to be glued to his Blackberry. But he is certainly seeing a lot of Cash now. This is a VC who believes in giving his CEO a hard time. Scoring points is what he loves best. 'Partnership is for wimps,' Cash struts around his Mayfair penthouse office saying to no one in particular. He prides himself generally on being 'ruthless' – in deal selection, in slashing costs at companies. Negotiating the deal is what he loves best, driving a real hard bargain, as his property tycoon father always taught him. Negotiating the terms with Doug, who had been rather worried about the provisions of what happened to his shares if he left, had been great fun. 'Don't worry about the terms,' he had said confidently, as he exerted his weight to bring the negotiations to a close. 'They don't matter. This agreement will be shoved in a desk drawer and never see the light of day. Trust me.' His favourite trick in follow-on rounds was to wait until the company was really desperate for cash and then go in for the kill.

Despite being in the business for a while now, he still thinks it's cool to have a $450m fund at his disposal (cut back admittedly more than a third from its full bubble splendour of $700m). Having money equals power, not that, with his upbringing in a Carmel mansion, he has much acquaintance with the reverse state. At the same time he and his partners have not done a new deal in a long time. The market is a lot hairier, and even with his MBA-honed analytical skills, it's tough sorting through those business plans. Indeed, as he doesn't admit to anyone, least of all himself, he is actually a bit lost. Being ruthless with the existing portfolio does make him feel a lot better, though.

'We have to let the guy down gently, soften the blow,' he says to his phone. He is talking to a prospective investor in the new round of financing the company is raising. Doug, it has been decided, is not up to it (despite, as any impartial observer would say, the company's main problem actually being the delayed roll-out of 3G). 'Otherwise the impact could be disastrous. We have to tell him this is the next phase of the company's life cycle. The condition for the new investors is,' he pauses, laughs, 'we want him out. We'll offer him a consultancy or something.'

Doug will soon be opening that drawer with the investment agreement and Cash may have to wait a little longer too to achieve his goal of the Stanfordization of Cambridge (whatever that may be).

What makes a good venture capitalist? Unfortunately, particularly since the boom, which drew scores of unqualified individuals into the area, most entrepreneurs are much more intimately acquainted with the traits of the reverse, the (entirely fictional) John Cash, the VC from hell. Choosing the right venture capitalist is absolutely pivotal. Few entrepreneurs will have the luxury of going out deliberately to pick the very 'best' VC, but you need to know some of the qualities you are looking for. The process is about so much more than just getting a signed cheque. It is the basis of a partnership that may last many years.

Says Hermann Hauser: 'If a company gets into trouble, whether it is refinanced or not has a lot to do with the existing shareholder base. If you have chosen supportive investors and negotiated a fair deal, it will be a very different experience from if you have cobbled together a group of incompetent VCs who have demanded tough terms, and who have proved fickle in their support of the company.' Far from being identikit sources of cash, VCs actually come in a bewildering number of guises and offer a service of extremely variable quality. In comparing a deal, you have to know what you are looking for – which, at its most basic level, is value as well as valuation.

Take Simon (not his real name), the founder of a niche retailing business who a few years ago secured two offers of venture capital, one from a large firm, the other from a small but well-connected boutique. 'We took what seemed like the best deal', says a colleague. The Firm was offering £2.3m for 27.5 per cent of the business, the Boutique, £2.1m for a 31 per cent stake. 'They were offering £200,000 more for 4 per cent less equity.' Moreover, the Boutique had sent round a retailing expert to do the due diligence who would also have sat on the board. 'He told us our warehousing was crap and we didn't know how to run a mail order business.'

The man from the Firm said everything looked fine 'which was another reason we chose them'. Simon and colleagues had given the term sheet – much of which had anyway been left 'subject to our usual terms and conditions' – the most cursory attention. That sounded 'boring', says the colleague, 'you know, like your credit card conditions or something'. One of the 'usual terms and conditions' was the appointment of a non-executive chairman, to whom Simon was more than a little surprised to discover he would be paying £18,000 a year for his services. The investor also insisted on a part-time finance director, who at £40,000 for three days, was easily the highest paid member of staff. 'These terms only came out when it was too late to do anything. Even [the high salaries] would have been sustainable if they had given us someone who was at all useful.'

Simon and his colleagues say they thought they were 'getting a partner' but found it very difficult attracting the attention of anyone at the Firm. When Simon rang up on one occasion, excited with the figures of the first month's turnover of a new shop, the immediate reaction, before he had said anything, was panic: 'What's the problem, what's wrong?' The non-executive chairman turned up to board meetings, but his experience was in a different area of retailing. The finance director was of limited use, being as he was a big company man.

When it came to the next tranche of funding, dependent on six milestones, the company had only hit four. The Firm refused to put in more cash 'but had no suggestions. All they said was "No no no", they didn't even bother to come and see us'. The non-executive chairman had already handed in his resignation by this point and the bank eventually called in the overdraft. The administrator was called in and the only people to get cash were him and the Inland Revenue. 'We thought we were getting a partner, but [the Firm] never introduced us to anyone, not to customers, suppliers, nobody.'

Simon is convinced that if he had gone with the Boutique he would still be in business. He knew he wanted a 'partner' but had been preoccupied with getting the best valuation for the business without thinking through what that partner might look like. The Boutique's expert had correctly identified the company's problems (the two missed milestones were in the mail order area) and the fact that he gave them a harder time during the due diligence probably indicates he would have been a much more effective board member.

Finding a good venture capitalist is not easy, particularly as no one can quite agree on the qualities that make a good VC. Certainly headhunters do not seem to have the definitive answer; nor do the senior partners of venture firms. Sir David Cooksey of Advent Venture Partners observes: 'It takes a hell of a time and costs a lot to teach someone the business. You have to learn by making mistakes. Virtually everyone in our firm has run a tech business. But we have found it quite difficult to spot people who are good at building a business *and* who will make good venture capitalists.' A venture capitalist is a particular character form that is not easy to spot, he says. 'You can get through a lot of investors' capital before you have determined whether they are any good. It's the most expensive business school going. My main objective is to make sure people never make the first four deals they want to do.' Successful firms are often made up of a small group of individuals who between them have a blend of skills, attributes and experiences.

VC qualities

Some of the qualities to look out for would include:

◆ knowledge and background
◆ operational experience

◆ vision

◆ instinct

◆ experience

◆ moderated ego

◆ commitment

◆ luck.

Knowledge and background

A VC is never going to know as much about your niche as you do, but you do not want to be responsible for having to educate him from first principles. This can be a particular problem at generalist investors like 3i, which has reorganized its technology group according to sector in recognition of the problem. A high turnover of account managers, which would be unusual at a small VC firm, exacerbates the problem. Says a non-executive at a 3i company, who had had six different account managers in four years: 'We are dealing with people who want to learn about the business over a long lunch.'

If yours is a technology business, you will be familiar with the cliché that US VCs are well versed in technology, while their European counterparts are not. It is a truism undermined not least by the fact that, during the bubble, the US VC industry certainly sucked in more than its fair share of non-technologist investment bankers, while there is also a growing number of more technically literate investors in Europe. At the same time, even in the mid- to late 1990s, most European VCs knew staggeringly little about technology. One software chief executive raising money in 1998 recalls: 'Every person I met had less experience of the tech industry than I did. That very fact, of course, gave me a lot of confidence. Which is very important in fundraising.' At the same time he expressed his frustrations at spending huge amounts of time doing the most basic education as the investment process advanced. The well-known venture firm from which he ended up taking money had already signed the term sheet when the main executive on the transaction enquired what a 'database' was.

At the same time, the European industry grew up populated by former accountants, and, more recently, management consultants and investment bankers, with financial and analytical skills, but not any deep understanding of technology. All one can say is that the level of technology literacy is improving. Cultural differences also play a part. Technology to a French venture capitalist who is a graduate of a leading engineering school will have an aesthetic quality – while the Brits persist in harbouring a slight disdain for geeks and their toys. Venture firms also hire in cycles. In Germany, one of the responses to the idiocies committed in the bubble has been to draw in partners with *Fachwissen*, deep scientific knowledge. Last time I was in Munich, nearly every new VC I met seemed to have a PhD in materials science.

You can tell a lot about a VC firm from the background of its partners and juniors. Analytical skills are certainly rated very highly, perhaps too highly, in the venture capital industry in Europe; hence the super intelligent, highly educated types who progress from investment banks and consultancy to venture capital. 'The first question will be what is my unit cost of client acquisition in year three – before they have understood what my business does,' says one entrepreneur. Alain Falys of Open Business Exchange agrees: 'Most European VCs take comfort in analyzing the numbers, yet that is precisely the least forecastable part of the business plan. What I want is someone with business experience, not necessarily VC experience.' The former bankers are prone to see a venture capital investment as a *deal*. 'Bankers are far too transaction oriented,' says one individual who worked at a VC firm in the bubble. 'I was always surprised, 90 per cent of the pre-investment activity was just doing the deal. Just at the point where you should be really pushing on finding out about the technology and the customers, [colleagues] were on the phone with our lawyer deep in negotiations. They were deal junkies; the huge celebration was when the deal closed. Which is actually when the real work begins.' In a downturn, these individuals can be excessively interested in protecting downside risk and entrepreneurs complain they tend to lack 'emotional intelligence'.

Operational experience

Operational experience is a quality much prized by entrepreneurs and the lack thereof equally lamented. A typical view: 'VCs have no idea how to run a business. Before we signed [the latest funding round] it was all about cutting costs, reducing headcount. As soon as the deal was done, they suggested we opened offices in Australia and New York.' So do former entrepreneurs make good VCs? 'If you have been on the pitch, you are more valuable on the terraces,' says James Dobree, former chief executive of Zygon, a software company. 'For MBAs, everything is about problem solving. As an entrepreneur it is about creating opportunities, even in a downturn, it is about regeneration. VCs [with too strong an analytical background] just focus on the short term and behave like accountants. People need to be motivated again and inspired.' Those who have been entrepreneurs may be better at that, he argues.

As already indicated (Chapter 5) a lot of nonsense is written about operational backgrounds. There are some very good investors who have operational backgrounds, such as Vinod Khosla, co-founder of Sun before he became a partner at Kleiner Perkins. There are others who do not; Jim Breyer, managing partner of Accel Partners, is a former management consultant; Mike Moritz of Sequoia was once a journalist at *Time* magazine. And what does operational mean? Ray Lane, the former number two at Oracle who joined Kleiner in August 2000, knows how to run things – but big corporations. Moreover, it is far from axiomatic that a strong business leader will make the transition into a flat, non-hierarchical partnership. In sum, there is no one 'right' background or range of knowledge, and getting a suitable blend of skills with an individual firm is also a delicate matter. Says one headhunter: 'You can do the analysis of the skill sets necessary to build a VC. The best management consultant on strategy, the best operational engineer, the best bankers. You may have really thought about it. But when you shake it all up, does the soufflé set?'

Vision

At the very top of the tree are individual venture capital investors who genuinely use their own ideas and thinking to create brand new markets, like Khosla who played a pivotal role in creating the optics sector. These individuals are rare indeed – non-existent in Europe, probably – although there is no shortage of VCs who would attempt to lay claim to such status. But there are also investors, and they can be very useful for your business, who possess vision in the sense of being able to raise their heads above the current 'noise'.

Prof. Richard Friend, who has worked with Hermann Hauser at two start-ups, identifies that quality in him. 'Hermann, with his love of genuine new technology, is very good at being expansive, of thinking how far something might really go one day. That is incredibly important. You need to keep having that conversation when you are being dragged down in the minutiae of running a start up.'

Instinct

There is far too little of it about. VCs certainly need the 'left brain' stuff, analytical equipment. But early stage investing is as much art as science. 'VCs are very good on the cost side. They find it very easy to figure out how any individual action will impact the bottom line. They find it much harder to predict, if something is yellow and this big, how much will it sell?' says one entrepreneur turned venture investor. One Sequoia portfolio company chief executive comments how Moritz, by contrast, is known for making snap – but very sound – judgements.

Whereas one might suppose that analytical minds would be good at filtering deals – a crucial part of the VC's repertoire – entrepreneurs often say they watch such VCs get bogged down and paralyzed by overanalysis. Hauser is certainly an instinctive investor, which in turn is a function of experience. Asked how he sizes up management teams, Hauser says: 'It is difficult to quantify, but "Do they get on, Can they work with each other?" . . . You simply get a feel for that after a while. That's experience.'

Experience

Da steh ich nun ich armer Tor and bin so klug also wie zuvor.
Here I am now, poor fool, no wiser than before

(Goethe, *Faust*, Part 1)

Investors need judgement, which, as Bruce Dunlevie of Benchmark Capital, says, is a product of experience and of making mistakes. Of course that assumes you learn from those mistakes. The industry is still replete with bull market types who do not seem to be doing much learning at all. Mark Suster of Build Online makes the point that entrepreneurship is like growing up, and while he talks from the point of view of the entrepreneur, it applies equally to investors.

"As a teenager, no matter how many times your parents tell you not to drink too much, you have to find out for yourself that drinking 12 shots of tequila will make you sick. You can know all the theory about running a start-up, but you can only develop wisdom by going through it. We signed dumb contracts, we expanded too much, we hired too many people, we developed too many products. The problem is people don't spot their mistakes and change and improve."

Lingering differences in attitude to failure also do not help, Suster believes. 'In the UK, failure proves you weren't any good. In the US, it's an acknowledgment that you've learnt.'

Dobree adds: 'I am looking for investors' pain because it makes them wiser. If they have been through the emotional rollercoaster before, they are less likely to panic.' Experienced VCs are long on pattern recognition. They have seen it before, and learnt from those failures. They are also good at instilling confidence. As the downturn hit in the last cycle, investors' lack of experience was one of the biggest problems for young VC-backed companies. 'We can see our VCs just don't know what to do,' one German entrepreneur lamented at the time.

Pat McGovern, chairman of IDG, the media group, and a long-time observer of the US venture industry, says: 'Great, as opposed to good, VCs act as a mentor. There are so many threats and choices for an entrepreneur. As a mentor you can say, eight of these nine things will never happen, focus on this.' Perhaps the main thing the best have, and develop through experience, is emotional intelligence, being good at dealing with people, which can help resolve rather than create conflict.

There is a paradox, though, Montanus at Atlas reckons: 'To have no experience is clearly bad. A lot is good. But too much also becomes a liability. If you have too many failures, you lose the enthusiasm to jump in. You have seen too much, you become risk averse. You can't bring the enthusiasm to believe in anything.'

A moderated ego?

A monstrous ego seems to go with the territory, but it is a defining rather than necessary quality and possessed in almost equal measure by good and bad VCs. VCs have the power because they hold the purse strings. The vicissitudes of the downturn have had some, but insufficient, moderating effect. Ego in Europe, where VCs have made less (though still a lot of) money than in the USA, tends to take the form of intellectual arrogance.

McGovern again: 'Young VCs are all intellectual analysis, but have no experience of dealing with people. They say: "Ah, you've not thought of that, you are missing the point." What they are really saying is, I'm smarter than you. This is inducing failure.' Playing hard ball negotiating a deal is a sign of immaturity, or perhaps not having mentally quit the world of banking.

Commitment

Anne Glover of Amadeus says she won't hire people who say they are 'considering venture capital or consulting' or 'venture capital or investment banking'. Commitment, she says, is a must, on account of the length and harshness of the cycles.

Luck

Has he luck? as Napoleon asked of his generals. There is plenty of luck involved in the venture game, as some practitioners are readier than others to acknowledge. The timing of fund raising, for instance, can make the difference between success and failure. Some young European venture firms made eye-catching paper gains at the top of the bubble – with investments in companies which later imploded – which enabled them to raise large new funds from investors. Without these one or two investments, they would probably be out of business.

VC road map

It will save a *huge* amount of time if you get to the right people. Do as much research as possible before making an approach. Venture capitalists' websites, trade associations, the entrepreneurial community, professional advisers are all good places to start. Talk to as many people as possible. It is a perplexingly fragmented industry. Even the venture firms themselves are not necessarily very clued up about their peers. Here are some of the lines along which the venture community divides.

Stage

As became clear in Chapter 3 on cycle psychology, the stage at which a venture capitalist is prepared to invest is not a constant. It depends on the state of the market. At the same time, appetite for risk is more than purely a function of the cycle, and there is absolutely no point in wasting time trying to sell the concept of a pre-revenue business to a late stage investor. The stage varies by expertise and also by size of the fund (see below). Seed investing is a highly specialized, risky and often thankless activity. Very few funds indeed will invest in a business to get it to 'proof of concept'. However, seed funds do exist, often clustered around universities. Specialist government funds are also available, such as the University Challenge seed fund in the UK (although it constitutes extremely expensive capital).

Beware the spin. Venture capitalists may present themselves as early stage investors when they are not. The term turns out to have entirely different connotations according to the firm and, to some degree, the stage of the cycle. Most VCs really did do 'early stage' in the bubble – the concept business plan produced by a couple of guys with an idea for a gardening website. In the downturn, early stage can, at one firm, mean being willing to back a company without a product and only part of a management team, whereas another firm might claim interest in 'early stage' businesses when it was really looking for companies that had €10m in revenues, a more or less complete management team and the prospect of profitability within a year.

Size

Size matters in venture capital, in a number of ways. Size is clearly related to stage – a proof of concept start-up may need just a few tens of thousands of euros, an expanding business with early revenues, several million, and so on. The size of investment any individual firm will make depends on the size of its fund. As already noted, very large funds find it uneconomical to invest small sums.

At the same time, funds can be too small. The worst thing, from a venture capitalist's point of view, is not being able to put more money behind a good investment, because his holding will get diluted as further funding comes in. A fund of less than, say, €30m is likely to encounter that problem. Moreover, management fees are calculated as a percentage of the money under management; a €20m fund might have just €400,000 in annual income, which would hamper its style considerably, most notably in the calibre of people it can recruit. This is a problem for many government-assisted regional funds. Venture capitalists turn distinctly shifty when asked what their minimum investment size is. The trade association handbooks will probably list a figure for member firms (as well as providing guidance on sector preferences), but the numbers may not be that meaningful. VCs often like to pretend they do half million chunks 'if a really exciting opportunity present itself' when in practice the smallest investment they have done for years is €8m.

Deep pockets, one might reasonably think, would be evidence of the ability to ride out cycles. Think again. Some of the biggest institutions have been the most fickle. Investment and commercial banks, large private equity firms, corporations all suddenly 'no longer do early stage' when there is a down turn in the market. Beware of the creatures of an up market who will, despite their protestations that 'this time it is different', make themselves very scarce when the climate turns frosty.

Sector

Alain Falys of Open Business Exchange, and one of the most confident and clued-up fund raisers around, acknowledges he wasted a lot of time on the wrong people initially: 'We made the mistake of talking to VCs who concentrate solely on very, very new technologies.' The new venture capitalist that eventually led the OBE financing was not looking 'whether technology protectable for the next 50 years' but rather 'understanding the capacity of management to deliver on a good idea'.

Research your prospective investors. When Accel Partners, the Silicon Valley venture firm, set up in London the firm – which specializes in communications and internet infrastructure, and invests in a select few western European countries – received a plethora of plans including one for a bowling alley complex south of Moscow. Many call themselves specialists when they are not and many of course rush from sector to sector. Beware the Fashionista that has moved from pet food online to nanotechnology via life sciences in the space of two years.

Excessively narrow specialization, even with real expertise, can also be dangerous – such as a very narrowly focused communications funds. If the sector your business is in is going through a tough time, it will not help if all the other portfolio companies in which the VC has invested are also struggling just at the same time. Broader VCs have their own issues too of course. During the IT boom firms covering IT and life sciences split apart because the life science guys were not doing well, and the IT guys resented sharing the rewards with them. Subsequently, the tables turned and tensions spilt over as life sciences flourished and the IT sector dived.

Geography

Venture capitalists come in all shapes and sizes, from small, regional operations in Grenoble, to national firms, to a few global operations such as Apax. The types of business they back, how they operate and what they offer will vary accordingly. International firms look at embryonic global industries, which is particularly appropriate for technology. Smaller regional players will have less of a view on the global evolution of an industry; local ties with the entrepreneur may be more important. If you have a business that can be a strong regional player but not more, or is a country specific niche market (such as retail), do not waste time with an international firm. Too many companies also squander time on a trip to Silicon Valley (or Boston). Heart of the VC community it may be, but those VCs who are interested in Europe (still a very small proportion) mostly have a presence in the region. Only if you have a very specific lead indeed is it worth the trip.

Once you have divided VCs into these rough categories there are three very important things you need to know about individual firms that often get overlooked. Do they have money, or is their ability to invest in you dependent on them raising a fund? Are they investing or are they sorting out a knackered portfolio? How long have they been around (have they ever *done* a second round and what is their track record?) In the Valley, the oldest firms are investing their twelfth fund. Many European investors are on their first or second.

You may not be able to answer these questions until the initial meeting, but these are areas where entrepreneurs frequently trip up. One London VC called the company in which it was poised to invest on the day of the signing, and explained that, since it had been unable to raise its own fund, the deal was off.

Now comes the interesting part of what exactly you *are* looking for beyond the cash. 'Adding value' is one of the most overworked phrases in the business, and yet more vacuous than its American equivalent of promising 'company building' expertise. Both, however, can be equally meaningless. 'Do VCs know how tiring it is, hearing again and again about adding value?' one entrepreneur asks. As a journalist, I found astonishing the degree to which VCs manage to make themselves sound the same in any given presentation, while actually being very different. They even differ in something as fundamental as the answer to the question: Who is the client? At Benchmark it is all about 'superior service to entrepreneurs'. PolyTechnos, a Munich-based VC, describes its objective on the home page of its website as 'to consistently provide superior returns to its investors'. Both raise money in exactly the same way, but think of themselves very differently and will behave accordingly (one not necessarily better or worse than the other).

What do they really offer? 'Connected money' is how Guy Kawasaki puts it. What he is saying is that much can be reduced to the value of the firm's network. Whom do they know – companies, customers, other VCs, potential new team members – and, importantly, whom will they actually introduce you to? The law of averages suggests that you are unlikely to get to one of the top brand name VCs, not least because they are almost all American, but knowing how they work can give you an indication of what you are aiming for. Joe Schoendorf at Accel, who handles corporate and strategic relationships for the firm, dines at Michael Dell's house; Steve Ballmer comes through the office once a month. Few VCs in Europe have anything like that level of contacts – including of course the Valley firms in Europe who are very much still in building mode. But the better firms are in a position to open plenty of doors.

The next question is whether the VC will actually pick up the phone to make the initial call on your behalf. One entrepreneur tells of getting an 'introduction' to the third most senior executive at Nokia. This consisted of an e-mail with the name of the executive and his phone number, both of which the entrepreneur had, but no introduction. 3i is an example of an investor that clearly has a huge portfolio of companies, but is often criticized for making far too little use of that enormous asset for the benefit of its investee companies – an area on which the group is now working hard.

Many of these are questions you will only be able to answer fully as you get more serious with a particular investor (Chapter 12). Connections with other VCs are very important too, in terms of the next round of funding. Are they respected? Do other VCs like working with them?

Perhaps the other big factor is quality of advice. An industry specialist can be pivotal in shaping the business. Sir Ronald Cohen says that when Mike Lynch (founder of Autonomy, believed to be Apax's most successful investment, and Britain's first technology billionaire on paper) walked into the office he was 'a very bright guy but the application of his technology was relatively narrow – using its pattern recognition software with the police to identify number plates and faces. Through interaction with John McMonigall [the firm's telecoms guru at the time] we developed an understanding of its application to the internet.'

The worst sort of VC is remote and out of touch. A French investor tells of a company that designed kitchens, in which he and a number of others had invested. A new catalogue had just been produced. 'Everyone had a view – about what was ugly, about which particular thing they would kill. Their views were completely unrepresentative, a sample of people earning in the top 0.1 per cent of the French population. Their views on the product were absolutely useless.'

Choose people who will challenge you. If they challenge you during the investment process, the chances are they will be helpful on your board too, as Simon and the niche retailer, above, learnt. While others plied Mark Suster with champagne and produced Formula One racing drivers on the phone to discuss sponsorship in an effort to get into his bubble era funding round, one VC courting him stood out – as being far the most awkward. GRP were 'just very difficult to deal with'. They wanted reams of extra figures and analysis, long lists of people to call as references. No one else was doing that and the hard-nosed Suster warmed to them for that. His attitude was based on a simple lesson from his days as a management consultant. It was the tough clients who forced him to stay up till the early hours, for whom he produced his best work. The rest of the management team did not agree and was disinclined to take GRP's money, but his view prevailed.

Will you get their attention? This comes down to style, which you will find out about as you go through the process. But you may get some idea of the basics from the website, such as the number of board seats per partner. Is it a firm that makes 50 $2m investments per fund with just five partners, suggesting an average of ten board seats per partner, or does it take larger stakes in fewer companies? In boom times, both will probably perform equally well in a financial sense. But don't go for the former if you expect the partner to return phone calls promptly or show up to board meetings. It also depends on what you are looking for. Says one entrepreneur with engaging honesty: 'Our VC turned out to be the right combination of hands-on, but not on our backs. It was a very fortuitous meeting because we would have taken the first person who gave us money.'

How will they behave when the going gets tough? A downturn can be the cue for massive interference. Finding out which ones help and which ones have a tendency to plain panic is part of your research task. Changing the management is a very tempting tool and a lever for which the John Cashes will reach far too frequently. An important element of the VC marketing pitch is that they increase a company's (not the founder's, note) chance of survival. But do they really? Where will VCs devote time in a portfolio made up of a mixture of winners and strugglers? A lot of VCs are not very clear on the answer. Says one investor: 'The secret is to maximize the value of the near winners and minimize the losses on those that don't work. You will have one big win out of ten. So you should spend time on numbers three and four and numbers eight and nine.' Others think they should devote all their time to the winners and, though they do not quite put it like that, abandon the losers.

Another big difference is between the approach of small independent firms, like Amadeus, and large institutions. 3i bashing is a very popular sport. It is the firm both entrepreneurs and rival venture capitalists love to hate. When 3i pulled back sharply from technology investing during 2001, it left a trail of extremely disgruntled companies in its wake. Centralized decision making leads to great unhappiness at company level when any individual situation is dismissed because 'it might set a precedent'. Guy Kawasaki, however, a dyed in the wool Silicon Valley type, had an interesting reaction to 3i. Introduced to its distinctly dreary London headquarters on the wrong side of the Thames he exclaimed 'This is the future of venture capital,' and started taking photographs. Why? Entire floors of VCs sitting at their desks spoke to him of a proper institutional firm by contrast with the fly by the seat of your pants Valley partnerships.

Making venture capital 'scale' is, as already indicated, a huge challenge. From the company's point of view you will want to think about the relationship you have with the investor. If your backer is an institutional VC, the relationship will be with the firm, rather than the account manager, who may change with alarming rapidity. 'If you have an issue with a smaller venture capital firm you go in and see the principals. I don't imagine entrepreneurs can go in and meet [3i chief executive] Brian Larcombe,' says one non-3i backed entrepreneur. Like any professional services firm, the quality of the individuals with which you deal is hugely variable. While 3i is a generally well-managed business, the investment procedure can also seem distinctly un-user-friendly from an entrepreneur's point of view. What the institution can bring, however, is global reach, access to a vast network of potential customers and suppliers and disciplined investment procedures – in theory at least.

In a smaller partnership, entrepreneurs may be inclined to choose at least partly on the basis of an individual, rather than the firm. That can be legitimate.

But consider what weight that person carries in the organization. Will they fight on your behalf? Mark Suster's analogy is again from his consulting days:

"Your mentor fought for you in promotion meetings. He would be arguing against someone else who wanted *his* guy promoted. It was not a case of who was best, but who had the best mentor. The VC you need is the one who will sit in the meeting and say: 'I know we are writing off ten companies but I am telling you X entrepreneur is the best.' A lot are too meek to say that. I know Pierre [the GRP partner who invested in Build-Online] will either fight for me to the grave if he is convinced. Or if he is not convinced, he'll shut me down in a second."

How many?

Funding structures change with the cycle. In the bubble, firms wanted to hog entire deals themselves; in the downturn they became much readier to syndicate their investments alongside one or more other venture capital firms. The number of investors you choose will depend how funding discussions evolve, but here are a few factors to bear in mind.

If you have just one venture capital backer, you clearly limit your options. Suppose they have run out of cash by the time you get to your next funding round. Ideally you will have picked a fund that has reserved enough money for follow-on investments, of course. But venture capital firms shift focus, as we have seen; they also shift geography (US investors pulling back home) or stage (moving much later stage). In a tough funding environment, you are at their mercy in any number of games they may play. One entrepreneur, with multiple venture capital backers, was raising follow-on funding while also pursuing merger discussions with an industry rival, which in turn had the backing of a single (large) VC: 'We were asking for 66 per cent [of the rival], so we were getting better terms. [The large VC] rang up our prospective lead investor and suggested they back [the rival] instead. Four weeks later [the rival] was bankrupt. [The large VC] played poker and lost.'

It is also possible to have too many investors, says Suster of Build Online, who has seven. 'Not all seven have the same appetite for our company. We have too many investors with not enough skin in the game.' It can increase the chances of complicated internal poker games, with multiple parties with different classes of shares, different rights, and different attitudes towards supporting the company (as will be seen in some detail in Chapter 17). Also reporting to and otherwise communicating with multiple parties becomes distinctly onerous. Suster's advice would be to aim for three investors:

'Losing one for a follow-on is not a show stopper. Each can have a significant stake, but not too much is required for follow-ons.'

Unattractive habits

There is no lack of unscrupulous VCs. A shortlist (the longer one would fill another volume) follows (with many more examples in later chapters). Only when entrepreneurs do a better job of researching their investors and finding out exactly how certain VCs behave will that behaviour perhaps be modified for the better.

◆ Stealing ideas/customers from an entrepreneur. A lot of this is myth. Ideas really are a dime a dozen and it is the execution that counts. That said, even otherwise reputable VCs undoubtedly forward business plans to portfolio companies on an 'FYI' basis. Some will also engage in due diligence purely for the purposes of finding out about a competitor to an existing investment, particularly its existing and prospective customers.

◆ Stringing along a prospective investment until it almost runs out of money in order to extract punitive terms. Very common practice, unfortunately.

◆ Not having the cash to make an investment, or support it further down the road. Not only are there scores of VCs who provide nothing but cash, there is the category that does not come up with the cash either (as above). One entrepreneur who had a signed deal spent an entire summer trying to extract the agreed investment from one well-known Swedish VC.

◆ Investing and immediately firing the founder. The more scrupulous VCs will indicate if they think immediate changes are necessary to the management team. Going for the silver-tongued option that suggests everything is wonderful is hence dangerous.

◆ Firing the management because things are not going according to plan and the VC can't think of anything else to do (as above).

10

The business plan

Je n'ai fait celle-ci plus longue parce que je n'ai pas eu le loisir de la faire plus courte. [I have made this letter longer than usual only because I have not had the time to make it shorter.]
(Blaise Pascal, *Lettres Provinciales*, 1657)

CLICKMANGO, THE HEALTH PRODUCTS WEBSITE briefly notorious for securing funding from Atlas Venture in eight days in the autumn of 1999, boasted a business plan based on a model involving 12 million calculations, co-founder Toby Rowland proudly related at the time. Atlas came to rue the publicity it had sought for its nimble footwork, as it later battled to shed a reputation for having rushed further and faster into the e-commerce fray than others. But when I spoke to Rob Zegelaar, Atlas partner, immediately after the funding he was at least clear that he had not invested on the back of the modelling. Zegelaar, who has since left Atlas, said he reckoned that 'real life' was 'quite complicated enough without trying to model it'.

What is a business plan?

A business plan serves a number of functions. First, writing the document will help you clarify and refine your thoughts. Most importantly, it serves as the core material that potential investors will use to get to know the company. But whether in the frenzy of a bubble period or in the depths of a downturn, the plan in itself will not secure venture capital funding.

Investors also vary considerably in their approach to a plan. Some will go through it with a fine toothcomb marking up questions before they meet you;

others will ask you for ten slides instead of a plan. Many will initially request an executive summary, and only ask for the plan if all goes well at the first meeting.

The details of a successful plan will also vary considerably according to the nature and stage of the business. The content you need for a biotechnology company will be very different from the material that investors will want to see in a business services start-up. Equally, a seed deal or pre-IPO financing will demand very different levels of detail. But some broad principles apply.

Who writes it?

Writing the business plan is not part of the process you should outsource. You cannot leave an accountant or consultant to articulate the DNA of your business for you, although specialists may well be helpful in fine-tuning or editing. Potential investors can also infer a lot about your style from the way you put together the business plan. A badly ordered plan suggests you may not be up to the rather larger challenge of organizing a company. Beware too of poor focus – venture capitalists like simplicity and will easily be put off a proposition that entails multiple products launched into multiple markets.

Keep it short

Size seems to be inversely proportionate to success. Bricks – the 100-page documents bulging with charts and multicoloured graphics – are the province of investment bankers. Venture capitalists are known to have very short attention spans when it comes to business plans. A two- or three-page executive summary and a 20-page business plan are all the venture capitalist is going to read. Mark Suster of BuildOnline is often asked for advice by others about their plan: 'Entrepreneurs say to me "Look my business plan is *that* thick." I simply think, *you* are that thick. Of course I'll help with an 85-page business plan; start by ripping out 70 pages. If you have time to spend writing 85 pages of business plan, you are not an entrepreneur. You should be taking that time refining the product or looking for customers.'

Forget the technology

Well almost. Giuseppe Zocco at Index Ventures says the typical European business plan devotes acres of space to an exhaustive description of the technology. VCs are not primarily interested in the features of the product, though they do need to see why it is unique and why it is defensible, but in the market; what is its value, how will you capture that value, and how will you develop it? Potential investors want to see you understand just how hard it is to get from an interesting product to a profitable company. Spend time explaining the market, the route to market, the business's financing needs, and the venture capitalist's prospective exit.

Executive summary

This is the document that you will be sending when you first make contact with the venture capital firm. Only if the executive plan grabs them will you even get a chance to produce the full business plan. Keep it short and keep it simple. Even in a downturn, venture capitalists are, and certainly regard themselves, as 'time poor'. They will also be looking to see whether you can distil the essence of your business and express it concisely. Some people are fluent when talking broadly about their vision, but find it very hard to concentrate the message into a pitch, a summary and a plan. Investors know businesses do not run on froth.

What do you do? Who do you do it for? And how do you do it? What makes it innovative? What is your unfair advantage? A surprising number of entrepreneurs cannot answer these basic questions. The first sentence needs to tell your audience what the company actually does and why. Venture capitalists complain that they regularly read through entire business plans without ending up any the wiser as to what the company actually does. In a theme that will be recurrent throughout this chapter, talk not about the features of the technology but the unmet customer need you are satisfying or problems you are solving. This is something that technologists find hard to do and can easily lead to a dialogue of the deaf between the founder, exasperated that the VC does not immediately fall for the features of his fabulous gizmo, and the VC who is only interested in the commercial application and an answer as to why and when customers will buy it.

Neil Rimer of Index stresses the importance of a business that is simple to understand, an idea that is compelling. Like many investors, he has a preference for something that is 'elegant enough to be described in two sentences. We have often found that if you can't do that, the idea is too derivative. You shouldn't need five paragraphs'.

What is the problem? People often give a wishy-washy answer, or something that is not a big problem. You have to come up with a pressing problem. Then, assuming it is such a big problem, it will be being addressed in *some* way at the moment. How is it being addressed? And why is your solution so much better?

Hermann Hauser, one of the founders of the Cambridge Entrepreneurship Centre, says: 'So many clever people, especially from academia, are like a fish out of water when it comes even to the basics.' Their business plans, he says, read like research grant applications. 'The problem is not one of intelligence, it is one of ignorance.'

Fathom the fashion

Don't forget the fashion victim element in the VC world. It pays at least to be aware of what the 'new black' of the moment is. What are investors really looking for? What are the buzz words? In the internet era, it was so-called 'land grab', 'first mover advantage', 'going global' on day one, and hence the (supposed) ability to 'execute' on that plan. In the downturn, customers suddenly mattered, so 'traction' (evidence the product was selling, aka revenues) and ROI (return on investment, from the customer's point of view, aka is it less than exorbitantly priced and does it work?) were the name of the game.

One good clue is the way in which the VCs' portfolio companies present themselves on their own website. When spending on information technology has slumped, it is all about ingenious ways to grab the customer's attention. So, every enterprise software company suddenly had on its home page separate tabs to click on, designed to appeal to specific job functions – IT managers, CRM managers and so on. Indirectly, this underlines the kind of criteria investors are looking for. Don't follow it slavishly, clearly, but do bear it in mind.

In sum

The executive summary is essentially a condensed form of the business plan. Explain how you are going to make money; describe the product; the size of the overall market, and your niche within it. What is the existing and future competition and how will your product or service differentiate itself?

A very short history and background of the company is helpful. Introduce the team, particularly if they have relevant experience in the industry – and even more so if they are serial entrepreneurs. Include headline financials – when do you make your first million in revenue, and when do you plan to reach break even in terms of cash flow? How much funding are you looking for? Including something on the likely exit route will impress investors that you understand the process. Don't forget your contact details.

Business plan

Do

◆ Make it accurate. Incorrect phone numbers, spelling errors and poor formatting look sloppy, and suggest worrying implications for the accuracy of the financial data.

◆ Be honest, including about what you don't know, about weaknesses, about gaps in the team.

◆ Be realistic. Over-optimism scares investors, and merely tells them you are out of touch with reality .

◆ Identify risks as well as potential rewards.

◆ Tell a story. Make it readable, hold the investor's attention, make him want to read on. As Neil Rimer at Index Ventures puts it: 'We don't need answers on everything. But we need enough to get us excited.'

◆ Put a fresh date on it. Investors don't want to think 50 other people have seen the document first.

◆ Get advisers, colleagues and friends to read it critically.

Don't

◆ Get preoccupied with the beauty of the technology to the exclusion of everything the investor is interested in, namely its potential market.

◆ Produce a brick with day-by-day spreadsheet analysis for the next five years.

◆ Contradict yourself – especially between the executive summary and the business plan.

◆ Hide behind reams of technical jargon. An excerpt from the executive summary for the Series E financing for Reef, a now defunct content management software company: 'Reef addresses a broader scope of markets than existing solutions – including the mid SMB market. Our sales strategy is indirect, delivering our product through VARs and VADs.'

◆ State the obvious, such as 'competent management'. To distinguish yourself from those who admit in their plan to being incompetent fools?

◆ Couch it all in a fancy binder.

◆ E-mail the entire business plan. Send a hard copy if invited to do so.

◆ Lie – at all, but especially about the team's background. Untruths may well be uncovered by the VC if he progresses to doing due diligence on the company.

◆ Include a figure for valuation because it will only box you in and commit you unnecessarily early, before you have had a chance to take proper soundings around the market.

Finally, to misquote Nike, just write it. Get it down – it will help crystal-lize your thoughts. You can always refine it later. On a daily newspaper, writer's block is not an option, but writing a book is an entirely different matter. When writing this one, I found a hundred reasons why not to start writing that particular day. Even my expenses got done.

Plan by section

The way in which you order your plan depends considerably on the business and is also a matter of personal taste. Below are the broad areas which should be covered and why. It primarily uses examples of technology companies sell-ing to large corporations, but can be easily adapted to other business models.

The opportunity

Anything that won't sell, I don't want to invent.

(Thomas Edison, 1847–1931)

Business models are, at heart stories – stories that explain how enterprises work.

(Joan Magretta, Harvard Business Review)

The story links together who your customer is, why they need your product and how you will make money delivering it to them. Thomas Edison was an innovating entrepreneur rather than a pure inventor. William Nordhaus (1997) argues that Edison did not in fact make any quantum leaps in electric technology when he discovered the carbon filament lamp in 1882, seeing that the first lighting by electricity took place with the electric arc lamp as early as 1845: 'Edison combined technical inspiration with commercial perspiration when he also generated electricity and distributed it from the Pearl Street sub-station in New York in 1882.'

During the bubble, Katia Verresen, formerly managing director for Garage Technology Ventures in Europe, saw more than her fair share of plans that 'spent pages telling you wireless internet is a huge opportunity'. But things were a lot vaguer when it came to how the business was going to exploit this opportunity, she says. Don't waste time proving the obvious.

Avoid the gunshot business model, which includes every way in which the business could possibly make money, somehow leaving the VC to divine which one of these is really important.

Make sure you answer the questions as to why people will actually buy it. Hans-Dieter Koch, former chief executive of of b-business partners, com-plained of countless propositions from entrepreneurs who said they wanted to deliver 'the Mercedes of security software'. 'What does that mean? To me that means that it is very expensive but tells me nothing about why customers will actually buy it.' Articulate the pressing problem. Anne Glover of Amadeus recalls a company called Bugs Buster, featured in a Harvard Business School case study, which rid commercial kitchens of cockroaches. The entrepreneur started off with the guarantee that the kitchens would never see a cockroach again. At the time he had no idea how he was going to do it – but he knew what the problem was.

If it is a technology business, is it potentially 'disruptive'? Or is it a better mousetrap? If it is the former, it will be harder to define the business model (though technology that is truly disruptive is a pretty rare beast). Stuart Evans, chief executive of Plastic Logic, which is using inkjet printing to pioneer plastic electronics, has a business that certainly has the potential to be disruptive. An immense amount of thought has been given, he says, to where the company is focused. 'As we scour the horizon it's fuzzy. Will [certain companies] be competitors, collaborators or customers, it is hard to see.' In the end, he narrowed his initial sites to two markets, one disruptive and the other not. For the display market – $50bn, almost entirely in Asia – Plastic Logic has 'the better mousetrap' because it offers incremental improvements. In electronic tags and labelling, however, the technology is 'completely disruptive'. Different sorts of markets appeal to different investors, he says: 'Some are excited by disruptive technology, some are slightly frightened. Nor was it Machiavellian [to focus on one example of each]. The essence of disruptive technology is that it takes a long time.'

Does the business model make sense? Danny Chapchal was brought in to turn around Cambridge Display Technology at a time when it was looking to raise around £10m to establish a factory to manufacture TV screens. The plan made no sense in a number of regards. To begin with, the manufacturing facility would have cost something closer to £200m. Chapchal also knew that TV screens constituted about the most difficult market to attack: 'No one had ever made money manufacturing screens.' So he changed the target to mobile phones, and adopted a licensing model (kicking off with a deal with Philips).

Finally, define how you will make money – including the timing of cash flow, when suppliers pay relative to when customers pay. As Bill Sahlman at Harvard Business School writes (1997):

Investors are looking for businesses which can buy low, sell high, collect early and pay late. The business plan needs to spell out how close to that ideal ... [the business] is expected to come. Even if the answer is 'not very' – and it usually is – at least the truth is out there to discuss.

The product

This should include a detailed description of the product or service, as it is now, and as it will develop. Be very clear as to the present state of the technology or service – do not confuse present reality with future expectations. How it is differentiated? What is your unique advantage, and what are the barriers to entry? Deep technical information belongs in a white paper – which the venture capitalist will ask for as he begins to get serious. If you are a raw start-up, how do you plan to get from prototype to production and launch? All plans need plenty of detail on how the product is to be built and manufactured, what is outsourced. Describe current and future research and development. What patents have been and will be filed? What regulatory approval may you need to secure?

History

Don't kick off the plan with the history of the company, or, even more tediously, a history of the sector. But it may be tucked in here – with details of who founded the company and when, what has been achieved so far, how much money has been raised. Don't be shy about problems. All young companies, especially technology companies, go through crises. A prospective investor will be interested to know what sort of hurdles you have vaulted and how.

Market

This is of consummate interest to the venture capitalists. Giuseppe Zocco at Index Ventures says: 'In a downturn, the real issue is less the team than market visibility. In a downturn you see better teams, so there is lower team risk. In an upturn, it is the opposite – a bunch of people chasing a great opportunity [or what looks like a great opportunity], but they are less prepared.'

How big is the market now and how do you expect it to grow?

You need to specify how much of the market you will serve. Small companies typically target niches. A tightly defined niche is much more attractive to venture capitalists than a vague proposal to chase a '$10bn space'. Are you forecasting rapid growth in the overall market or your particular part of it? Give an indication of what sort of scale the business will reach in terms of revenues.

How does your product fit into the market?

Guy Kawasaki of Garage Technology Ventures says he wants to be able to 'fantasize' about the size of the market, not to be 'bludgeoned over the head with proof'. Don't, he advises, tell investors you plan to capture 1 per cent of the $300bn medical devices market. 'Tell me instead,' he says, 'there are 65m people with diabetes and everyone needs one of your scanners.'

Expensive pieces of independent market analysis are certainly discredited following the bubble era. At that time, companies could virtually 'rent a statistic' from the big research groups. It became a meaningless circular process, as analysts gathered their numbers by talking to entrepreneurs, and then produced their forecasts, which the entrepreneurs duly fed into their business plans to show to the venture capitalists.

Many venture capitalists will say they prefer 'bottom-up' analysis to a 'top-down' approach; they would rather see a 'real world' analysis built up from assumptions about the price of the initial unit sold. They will also want to know why the market structure is attractive for a small company to make money. A section on pricing strategy, and the margins you intend to achieve is essential. Are they realistic in the context of the industry in which you are operating? Bear in mind that pricing is dynamic, rather than static, so account for the fact that prices will decline as competitors enter the market.

Customers

As Armand Hammer used to say: 'A product isn't a product until someone agrees to pay something for it.' Who are your customers and why will they buy? In the bubble, people managed to get funded by claiming to be 'in discussions with Tesco'. This sometimes meant they were waiting for their call to the switchboard to be returned. Today, rather more precision is required. Throwing in a few company names will not do. Who have you talked to within the respective organizations? How do they make buying decisions? What is the size of their budgets? VCs will often know (or should know) the key people at these companies, so it is not wise to bluff.

Venture capitalists complain that many European business presentations lack what in the USA is called a 'strategic marketing' plan. Exactly which needs are you setting out to satisfy? Segment the market. Which subsector of customers will you target first and how will you expand? One venture capitalist reiterates in this context the importance of the customer, not the technology: 'We are looking for people who know what they are good at and know how they plan to grow from there. That is pretty rare. Often entrepreneurs cannot tell you how they are going to make the first million of sales or how the product is matched to the customer.' Mark Suster of BuildOnline thinks of prospective customers as either rabbits, deer or elephants:

"The thing about rabbits [small, $2,000 contracts], is that there are lots of them, you see them everywhere. So it is tempting to go after rabbits. In fact, they are not that easy to catch, and when you do, there is not much meat. Catching an elephant, on the other hand, may take six months or more, it sounds much more intimidating, but there is a lot of meat. You need a mix of elephants [$200,000 contracts] and deer (mid-size contracts which provide good 'meat' but balance out the elephants so that they do not have too much leverage)."

What is the customer's return on investment? In a downturn the 'experiments' budget has been axed. Companies no longer feel compelled to be testing technology purely to maintain their strategic lead. Define the payback for a corporate buyer. Ideally, the product should be generating savings within three months, certainly within a year.

Distribution

How will you get to market and at what cost? As Zocco points out: 'All the best companies created in the past – the Oracles and Ciscos – underestimated the opportunity by a large factor – and overestimated how quickly they would get there.' Investors will be looking for a detailed description of distribution channels. Are you selling directly or indirectly. If you opt for the direct route, how big will the sales team be? If you choose to operate through distributors, how much will you pay them? If you are a technology company opting for the licensing route, why have you decided to do that and how will you achieve it? What sort of partnerships are you contemplating? How about promotion – advertising, PR and, if appropriate, brand strategy?

Competition

Perhaps counter-intuitively, the more you say about it, the better. It shows a depth of understanding about your market. As Kawasaki likes to say: 'If you claim there is no competition, it means one of two things; there is no market, or you are a clueless bozo who doesn't know how to [use] Google.'

Who are your competitors? What are their strengths and weaknesses? How will they respond? What are the barriers to entry? With enough money most things can be duplicated. What is your unfair advantage?

The people

VCs, as the cliché goes, bet on the jockey, not the horse, so the people section is clearly crucial. The theory is that great entrepreneurs select great opportunities; that you won't get a great entrepreneur looking at a stupid idea, whereas there are plenty of stupid entrepreneurs looking at great ideas. If the model does not work initially, a great entrepreneur will change the model. Bill Sahlman (1997) says he always reads this part of a plan first, with three basic questions in his mind: 'What do they know? Whom do they know? How well are they known?'

The venture capitalist should be more interested in the team's experience and achievements – how they executed in the past – than which university they attended. Emphasize those factors and keep education to the minimum, except where it is of particular relevance (such as in the case of a scientific founder). Be specific: '12 years of marketing experience' tells a prospective investor absolutely nothing. Highlight experience in similar lines of business. If members of the team have worked together previously, so much the better. How well are the individuals known in the industry – by customers and suppliers? This helps a small company overcome the massive challenge of getting attention. Acknowledge any gaps in the team, where you still need to recruit. Having introduced the principal members of the management team, you should also describe the board of directors (to the extent that is in place).

Finally, do not rule out unusual ways of getting an investor's attention. Charles Irving of Pond remembers a plan where one feature that leapt off the page was the individual's past as a barefoot water-ski champion: 'I kept looking at his feet in the first meeting.'

Financials

In the bubble, Kawasaki used to complain that every business plan he saw had revenues of $75m in the third year (no matter whether it was semiconductors or organic farming). Five-year predictions of sales, let alone profit, clearly enter fantasy territory. Particularly in tough and volatile markets. So the plan loses credibility rapidly if you include down to the nearest cent your predicted profit in the third quarter of the year after next. The younger the company, the less meaningful the numbers. Irving at Pond, a venture firm which looks at opportunities as early as university spin-outs before a company has even formed, says: 'There are no financials at our stage, it is a judgement call. We look at the team, the technology, the global potential of the market.'

Evans of Plastic Logic included financial terms only until the end of the following year when he last raised funding. 'Spreadsheets can be a substitute for thought,' he avers. What particularly interests a good venture capitalist is the underlying assumptions – the metrics that drive the company.

If there is historic data, then include annual balance sheets, profit and loss, and cash flow statements. As for projections, you should include a current balance sheet, together with monthly P&L and cash flow statements for the first two years, or perhaps monthly for the first year, and quarterly for the next two. Be prepared to discuss years three to five. VCs like a model where all the assumptions can be changed. They will also be looking for detail including projected head count by area (research and development, marketing, and so on). Do not construct a model by working back from the numbers you guess they might want to see, because that approach tends to be pretty transparent. An honest assessment of risks is also important – their nature, and how probable you judge them to be. Again, investors today are looking for realism.

Share capital structure

Assuming you are not a pure start-up, investors will need to see who owns what. The cleaner the share capital structure, the better – no warrants to the web designer, options to the doctor, huge numbers of different classes of shares to several rounds of angel investors. VCs also dislike businesses which give 98 per cent to the founder and nothing to the other members of the team.

How much are you raising?

In a downturn when valuations are low and exit possibilities capped, business models which consume a lot of capital are very hard to fund at all. The following example, from Gerry Montanus at Atlas, gives an indication why on page 166. Assume the venture capitalist thinks the company can, in time, be sold for as much as $150m.

The model shows three rounds of funding – series A, B and C. The pre-money valuation denotes the value ascribed to the company before the investment is made, the post-money valuation after. The latter is arrived at by adding the cash invested, in this case $8m, to the pre-money valuation. If a venture firm invests $8m, at '$8m pre' it will own 50 per cent of the company whose post money valuation is $16m.

	New money	Pre-money valuation	Post-money valuation
Series A	$8m	$8m	$16m
Series B	$15m	$32m	$47m
Series C	$25m	$70m	$95m

A series B pre-money valuation of $32m would give the series A investor a theoretical return of 100 per cent. If the series B investor invests at $32m pre, that is twice the post-money valuation of series A. The 100 per cent theoretical return accounts for the fact that he is putting money in at the earliest, riskiest stage. The series B investor then receives a (theoretical) return of less than two times his money between series B and series C. The series C investor also receives less than two times on a putative exit at $150m. This is not the exceptional return a VC is looking for.

The other problem is that VCs are reluctant to take a majority stake in a company at the outset. Often this affects their tax structure. They recognize it is demotivating, and steadily more so as future funding rounds further dilute the founder or founders.

If you think you need to raise $40m or $50m to reach profitability, remember to look at the capital requirement in the context of the venture capitalist's exit. In an up market, people will tell you to ask for less than you need as a tactic to get as much as possible at as high a valuation as possible. If you say you are fully funded it creates the illusion of scarcity and may generate extra interest. In the downturn, the situation is more or less the opposite and a heavy dose of realism is needed as to how much cash you can get by on – at the low valuation that you are going to be given. This section of the plan needs to detail how much you are looking for – a range is OK – and how you intend to use the cash. If you ask for too much, investors will balk because they worry you will fritter it away. At the same time, there is a balance. If you ask for too little, it shows ignorance of what it takes to build a company to profitability ($20m to $30m for a software company, for instance). Risk-shy VCs also seem to be in danger of forgetting that, to generate a significant win, a company has to be spending money fast enough that it is loss making for two or three years.

Give an indication of the further funding rounds you anticipate to get to profitability. This is tricky. In boom times, there may be days when the elapse of time is sufficient to secure more cash from new investors at steadily higher valuations. The post-bubble period has ushered in 'flat' or 'down' rounds and made venture capitalists highly suspicious of each other's deals. Further funding is very much tied to achievements of specific milestones – proving the product works, generating initial revenues, broadening the customer base, becoming cash flow positive, and so on.

Exit

'Our exit strategy is an IPO at £100m or £150m' is the *wrong* thing to say, especially in a period when the initial public offering markets are closed. Any mention of an IPO needs to give heavy acknowledgement of the fickleness of public markets, while such a precise number simply smacks of naivety. Concentrate, rather, on what sort of trade buyers might acquire you.

Times frames have extended dramatically. During the bubble (when businesses were going public within two years, and the public markets were playing at being venture capitalists) the cliché used to be 'an exit within three to five years'. Now that venture capitalists are back to building real businesses, a more realistic assumption might be four to seven years. But mentioning the exit will help you stand out from the crowd. Peter Englander at Apax Partners says that most business plans omit the subject entirely: 'They all leave us to figure it out, because they are so sure it is going to be a great business.'

Valuation

While it is important to be thinking about the valuation at this stage, you are unlikely to want to put it down in black and white in either the executive summary or the business plan (although plenty of entrepreneurs certainly did that in the bubble, when everyone had very definite, hugely inflated ideas about what their business was worth). If the number you pick is far too high, you get dismissed as unrealistic. But if you are too conservative, you might end up aiming lower than the figure the VC had actually been prepared to pay.

As discussions progress, you might give a range – 'we need $5m to $8m and are thinking of giving away between a quarter and a third of the company', for instance. But do so only after you have tested the temperature around the market. Most VCs are put off by entrepreneurs who are too fixed on valuation. At the same time you don't want to be clueless, which Gerry Montanus warns is a big mistake: 'If someone says to me, what do you think I'm worth, it doesn't make a strong impression.'

The first to remember, though, is that valuation is art, not science. Shortly after Elderstreet, a small freewheeling and quintessentially English VC, had been acquired by Dresdner Kleinwort Wasserstein, Michael Jackson, its founder, was joking with colleagues about the new owners. The Germans had been asking about Elderstreet's systems, he told them. There had been a series of questions about how the firm operated: What for example was 'the valuation process'? Jackson laughed – and did an elaborate finger in the air gesture.

At the earliest stages of a company, the price is, in the absence of any concrete metrics, basically what someone is willing to pay. In the downturn, the fundamental question for a VC is whether something is worth investing in. Valuations are so low that price barely enters the equation. This is in stark contrast to bubble behaviour when everyone thought they knew what to invest in, and the decision came down much more to one of price. Mark Suster puts the entrepreneur's point of view: 'You can do all the spreadsheets in the world – calculations based on multiple of revenues or discounted cash flow. But if you are a start-up and have no track record, the VCs will say: 'We don't believe your numbers, most early stage businesses are £3m post-money.' Valuation is about the market. It is a question of listening. You need to see enough investors to get an idea of value.' And remember, as this book repeatedly stresses, valuation is far from the only consideration – it is the overall package, including the quality of the investor and the terms of the agreement that matters.

Valuations during the late 1990s bubble were not only unrelated to profits, which, if anyone talked about them, were years in the future, but assigned numbers to business models and brands that did not yet exist. As Chris Grew, senior partner at lawyers Hale and Dorr, remarked in the autumn of 1999 (*Financial Times*, 1999): 'Any venture capitalist who says they have a definitive way of valuing an internet start-up is lying through their teeth or smoking an illegal substance.' If any science is applied to the art of valuation it comes in a number of forms. A (by no means complete) list follows.

Comparables

Hermann Hauser says that during 2000 'everyone' worked off revenue multiples, and when there were no revenues, then some surrogate or other was roped in such as multiples of 'eyeballs'. In January 2000 he sold E*Trade UK to E*Trade US – which he characterizes as 'one of my better deals'. The initial offer from the US part of the online investment group (which was of course the only buyer) had valued the UK operation at $80m. As Hauser tells the story, he commissioned an investment banker to dig around and find whichever metric would allow E*Trade UK to put the highest price on its head. Some handy metric which valued the business at $450m was duly produced and E*Trade US agreed to split the difference, settling on a figure of around $200m. In the minor biotechnology bubble that occurred in the early 1990s, companies would be valued on multiples of PhDs. If a comparable business was valued at $50m and had 50 PhDs, then a start-up with 10 PhDs was worth $10m, is how the 'logic' ran.

Venture capitalists have now moved away from the eyeballs which were (an exceptionally poor) proxy for revenues, which in turn were a proxy for free cash flow or profits. Some say they are looking for more concrete metrics – but what can they look at?

The earlier the stage, the less any sort of metric can apply. Says one investor that specializes in university spin-outs: 'We will sit down and figure out together with the team how much money they need. Say they need $5m. We will then figure out what sort of stake motivates everyone – us, the founders (including the university), and an option pool of 25 per cent if we need to recruit a chief executive.' But taking some form of comparable – either private financings for similar businesses, or public market valuations, or a combination – is still a quick and dirty way to come up with a rough valuation. However, by definition, little information is available on private companies. Even if the valuation is known, the financials will not be. Also, there are huge regional distortions. For instance, the weight of a lot of unsophisticated venture capital euros pushed valuations in Germany vertiginously, not just during the bubble but for a considerable period thereafter. Meanwhile, there are clearly plenty of problems with taking public market valuations, including the need to take a sizeable discount for the illiquidity of a private company.

Venture capital method

This method (adapted from a Harvard Business School note, 1998) tries to determine the value of the company at exit and then discount back to a present day value. The calculation is as follows:

$$\text{Discounted terminal value} = \frac{\text{Terminal value}}{(1 + \text{Target rate of return})^{\text{years}}}$$

A VC plans to invest $5m in a start-up biotechnology company, and needs to determine what size stake he takes. After working through projections with the company, each side is happy with forecast net earnings of $20m in year seven. The average PE for (the few) profitable publicly listed biotech companies is 15, so the VC makes the assumption that the terminal value can be estimated as net earnings times the PE multiple. There are 500,000 shares outstanding. The VC believes 50 per cent is an appropriate target rate of return for the risk he is assuming. Putting those numbers into the above formula:

$$\text{Discounted terminal value} \quad = \quad \frac{20 * 15}{(1 + 50\,\%)^7} \quad = \quad \$17.5\text{m}$$

His required stake is therefore the value of his investment ($5m) divided by the discounted terminal value ($17.5m), namely 28.5 per cent. Hence the number of new shares will be:

$$\frac{500,000}{(1-28.5\%)} - 500,000 = 200,000$$

The price per new share is therefore $5m divided by 200,000, or $25 per share.

Hence the pre-money valuation would be $12.5m (500,000 * $25 per cent share) and the post-money valuation $17.5m. The calculation would need to be amended to take account of the dilution effect of further financings rounds. The drawbacks to this method include the fact that today's multiples are an extremely bad guide to values ascribed by the market to businesses in five years' time – as recent history has amply demonstrated. Moreover, the discount factor applied is, as the HBS study points out, the 'fudge' factor – it changes everything.

Discounted cash flow or net present value method

'This is the only methodology that has any mathematical rigour,' says one venture capitalist. 'The mistake we made in the bubble was paying too much attention to revenue multiples at exit. And we also did it without perspective. We accepted the "paradigm shift" argument, so we didn't look at revenue multiples over a long period of time.'

Yet predicting the cash flow on an early stage loss-making business is itself such a wild stab that any 'mathematical rigour' would seem to be quite limited. Certainly at the earliest stage, the uncertainty is so great that you can basically pick any number you want. In addition, this method suffers from the same problem as the so-called venture capital model in terms of its dependence on what discount factor is applied.

Triangulation

In practice, venture capitalists will often arrive at a number by a process of 'triangulation'. They will consider the potential exit valuation. They will look at current valuations in the public and private markets. And they will try to work out the prices they might achieve for future private funding rounds – can they sensibly achieve a premium each time (the 'staircase' effect)? As I said, this process resembles art more than science.

References

Campbell, K. *Europe Seeks Strands of Gold in the Web*, Financial Times, October 14, 1999.

Magretta, J. (2002) *Why Business Models Matter*, Harvard Business Review.

Nordhaus, W. *The Economics of New Goods* by Timothy F. Bresnahan and Robert J. Gordon University of Chicago Press 1997 as quoted in William Baumol *The free-market innovation machine. Analyzing the growth miracle of capitalism*, Princeton University Press, 2002.

Sahlman, W. A. (1997) *How to Write a Great Business Plan*, Harvard Business Review.

Willinge, J. (1996, rev. 1998) "A note on valuation in private equity settigs", the President and Fellows of Harvard College, Harvard Business School teaching note. This note was prepared under the supervision of Professor Josh Lerner. Reprinted by permission of Harvard Business School.

Links

Sequoia
(Some VC firms have outline (often quite sketchy) business plan requirements on their websites. One of the best Silicon Valley VCs, Sequoia has a simple but highly intelligent road map of what they expect to see.)

www.sequoiacap.com

Index Ventures
(A pan European VC based in Geneva, has a European version.)

www.indexventures.com

Top Technology
(A UK VC, has a very good set of links for business plans.)

www.toptechnology.co.uk

MIT's enterprise forum has a good business plan resources section

http://web.mit.edu/entforum

A handy spreadsheet tool can be found at

www.accountingweb.co.uk/spreadsheetbuilder

11

Early meetings

I like to listen. I have learned a great deal from listening carefully.
Most people never listen.
(Ernest Hemingway)

PIERRE OMIDYAR, founder of eBay, turned up to the offices of Silicon Valley venture capitalist Benchmark to pitch his online flea market without a laptop, PowerPoint slides or a business plan. When he logged on, courtesy of Benchmark's hardware, his site was down. Breaking all the rules does not, unfortunately, guarantee a one-way ticket to presiding over one of the most lucrative investments in venture capital history. And Omidyar did have a couple of secret weapons. The company had the merit of being already profitable and Benchmark partner Bruce Dunlevie had, in his earlier life at venture firm Merrill, Pickard, Anderson & Eyre, backed Omidyar's previous company Ink Development, one of the few pen computing companies to reach profitability.

It is easy to be intimidated by the first meeting. Indeed, most VCs' offices seem designed to do just that. In mainland Europe, the natural habitat of the venture capitalist is often some palatial eighteenth-century building – all elegant stairways and vaulting ceilings on the outside, *'chic-er* than thou' twenty-first century design and gadgets within. In London, venture firms cluster in Mayfair and St James's occupying some of the most expensive real estate in the capital. The power statements are loud and unmissable and the settings vastly more intimidating than the comparatively casual shacks on Sand Hill Road in which the Valley's elite financiers are housed.

Ignore all that. Rid your mind, too, of any notion that you are the supplicant. 'People who turn up to a VC feeling awkward are going about it the wrong way,' says Stuart Evans, chief executive of Plastic Logic in Cambridge. 'You need to get away from the thought that they are somehow doing you a favour. No. You are doing *them* a favour. You are a solution to their problem, which is where do they find good companies?' Confidence is infectious. Alain Falys at Open Business Exchange claims he scarcely had a bad moment even raising money in the teeth of a bear market, and one almost believes him. Was there any point, I ask, at which he thought he wouldn't raise the money? ' No.' He pauses. 'Not a chance. You have to have the mindset that you will win. I was absolutely convinced I would get *some* money. Of course, what goes through your mind is the amount and from whom. But not whether.' He started fund raising in early September 2001. 'This was exactly the time the VCs were pretending they were investing, but they weren't. They suddenly wanted three successive quarters of revenues. We had just released the service but couldn't show tangible usage. The so-called early stage VCs were disappearing by the day.' He conceded the negotiations were 'tough'; but then that is what business is about he says with a gallic shrug.

Look at fund raising as the ultimate selling job – selling yourself, your idea and your team. Do not drop your guard because of nervousness or a setback. Following the arrival of a vicious term sheet from one investor, the chairman of a young software company lost confidence entirely at his next meeting, which was with a Scottish venture capitalist. Barely in through the door, he started enthusing about how he had always banked with a Scottish bank, because he considered the Scots 'good with money'. Be rehearsed and professional. And, whatever venture capitalists may say about being astute about penetrating facades, first impressions count. Just as with a job interview, turn up on time, and look presentable. As for the formality of business attire, it is hard to generalize. While the rest of the business world put its ties back on in mid-2000 as the dress-down dotcom wave evaporated, venture capitalists have largely kept their Prada shirts open at the neck. But opinions certainly differ. Says one continental European investor: 'In Europe, you can only do the casual thing on your home turf. Depending where you are, it could be taken as a lack of respect. I think the safe bet is to wear a tie.' Contrast a US VC in London: 'In the Valley, a suit and tie would be taboo. Here it is a bit more formal. We see ties and we are not put off at all.'

If the first meeting is with a partner of the firm, so much the better. But in the larger organizations you are quite likely to start off at associate level, even if your initial introduction was to a partner. Remember that, assuming he likes the proposition, the associate has to sell it internally himself, so concentrate on making his life easy for him. He is likely to be an extremely bright individual, but cannot be expected to perform some sort of translation Houdini job on a still poorly articulated grand vision. Meetings in Europe tend to be rather longer than in the USA, where 30 or 40 minutes is all you are likely to get. When 3i executives moved to the USA at the end of the 1990s, they found entrepreneurs would be amazed they had been allocated an hour and a half for a meeting. And there will be little preamble – save, perhaps a brief aside on sport. European VCs may well give you an hour, occasionally more, and the whole process is more relationship driven. Charles Irving, co-founder of UK-based Pond Ventures with his techie brother Richard who operates from San Jose, California, adds: 'I'm being all smooth and warm and I can just see him [Richard] fiddling around, dying for the entrepreneur to get to the white boards and put the formulas down.'

But that does not give you carte blanche to meander. Annoying but true, Americans are much crisper at presenting. So cut the leisurely stroll through how you founded the company ten years ago and dispense with the tangle of technical specifications that make your product the best thing since sliced widgets. Instead, distil your message into ten or a dozen PowerPoint slides. The trick is to tease your audience into wanting to know more, not to suffocate them. Plan on presenting for perhaps a quarter of an hour, with the rest of the time left for questions and answers. Practise beforehand – to friends and colleagues. Respond to their feedback. Much as it may go against the grain, consider going on a course to learn how to present. Venture capitalists know perfectly well that good presenters are not necessarily gifted entrepreneurs, and vice versa. But packaging is pretty important. Kicking off with a bad presentation is an unnecessary and possibly fatal handicap.

Do the homework on your audience too. Venture capitalists will be very disappointed if you don't know who they are and which (successful) companies they backed. Remember flattery gets you everywhere. Express enthusiasm (provided it is genuine) for a company the VC has backed.

Give careful consideration to whom you take along. For the initial meeting regarding an early stage business, the venture capitalist will only be interested in seeing the core founders or, in a more mature company, the chief executive. Leave the team for later, because the larger the number of people, the greater the scope for contradiction. A software company struggling to raise second-round funding wheeled out the chairman, the managing director and the chief technology officer on every occasion. The three spent their entire time chipping in and contradicting each other about the most trivial matters. 'No we didn't sign the contract on April 5, it was April 3,' one would say, and a long discussion would ensue. Says a consultant who was called in mid-fund raising: 'Venture capitalists are trying to rate how professional the business is. It was a disaster. My main aim now? To keep them all on message, and stop them going off piste.'

It is a good idea to have someone in the meeting solely to observe – to give you feedback, but also to watch (unobtrusively) the venture capitalists. At what points do they look interested? When are they frowning – or worse, nodding off?

In terms of the content of the presentation, many of the principles applied to a successful business plan are once again relevant. Here are some basic dos and don'ts (see box).

Presentation

Do

◆ Explain straight away what the company does. Do not leave the investor puzzling eight slides in – which happens quite frequently. And say what you do rather than what you don't. In the fashion-driven venture world companies sometimes get sucked into distancing themselves from the last year's fashion – 'we are not an e-commerce company' – neglecting to describe positively what they themselves are up to.

◆ Keep it simple. Complexity merely suggests to the venture capitalist that you have not entirely mastered your subject.

◆ Find the burning problem and articulate it forcefully. Too many start-ups are a solution looking for a problem. A service offering mobile messaging at 6pm every evening detailing films showing in the user's neighbourhood does not address a pressing need.

◆ Tell a story – and, as in any form of public speaking, play with pitch, volume and speed to hold your audience's attention. Garage Technology Ventures, which coaches entrepreneurs in Silicon Valley on how to raise venture capital, went as far as employing a director of storytelling to coach on pitches.

◆ Avoid so-what statements. 'Our distribution costs are 15 per cent.' Without a relevant comparison to traditional costs in the industry concerned (or the nearest equivalent if it is an entirely new sector) this remains a meaningless piece of information.

◆ Acknowledge you have been lucky when talking about past success. VCs (not all of whom are quite as ready to acknowledge their own luck) are long on this. 'Being in the right place in a bull market is different from being good,' says one venture capitalist. Er, yes.

◆ Watch and *listen*. 'Sometimes we see people who are really well prepared, really in tune with the market and their customers and they
don't listen to anyone,' complains one Italian investor. 'For us the last
thing we want to have is a powerful strong machine on autopilot that
you cannot change. If we feel we have zero influence we don't want to
be a partner. We would rather take someone who was a little bit less
prepared but who was more flexible and who listened.'

◆ Be receptive, too, to signals. Even the location of the first meeting will
tell you something about the firm's style – if held in the associate or
partner's office, this may suggest the firm is a more informal set-up
than if you all troop off to the boardroom.

◆ Think of the investor as a future evangelist for your deal within his
own firm and start giving him the right ammunition.

Don't

◆ Assume the venture capitalist has read anything you have sent in. They
are busy people and often will either not have got round to reading you
materials at all, or have only glanced at it.

◆ Produce a set of excessively decorative slides. As Guy Kawasaki, chief
executive of Garage Technology Ventures, told one unfortunate team
attending after a presentation at the end of their summer entrepreneurship class at London Business School: 'First, I wish I was colour
blind. And second, what you've mostly told me [in the course of the
presentation] is you just got a Mac for the first time.'

◆ Undersell. PDAs are the second fastest consumer electronics market in
the UK, says the entrepreneur, pointing to a chart showing digital
cameras prominently as number one – which would mainly suggest to
most VCs that they should go and fund something in the digital
camera sector. Have the chart showing PDA volumes as the biggest
bar. Then you can say: 'PDAs, after digital cameras, are the second
fastest growing . . .' Again, if you have a slide showing your 'unfair
advantage' with just a pair of rather limp and lonely bullet points, it
will not look all that unfair.

◆ Lie. If you neglect to tell investors about something dodgy or if you
tell them the opposite of the truth, it is the kiss of death when they find
it out for themselves during their due diligence process. Imagine you
claim to have 'great traction with Cisco'. The venture capitalist subsequently rings up. 'Oh yes,' says the executive, 'those bunch of jokers.
We'd never buy their X.'

◆ Attempt to negotiate. It is far too early; both sides are simply getting to know each other at this stage.

◆ Dismiss the VCs as stupid if they reject the idea, not least because most are not. Treat the meeting as an opportunity to learn – from their reaction to the presentation, from the questions asked. Make sure you have pumped them for information too. On the basis of what you have gleaned, change the pitch as you go along. Neil Rimer at Index Ventures says that good teams learn from good investors and vice versa. Teams that Index has turned down come back to the firm for advice, he says. 'People can be bogged down in the details and be missing out on larger trends.'

Figuring out which buttons to press is an important part of the game. Alain Falys at OBE says that in hindsight he focused in meetings too much on how his electronic invoicing process worked and spent too little time explaining the business model itself: 'We would start too many meetings saying: 'Let's show you how we do it' and we would then go into this elaborate whiteboard exercise on electronic invoicing. If you are selling to the CFO of a large corporation, that is absolutely the right thing to do. He knows he receives a million paper invoices a year. But VCs may never have *seen* a paper invoice.' To capture an investor's attention, however, the more appropriate approach is to focus on the nitty-gritty of how you are going to make money – in OBE's case, using the internet to facilitate cheap transactions in a virtuous circle.

The big communication challenge is bridging the knowledge gap – the entrepreneur is intimately familiar with his business, his audience is not. Be quick to calibrate the presentation to the audience's level. Jim Swartz at Accel Partners takes the view that his partners are not doing their job if they do not already know '80 or 90 per cent' of what is in any individual presentation. In Europe, such levels of knowledge would be rare, with the possible exception of biotechnology and, while levels of expertise have improved greatly in the past few years, the ignorant – and often equally arrogant – investor is alive and well. Differences in knowledge and preparation come down to individuals too as much as to firms.

Meanwhile, you need to control the meeting – as senior executives are taught in media training sessions on how to handle journalists. Work out the key messages you want to get across, know your agenda and stick to it. Venture capitalists can be easily distracted by their own assumptions and may have rather too many preconceived ideas about which box to put your business in, and of course they like the buzz words. 'So won't web services knock this out?' they will ask. Do not be deflected. Explaining that you will get to web services later, continue teaching them about your market and product.

In assembling the agenda, you will need to think carefully about the venture capitalist's priorities. If you are selling a product or service aimed at large enterprises in a downturn when corporations' budgets are pared to the bone, you will want to start off (as related in Chapter 10) by convincing investors this is a 'must-have', not a 'nice-to-have' item for customers. Give them a graphic illustration in the meeting of the sort of payback a customer can expect. Falys would run through a large customer with 15,000 suppliers. For every 10,000 invoices received, this service would allow the corporation to dispense with one clerk, his argument ran.

Plan for what one might term 'pitch decay'. People recall on average 50 per cent of the information put across in a presentation after one hour, 20 per cent the next day and 10 per cent after a week, according to research by Garage Technology Ventures. Figure out the 10 per cent you want your investors to remember and tell them three times.

Identify strengths and weaknesses of the business, and make sure you address the weaknesses adequately. Being up front and realistic about the competition and short-term challenges is not a mistake. Realism will be valued. One venture capitalist revealed a discussion with one entrepreneur he had recently backed operating in the hard-pressed telecommunications industry: 'He is extremely enthusiastic, but there is an element of naivety. We had a frank discussion. I said I recognized perfectly well that an absolute key personality trait of the entrepreneur is that the glass is always half full. But if the glass is nearly always almost full, the attitude becomes dangerous. What you actually need is that rare mix of the glass being half full combined with paranoia. You need sleepless nights.'

Giuseppe Zocco at Index Ventures observes: 'So many people think they have to oversell. That if they show weakness they will be out of here. But the better and more mature investors love entrepreneurs who are open. You should level with the investor as a partner.' More broadly, investors will be beginning to make an assessment of your qualities as an entrepreneur. Remember that many subscribe to the thesis that investment success derives from paying attention to three basic principles – management, management and management.

Jim Swartz, a veteran VC, gives the five enduring traits he seeks in an entrepreneur (1990). In order of importance, these are leadership, vision, integrity, openness and dedication. Leadership speaks for itself, though not everyone has it. Vision, Swartz points out, doesn't come magically, but is hard work. Integrity is nearly impossible to assess on first impressions. That is something you know about after six months of working closely. Openness is something he describes as 'constantly reassessing, becoming your own management consultant'. But there is a fine line: 'Flexibility can be insecurity in disguise. You don't want a plan that is simply the VC's vision.' Dedication and perseverance speak for themselves – and qualities that were conspicuously missing in many would-be entrepreneurs in the late 1990s. 'Are all of these qualities always there,' Swartz asks rhetorically. 'No. Are VCs always right? Clearly not.'

Knowledge of the venture process is another trait that will tend to impress. Show you understand the venture capitalist's need for an exit and that you have thought about it sufficiently to enumerate possible (realistic) alternatives. Perhaps the thorniest issue to consider is what you will say about whether you, as founder, may need to make way for a professional chief executive at some later date. As already suggested, venture capitalists can legitimately be criticized for being far too trigger-happy with management changes – and it may seem more than a trifle contradictory given the management times three mantra. But it is accepted wisdom in the business that different skills are needed at the various stages in a company's evolution. However you may look at it, a venture capitalist will see it as evidence of 'maturity' that you can encompass that option.

Meanwhile, if three-quarters of the meeting is to be devoted to questions, prepare for those just as – if not more – thoroughly as for the presentation. 'People are far too often thrown by the questions and answers,' says one adviser. 'But that is arguably the most important part.' If the VCs are letting you deliver a monologue, things are probably not going well. A good meeting is likely to be very interactive. Make a list of all the questions you least want to be asked, and work out careful answers. When they come up, you can then respond easily and casually. Remain open and friendly. VCs have seen more than their fill of negative and defensive types as the bubble evaporated. Consider what the VCs' biggest fears are – putting money into the wrong deal, or missing out on a hot deal – and what they are best at – sitting on the fence. Do your best to answer their questions.

The nature of the questioning will revolve around their investment precepts and their attempts to avoid past mistakes. Do you have a sustainable competitive advantage? Is your intellectual property defensible? What is unique about it? Has it been patented or is it patentable? Or does the defensibility of the business lie in the fact that you think you are two years ahead because it took you two years to build the software? Expect probing, clearly, on your customers and the size of the opportunity. 'How entrepreneurs answer questions is a key part of our assessment,' says Anne Glover of

Amadeus. She goes back to the 'burning problem' question. 'I always ask, what problem are you solving? It is amazing how many people cannot answer that. Or they give a technical response – "well, it's the hardest mathematical problem that's left". Or an engineering answer: "There's this Intel product that does this that's missing that component."'

What can VCs see past?

'We *should* be able to see past the great product engineer who doesn't know how to sell. I wish we always did, but we don't,' says Glover. 'If an engineer really understands the problem, then the salesman can deliver. But if the engineering team can't articulate what problem they are solving, the sales guy can't develop the sales message.' She cites one entrepreneur who succeeding in raising large sums of capital during the bubble. 'He could explain the problem. That's why he got the money. What he didn't have was the solution – for about three years – but no one had figured that out at that stage.' And in terms of the buying decision, investors want a lot of detail. 'Who is going to champion your product within the organization and who is the specific decision maker who authorizes it? Invariably people haven't thought in terms of the organization they are selling to,' says Glover.

One thing venture capitalists often get wrong is the size of the opportunity. The company may have got the customer need exactly right, but there may be only six customers with that particular need on the planet.

Can the management team execute? Burnt by immature 'boy band' management teams learning on venture capital money during the bubble, investors became much more concerned, paranoid, even, about this. They will want to see extensive evidence of the team's experience. 'As a mature [for which read, battle-scarred] investor you start being very sceptical on markets and execution,' says one venture capitalist sporting new grey hairs. 'You tend to be quite demanding on their analysis, why they should succeed, how they will get it done. At the same time, in the first meeting you will probably give the benefit of the doubt to the entrepreneur, you won't discount everything at first swallow.'

Expect plenty of questions about the competition. Will Microsoft do this? And don't trash competitors potential or actual. After all, Microsoft could be a potential acquirer of the business as well as a competitor. Given the analytical bent of many venture capitalists, detailed financial questions will clearly be on the menu. Most will take comfort from a lot of figures. Have three or four financial metrics that are very concrete. How many customers do you need to get to break even in two years time, and what are your assumptions? Don't guess. 'I need 20 customers to get to break even with an average of x transactions each and a sales lead time of five months.' Why a sales lead time of five months? 'Because in X [comparable] industry I worked in, it was three months and I'm being conservative.' A more intangible point, but, after squandering their dotcom dollars, VCs are now very keen on fiscal responsibility and doing things within a tight budget. The opposite sets alarm bells ringing.

The first meeting should also be a chance to ask the VCs questions (treated in greater detail in the next chapter). For instance, since you are unlikely to have secured a non-disclosure agreement, it will be useful to try and determine whether the investor is evaluating other companies in your area.

Results

One software entrepreneur, who worked with an adviser on a second round financing, says he could invariably tell which investors were seriously interested – which the adviser could not. Some VCs will only be holding the meeting to find out more about the industry – the equivalent of apartment hunting in Paris, when you have not yet figured out if you want to live in the sixth arrondissement or the Marais. They will tend to ask general questions, and will tend not to drill down to the strengths and weaknesses of the business.

Those VCs that are effective at filtering (see Chapter 9) know what questions to ask, which boxes to tick – and tend to respond quickly. 'I divide investors into three categories,' this entrepreneur says. 'Lost, shopping for information, or actually serious.'

Second meeting

The principal aim of the first meeting is to get a second meeting which is likely to be considerably longer. Says one French VC: 'In the first meeting, I challenge them a bit on two or three points, to see whether they are really in command of their topic, but mostly I let them talk. Maybe this lasts an hour. Then the second meeting will be longer. Sometimes people start strongly for an hour. But then in a longer meeting they appear how they are, they falter. At the end of the meeting, they may have gone down so much that I say: "Thank you guys I am not interested."'

Investors may well want to meet the entire senior management team (if there is one). Agree what everybody will say, and emphasize consistency. Consider bringing them on one at a time so they do not contradict each other. Some investors may of course insist on seeing the team together so that they get an idea of chemistry. Be consistent – within meetings, within the team, and between meetings. For instance, perhaps you told the prospective investor at the first meeting that you were not proposing to follow an indirect sales strategy. At a later meeting, someone mentions the company is talking to Accenture (because you met an executive from Accenture at a recent trade fair). This suggests that, at best, you are excessively opportunistic. And beware 'casual' meetings. Never drop your guard throughout this process.

Finally, it is worth bearing in mind the most frequent reasons VCs cite for *not* investing. Lack of trust of the individuals invariably comes near or top of the list. Insufficient market potential is another bugbear; even at the level the entrepreneur perceives it, there is simply not a large enough market. 'Crazy' valuation expectations are another killer, even if the team and the proposition have gone down well. Just as in a job interview, you don't negotiate salary until you gauge the prospective employer definitely wants you, so you should not introduce valuation, certainly not any fixed level of valuation, at the early meetings. In a bear market, valuations are so low anyway as to be virtually an irrelevance: it is the terms and the nature of the post-investment relationship that counts.

Reference

Swartz, J. (1990) *Computer Systems News*, 30 July.

12

Due diligence

La diligencia es madre de la buena ventura.
[Diligence is the mother of good fortune.]
(Miguel de Cervantes, *Don Quixote*, 1605)

DUE DILIGENCE IS A fancy phrase denoting research. It involves the venture capitalist coming into the business and peering under every stone – assuming, that is, they are doing their job properly. Firms differ in their policy as to whether they do the bulk of the work before or after issuing the term sheet. Giuseppe Zocco at Index Ventures in Geneva says: 'We do most *before* the term sheet. We want to be 80 or 90 per cent sure we are going to do the deal, because we don't want to give false hopes to the team.' Investors also want, as far as possible, to prevent the company from hawking their term sheet around to competitors. The more prominent the fund, the more sensitive its partners will be to having its name used to solicit other offers. Moreover, as a matter of credibility, a good venture capitalist does not want to issue a term sheet that is not accepted. 'But it is a balance,' says Zocco. 'If you produce it earlier, it may make the team more relaxed. Things are pretty tense [in a bear funding market] and every day counts.' By contrast, firms which carry out the bulk of the due diligence afterwards are often simply trying to lock up the deal. Their aim is to get the entrepreneur to sign up to exclusivity, and thereby try and stop a 'better' investor getting involved. They may well then attempt to negotiate the price down based on their 'findings' in due diligence.

From the entrepreneur's point of view, it is clearly undesirable to get locked up in exclusivity with an early term sheet because you back yourself into a weak negotiating position. If that deal then falls through, you have cut yourself off from other investors. The timing of the work in relation to issuance of the term sheet also depends on how much the venture capitalist is carrying out in-house. Those without deep technical backgrounds, for instance, would farm out the technical report to a consultant, which costs money. So they may not want to start the meter running until the company has signed a term sheet and (effectively) agreed to pay those costs. Legal and accounting due diligence on which money has to be spent are typically carried out post-term sheet. The curiosity that most venture firms expect you to pay *their* research costs will be dealt with below. Obviously, the earlier stage the business, the less due diligence can sensibly be done.

In the frenzied bubble period, of course, when venture capitalists were falling over each other to muscle their way into 'unmissable' deals, due diligence was skimpy in the extreme. John McMonigall, director of Apax Partners, says he heard plenty of 'horror stories' of firms literally not carrying out any: 'Entrepreneurs would say to us indignantly: "Why are you asking all these questions?" We tried to stick to our process – although we did do some deals more quickly.' Most venture firms will now claim it was always 'the other guy' who skimped. In Apax's cases it happens to be more than spin (not that they entirely avoided the bad investments). Says one entrepreneur raising funds during the bubble, who went elsewhere for funding: 'Apax was frustrating at the time – but smart in hindsight. They wanted us to take less money, to focus on one country and were slow in their decision making – with loads of analysis. Apax wanted personal references, people I'd worked with in the past, what they said about me.'

More typical was one of the many late stage buy-out firms that had secured permission from its limited partners to stray from what it knew best in order to play at some early stage internet investing. One of its senior directors remembers pitching up to an investment committee meeting where a younger colleague was presenting a proposal. The colleague, excited and close to making the investment, waxed lyrical on the idea, the team, the likely exit valuation. 'And what are they going to spend the money on?' the director enquired. There was a deathly hush. No one had thought to ask.

A headhunter who worked in venture capital during the bubble, reflects: 'It always used to surprise me that people spent 95 per cent of their time – and this was particularly true in Europe – structuring a deal. They did so little checking of the background of entrepreneurs, how people react in certain situations, and so on.' The areas on which an investor will concentrate are likely to be related to their previous background. Structuring deals is what bankers do, and many venture capitalists are former bankers. Ex-management consultants may be more inclined to spend time phoning customers to ask about arcane aspects of the market rather than probing a management team's background. Following the April 2000 Nasdaq slide, Anne Glover of Amadeus was quick to spot a silver lining to the end of the euphoria: 'It means we can go back to doing our job properly,' she said.

During the downturn, however, investors seem to have gone to the other extreme, and are spending many months over the process. What can possibly take all that time, you may well ask. Why spend four months of due diligence on a piece of technology if the venture capitalist is in the end really backing *me*? Well, investors are certainly doing the job somewhat more thoroughly. They are making more customer calls to try and satisfy themselves about who will actually buy the product. They are seeking more extensive validation of the technology from third party experts. There are more checks concerning who else has invested in the area. Their internal decision making may well be more standardized and formal. And, very importantly, they are not working 14-hour days; the power is in their hands and they do not feel in a hurry. If you calculate that might add up to an extra three or four weeks, the only answer can be that most of the rest of the time is spent fence sitting and pre-varicating.

They may be prevaricating, but the last thing you want to do is to add to the delays. So one of the main tricks is to get back quickly to your potential investors, with good quality information. Make life as easy for them as possible. It makes you look professional, which in turn should give them additional confidence. Rather than taking weeks to reply to a particular question, try and exceed their expectations by producing facts and figures which are perhaps more comprehensive than those actually requested. Prepare as much paperwork as possible in advance – have copies of all contracts (employment and customer agreements and so on) well organised and ready to send out. As they pull apart your carefully constructed business plan, remember they are not going through the exercise just for fun. Many will be compiling an internal proposal (which you will never see – saying things, as it may, about the weaknesses of the team or such like) probably thicker than your original plan to put to their investment committee, or their fellow partners.

At the same time, the process is also about getting to know each other – and seeing if there is mutual chemistry. Christopher Spray, principal at Atlas Venture, says: 'There has to be – and I know it sounds trivial – mutual trust. You have to feel you understand each other, that there is going to be a real conversation, rather than talking past each other. However gifted the entrepreneur, if you have no real chemistry, or if you feel you will have no influence on him, it is going to be a struggle.' Spray mentions one Atlas portfolio company where the CEO is 'very talented, but it's very hard to have any influence on him'. On occasion a venture capitalist will decide to go along for the ride anyway – or just find out when it is too late. But, rightly, the better ones are looking for a proper partnership.

The exercise will of course demand more of your time than you possibly imagine, and the danger is that for months you are distracted from the business. It will also place demands on the company at all levels. Says one investor: 'We expect to know half the staff [of a larger 30- or 40-man business] by name.' One entrepreneur complains of armies of consultants camped out in his small offices following the term sheet signing. He had a syndicate of several investors, and while they had agreed in theory to divide the work between themselves, that had not happened in practice. (One reason, incidentally, to limit the size of any syndicate – and certainly to insist there is division of labour in the process.) Meanwhile, given the time you will be spending, you might as well make sure you get as much out of it all as possible. Pump the various parties for information and listen to useful feedback. Then at least you will have some positive benefits even if that firm does not invest.

Finally, be prepared to answer the inevitable stupid questions patiently – the venture capitalist is doing his best to understand your business in a pretty short time frame, and it will certainly not advance your cause to make him feel in any way dumb.

The process

The areas investors will be probing break down broadly as follows: technology, market, people, financials, and legal and accounting.

The technology

Just because you have a few patents, it does not mean your technology is interesting, unique or defensible. So for a technology business this is one of the areas where the venture capitalist will be keenest to dig. A distinguished Cambridge scientist who knows the UK venture community well observes: 'One thing that has always fascinated me is what incredibly crappy bits of technology VCs back, how dumb their technical due diligence is. There is nothing like the level of technical competence there is in the US, even if it is getting better.' It is traditional to knock European venture capitalists' knowledge of technology (not that the Americans' supposed technical competence saved them from folly in the bubble). In the pre-bubble era, that was certainly true. James Dobree, former chief executive of content management software company Zygon, recalls one of his investors sending in a so-called technical consultant. The questions, he says, were more about the team – or him. The fact that he was a former Oracle executive, even though (if anyone bothered to ask) on the strategy planning side, was more or less enough: 'Because I'd been at Oracle I had this aura. These were very early days in entrepreneurship in Britain.'

Clearly the process tends to be a good deal more sophisticated these days. An important part of the quality of a venture capitalist's network resides in the resources he can draw on to stress-test the technology. The best investors will call on a wide variety of sources, starting with their contacts at big corporations. As Kevin Comolli, managing general partner of Accel in Europe, puts it: 'If it is something new in the software space, we will want to know if it links up, say, with IBM's view of the future.' Chief technology officers or vice presidents of engineering at other portfolio companies will often also be asked to proffer an opinion. This works both ways, and can be a useful way for portfolio companies to keep abreast of new developments. And the technology community is quite small. Christopher Spray of Atlas tells the story of Systemonic, one of the first companies to be spun out of a German university. His Munich-based colleague Alex Brühl had had a couple of meetings with founder Professor Gerhard Fettweis and other members of the team from the Dresden University of Technology. There were the rudiments of a business plan. So Atlas principals started asking around their wider network to get an idea of who might be able to do due diligence on this type of technology. 'The answer kept coming back, Fettweis. We knew we were on to a leader,' says Spray. The man knew more about the subject [specialist silicon systems for the wireless sector] than anyone else they could find. Some venture firms also have technical advisory board members – who vary in their availability and effectiveness when it comes to reviewing potential investments. On the whole it is the weaker VCs who outsource technology due diligence. 'You can push a button and generate a report, but in most cases it will be totally inconclusive. It ends up being a judgement call anyway,' observes one VC who is not a friend of that approach.

The market

Probing the market entails a broad study of the industry. Venture capitalists will vary enormously in terms of where they start on the learning curve. And the process will vary greatly according to the stage and nature of the business; if it is a new sector, for instance, the VCs will be much more limited in what they can do. Investors will look at a wide range of things, including public company comparables. But the most important factor will be what individual

customers have to say. A high technology recession in which large corporations have slashed their budgets while they digest the mammoth binge of
the late 1990s has made venture capitalists paranoid about ensuring they do
adequate customer calls. 'It is down to the level of: "Show me the line on
the budget that allows you to buy this thing",' says one newly diligent
investor.

Venture firms may want to talk to any category of customer – existing customers, prospective customers, customers lost, those who decided not to
progress from pilot stage to full commercial deployment. They will want to
know why the company is buying the product (or has stopped buying it), sat-
isfaction levels, views on pricing, and so on. 'You want to push people a bit,'
says one investor, noting that this is easier said than done in some countries.
'In southern Europe – France, Spain, Italy – this is more difficult. You have to
read much more between the lines. People prefer not to talk about challeng-
ing issues. They will tell you that everything is fine – with a commercial relationship or with the management [when doing personal background checks]
and afterwards you discover this is not the case at all.'

So how do you manage the process of the venture capitalist crawling over
your customers? Suppose they want to spend an hour and a half being sceptical on the phone to a prospective client? Will this damage your prospects of
making the sale? Well, clearly it may. You certainly do not want ten venture capitalists calling and stretching the relationship, and then not investing. Some
companies will forbid prospective investors from making customer calls until
they have received a signed term sheet. But this is not necessarily the answer.
Says one venture capitalist considering an investment in a pre-revenue company in a new area: 'We had serious questions about certain aspects of the business model. But [the entrepreneur] said he wouldn't offer us access until he got
a term sheet and an idea of our valuation. It is chicken and egg. We didn't want
to provide a speculative term sheet. We present term sheets when we are
roughly 80 per cent certain of investing and have done quite significant due
diligence. We will have discussed the deal at investment committee level. [The
entrepreneur's] point was that these people were very high level, the company
was very dependent on their goodwill, and they would only take a few calls
from VCs.'

The VC says he understands the dilemma: 'You obviously don't want to
give access to customers too early, the VCs need to understand your business.
Normally you believe in the proposition [by the time you are making customer calls]; in this case he knew I was sceptical. The entrepreneur has to
filter. But you don't want to encourage speculative term sheets. In the bubble,
people would put in speculative term sheets at a high valuation to get access

to deals, then do due diligence and drop away, or lower the valuation. In the meantime, management has focused on the wrong party, and the company is tainted.'

It comes down partly to judging your venture capitalist. In the case just mentioned, there was more to the story. The company had been warming to another party, hoping to do an interim smaller round and keep the other, larger investor, for a later round, a strategy it then decided against. While the latter was somewhat miffed, the company was able to bring the firm round – and, although a good deal of time was lost, the larger venture capital firm did eventually invest.

You also need to judge the customer. Among other things, you will want to avoid unsettling existing customers with the fact that you are fund raising in the first place. Alain Falys at Open Business Exchange advises: 'You need to agree it with those you have confidence in. Some customers you will want to "protect" from the fact you are raising money; in the case of others, you will trust their judgement better. You have to bite the bullet – but be careful how you tell them. Say something about "raising more money to expand".'

For some investors, customer calls are an integral part not just of the due diligence exercise but of the formulation and refining of the business plan. Pond Ventures is an example of a firm with a particularly hands-on approach to due diligence – with the aim of addressing one of the principal shortcomings of European technology companies, namely their failure to adapt the product to the customer's need, and their weakness at selling. So Richard Irving, Pond partner, will accompany founders on a week of calls to potential customers and strategic partners in the USA – taking economy class flights and staying in bed and breakfast places from coast to coast: 'What we are looking for is a nod from most of these people that it's cool stuff, that it solves problems that concern them,' he says, explaining that customer feedback is an integral part of refining the sales strategy.

Alain Falys, by contrast, suggested joint customer calls with his prospective investors, with a resounding lack of success. 'We said: "Instead of us trying to convince you of the viability of our product why don't you pick a client, and we will go and see the client together?" None of them took us up on this.'

The people

'If a US entrepreneur comes to you with a business plan,' says Charles Irving of Pond, 'it is assumed he or she understands the rules, what it takes [to be a

venture-backed company]. In Europe the entrepreneur is still more of a maverick, it is less the norm. We spend a hell of a lot of time checking people out.
There is no point in backing them unless they understand the risks. We want
to know how people behave, can we trust them, do they get drunk on the
plane [on the way to joint customer calls]?' Getting founders drunk *off* the
plane, though, may be part of the process – and the occasion to pose the
golden question: 'You are the founder, but during the trip to the moon it's
very likely you are not the person qualified to be CEO. What do you think
about that?' Irving says Pond walks away if the response is along the lines: I'm
the founder, I'm the CEO, it's my company.

The answer the VC wants to hear? 'Yeah I'm the founder, but I'm interested in the creation of wealth rather than the title.' This is of course only any
good if you believe it. For venture capitalists like Pond, which deals with very
early stage companies where the founder will often be the scientist who has
invented the technology, the question is all the more relevant. The motto is,
in all cases though, do not drop your guard at the 'casual' or 'informal' meeting or dinner.

Giuseppe Zocco at Index cites another reason why performing due diligence on the team is harder in Europe than the USA: 'In Silicon Valley everyone knows everyone and so personal background checks are straightforward.'
Investors who operate across Europe are constantly having to make multicultural adjustments of all kinds. 'One day we may be dealing with an introverted
Finn, the next with an exuberant Spaniard. They may both be at the same
point in their business – but it won't sound like it.' Local rules, regulations
and cultural attitudes are an extra impediment. In the Netherlands, for
instance, complains one venture capitalist, it is illegal to ask for someone's
health records: 'Oh yes, we like to know *everything*, which is why we prefer
doing business with people we know,' he adds. Whereas some venture capitalists in the USA even demand an entrepreneur's tax returns, that would still
be regarded as unusual in Europe.

For the key people in the business venture capitalists will pursue a mixture
of personal and professional references – with the professional including
people you have hired, as well as people for whom you have worked. They
will be endeavouring to find out everything from whether you have a stable
family situation – very important in helping balance the stresses and strains of
the business – to how you reacted under pressure in previous work crises.
They are entrusting you with their money so feel entitled to get very nosey.
Some even resort to forms of psychometric testing such as Brigg Myers –
something that would be frowned upon by many, especially US venture capitalists, who would have little confidence in or respect for people who did not

trust their gut feeling. 'Either you can judge people or you can't. If you have to rely on Brigg Myers maybe you shouldn't be a VC,' sniffs one.

A little known fact, investors will not infrequently use personal investigators. 'Informal referencing sometimes turns up stuff like sexual harassment cases. We had that once, we did a lot of to-ing and fro-ing on that,' one venture capitalist told me before, understandably, declining to elaborate on whether the investment got done.

'Yes, you maybe use an investigation firm,' says a French venture capitalist, 'to understand whether there has been litigation against the management. Or maybe there is something funky that you feel. You can definitely dig way, way further (than the reference calls) – problems with the tax authorities, that sort of thing.' Given the possibility of a pretty thorough checking out, it is clearly foolish to lie about anything from university qualifications to the especially difficult stuff such as any previous bankruptcies, law suits or criminal offences. Even if you somehow manage to bamboozle the investors on the way in, these are the sorts of things about which you will be giving warranties (see Chapter 13) and any later discoveries could prove financially very costly. The last thing a venture capitalist wants is surprises. That is the quickest way to kill the deal.

Of course, despite the VCs' best endeavours, things still go wrong. Says someone from one of Europe's most disciplined private equity houses: 'We always try to derisk any investment. One risk we hadn't anticipated [in one particular failed investment] was that the two entrepreneurs couldn't stand the sight of each other.'

The financials

Here the venture investor will be ripping into the business plan and looking at historic performance (if any) and future projections. Investors will approach this in different ways. 'Talking with the management about the model is not about trying to predict where the company will be in five years,' says one investor. 'In an early stage company, that makes no sense. For me it is more about understanding the level of their sophistication. How do they look at the business, do they really understand the drivers of growth and profitability. How sophisticated, how practical, how realistic are they?'

Legal and accounting

Before the draft term sheet is drawn up, the VC will need to know how the share capital is organized, and the nuances of the structures of any earlier investment rounds. But the bulk of legal due diligence will come after the term sheet is signed – when lawyers will comb through all aspects of the intellectual property such as patents, will look at existing contracts, and at any past or current litigation.

Accounting due diligence, meanwhile, depends on the stage of the company. In the earliest days, there is nothing to look at. If there is a financial record, VCs will want to make sure the accounts are sound.

Something wrong?

It is more or less inevitable that an investor will discover something they do not like. There is no such thing as a perfect investment. If you have done a good job at setting out the risks of the business in the original plan, and been honest in compiling it and answering the questions this far, there should be fewer surprises.

A few factors will clearly be deal breakers. The VC may take the view that the technology is not as fully developed as the entrepreneur claims, and therefore that there is undue technical risk. Customer references may suggest the market is not large enough, or that demand is too distant for that investor's tastes. Deal breakers may of course be advanced in brinkmanship exercises, particularly if a term sheet has been signed early in the process.

You on them

While the venture capitalist is sizing you up, you should be doing your own due diligence on them. Entrepreneurs often fail to pay nearly enough attention to this. If an employee is no good, you can fire them. If you take on a venture capitalist, you cannot just boot them out. 'Some people are too meek to do proper due diligence, they are on their knees to these people with a tin cup,' says one chief executive who is not burdened by any such proclivities.

Start with the basics. Does the fund have money? This may sound like an exceptionally stupid question. Having money is the venture capitalist's business. But the deal is not done until the cash has hit the bank account. One company which found out the hard way had been raising money from a London-based firm. It had gone through the entire process, and all the investment documentation was complete. The day the funds were due to be transferred, the venture capitalist rang to say the deal was off – the firm had not managed to raise its own fund. Or take Agincourt, an Irish fund launched a few years ago boasting a roster of luminaries on its board and, supposedly, €200m to invest. It failed to close the first investment because the so-called commitments mysteriously evaporated when it came down to producing the cheque.

So do some digging as to the firm's funding situation. Even an established, respectable venture capitalist will be likely to behave very differently according to its position in its own funding cycle. Has it just raised new cash, or is it nearing the end of the fund? How much does the firm set aside for follow-on investments? One cause of the demise of many small funds during the boom was that they invested their entire resources without reserving any cash for their portfolio companies' next funding round. Even if they manage to raise another fund – and many do not – there are complicated issues that arise, especially concerning valuation, when venture firms deploy a new fund, with a different set of limited partners, to support existing investments. With exit markets difficult in a downturn, firms need to be much more conservative these days as to how much they set aside. The cautious might put by more than half the fund for follow-on investments.

Other basics include the level of interest in your sector. Has the firm done other deals in the area? If they know nothing about the industry, persuading them to invest is going to be an uphill battle at best, and probably an entirely fruitless exercise. More broadly, what does an investment in your company mean to them? If a past fund has done very well, the partners may have got fat and happy. Past poor performance may mean the firm is working hard to re-establish credibility – or alternatively, the partners may be so preoccupied with trying to rescue the disasters that they cannot muster enthusiasm for new deals.

You will be learning much about the style of the firm simply by the questions that are being asked. Michael Ledzion of Polight, a very early stage spin-out from the Department of Chemistry at Cambridge University, says: 'Investors can give themselves away by the questions they ask. One had said to us: "I really want to understand the nitty-gritty of how you are going to get to market." In Ledzion's view, this was ludicrous for such an early stage operation. 'If they ask about the ins and outs of an operational marketing plan, then they are the wrong people. To my mind, that simply flags them up as unconfident. At our stage, the questions are: Do you believe it is a good market, do you believe our product can achieve higher performance at lower cost and do you believe in the management?'

Other chief executives in the portfolio, as well as entrepreneurs who have had backing from the firm in the past (including the failures) will be one of the best sources for information on how the firm behaves. Ask the VC for an initial list. Use that to broaden your sources. And how do you get people to say anything other than the bland? As a journalist one learns the odd trick; one of the most effective is simply letting people talk. And when they stop, do not fill in the silence. Wait it out. They will fill the silence – 'Oh well, there was just . . .' Then they will start telling you what you really want to hear.

Remember that, while the culture of a firm is important, styles of operating often come down to individual partners. What was promised before the investment – and what was actually delivered. Do they really add value? Do they interfere? How much time do they spend? Beware of the honeymoon period, though, experienced by entrepreneurs who have just got funded. Find out how the VC behave when the going gets tough. Does he get emotional and personal? Plenty more questions will occur from re-reading Chapter 9.

Get as deep an understanding as possible of how the firm operates, how it makes decisions (see Chapter 14), who has influence. As well as examining the backgrounds of the team, look at the wider network. Is there a supervisory or a scientific advisory board, and if so who is on it? Are they effective (many are not)? One of the many questions that tends to go unasked is: How will your VC be rewarded? In a captive venture capital firm, executives may well not have a traditional carried interest scheme, but instead receive bonuses for completed deals. This is well worth knowing about, because it could affect their willingness to exert themselves after the investment is done (and bonus paid).

Cost

So who pays for all these consultants running around your business? The answer is, in most cases, you of course. 'Why should we pay for their due diligence?' asks one entrepreneur indignantly. 'It would be called "cost of sales" in any other business.' It all comes down to negotiation – and his righteous indignation was obviously effective. In his case, most unusually, the venture capitalist paid his own costs.

Another chief executive spots something of a conflict of interest. 'So much of it is arse-covering anyway. But when you think about it, the consultant is working for [the venture firm] to validate the business plan, but it is us that is paying them. Where exactly do their interests lie?'

It is an excellent idea to put a cap on due diligence costs. Some firms will run up vast bills – £50,000 or £60,000 on market analysis, for instance. (On the whole the better the venture capitalist, the more they will do in-house.) What you do not want to be doing is paying the venture capitalist if he pulls out. Resist that, although plenty of firms will try it on. You must have a clear agreement on costs by the time you sign the term sheet: who pays what, and up to what cap, should be clearly set out in the document.

The next chapter (Chapter 13) deals with the term sheet because, while you will already be starting negotiating (Chapter 14), you need to know the kind of deal you will be aiming at.

13

Term sheets

Nothing in fine print is ever good news.
(Unknown)

ALAIN FALYS, a senior executive at Visa International before he founded Open Business Exchange, an electronic invoicing system, points out just how foreign some of the elements of a term sheet can be, even for seasoned executives: 'You think you know a lot when you have worked at a senior level in a corporation. But there is no reason why you would ever have seen a shareholder agreement . You just don't know about such things as liquidation preferences.'

Not every venture capitalist necessarily regards term sheets as ideal bedtime reading either. Barry Maloney is an operating partner at Benchmark in London, who started Irish telecoms company Esat and sold the 1200-people business to British Telecom for £1bn, and sees himself firmly as 'an operating guy'. He admits that all the 'complex wording and mumbo jumbo' drives him crazy. 'It's like root canal treatment.' Luckily the London team has an in-house legal expert who handles such matters. 'The danger is the entrepreneur feels so piddled off that you start the relationship on the wrong footing. It is a law of diminishing returns, it's supposed to be risk capital. The way [some of the terms] are drawn up you might as well be a bank.'

The term sheet is a letter of intent, a sort of 'prenup' between entrepreneur and venture capitalist. It outlines the framework for the final deal, but, with only minor exceptions, it is not binding. The venture capitalist is at liberty to change anything as negotiations progress – and often does, especially the valuation. From the VC's point of view, the terms constitute protection for what is generally a minority position, facilitating his ultimate goal, namely an exit and a return on his investment. At the end of negotiations, the terms will be incorporated into the final documentation – the articles of association and the shareholders' agreement. Mark Suster of BuildOnline has after several financing rounds developed a healthy cynicism regarding the power of the terms: 'Every term in your term sheet is for investors to extract more value from you or from the other investors. No one ever told me that. Entrepreneurs are obsessed with the valuation itself, not realizing there are all these bombs in the terms.'

Look on the gloomy side of life

Entrepreneurs would never get anything accomplished if they were not natural optimists, but a portion of that optimism has to be suspended for the length of time it takes to grapple with the term sheet. It is essential to scrutinize the details. The term sheet is drafted by the venture capitalist and hence represents *their* preferred terms, including all sorts of provisions covering what is to happen if things go wrong. Entering a deal, no entrepreneur wants to think about such eventualities, but not to do so is merely storing up trouble. The good news is that there is room for negotiation.

Max Cartellieri of Munich-based Ciao.com, a consumer choice site launched during what the Germans now term the 'hype' years, stresses the importance of not getting hung up on valuation alone. 'Look at the rest of the terms,' he advises. 'Every entrepreneur thinks they will be wildly successful. So force yourself to make sure you are covered if things do not go according to plan.' Remember that subsequent rounds of financing, future hirings, and other events up to and including the sale of the business, will be also heavily influenced, if not dictated, by the initial agreement. The term sheet may be intended to align both party's interests, but harsh clauses at the outset will end up pitting one side against the other, and lead to endless acrimony with future investors, employees and possible purchasers into the bargain.

In the USA, where there is a smooth, well-oiled venture process that has evolved over many years, documentation is relatively standard (although there have been some changes, see below, in the post-bubble fall-out). There are only a handful of basic templates, representing the house styles of a few leading venture law firms – with some minor variations between east and west coast practice. In the still relatively immature European market, by contrast, a cacophony of confusion reigns, with a huge disparity between the term sheets and legal documentation that may be doled out. There is sometimes not even a standard within individual firms. One of Europe's largest private equity houses deals with at least three different sets of law firms, and multiple partners within each firm, all using their own pet format (or that of the VC partner concerned).

US-style term sheets came to Europe with a vengeance during the bubble. But, given the differing legal systems, this is inevitably a complicated translation exercise. At the most basic level, European legal frameworks are designed to protect creditors, whereas US law is all about protecting shareholders. For instance, in Europe, a company can only buy back its shares if it has distributable reserves; in the USA it can do so if it simply has the cash. So complex mechanisms are needed by European lawyers to replicate something which is pretty straightforward in the USA. To make matters worse, too few European advisers have a good understanding of term sheet structures, and even fewer command a working knowledge of the differences between European and US practice. There are philosophical differences too. At least until recently, the US ethos was to make the term sheet a straightforward affair, and to exercise influence on the company through the venture capitalist's presence on the board. It was much more about the spirit of a partnership; both sides were in this together and there were only two possible outcomes. Everyone made masses of money or they lost the lot. Either way, the terms would not make much difference.

In Europe, by contrast, management buy-out type thinking has been dominant. This means, among other things, that investors were traditionally less concerned with board seats, and more concerned with complicated investment agreements in what came to look more like a contractual banking relationship, full of negative controls (long lists of things over which the VC wants to be able to exercise a veto). It is striking just how pervasive that buy-out thinking still is. The relevant section of the otherwise excellent European Venture Capital Association training materials, for instance, is written by a management buy-out specialist, with the financing structures of buy-outs and start-ups more or less muddled up together.

The reasons are largely historical. In the USA, venture capital and leveraged buy-outs are two entirely different industries. In Europe, by contrast, 3i, which from the 1950s onwards structured investments as loans with cheap equity, has been the dominant influence. It was a cautious investment strategy – from the group's point of view, at least it should get its cash back, with an interest coupon. For the company, it was considerably less attractive, but these structures simply became accepted by the accountants and lawyers advising entrepreneurs. In the USA entrepreneurs would not tolerate such structures, not least because they weaken the balance sheet – but then they have had more bargaining power because there were always more venture capitalists around.

Also, the USA has something called 'thin capitalization' rules. If the IRS deems a balance sheet thinly capitalized, it will argue that the loans are really equity so do not warrant tax relief. In the UK, companies can generally obtain tax relief on the interest payments.

Again, before the bubble, Europe had fewer of the multiple rounds of financings bringing in new outside investors that are established US practice, which made some of the protection such as anti-dilution (see below) seem less relevant. If there were second and third rounds, it was often the same investors who participated.

At the same time, term sheet content is about as cyclical as everything else in the venture industry – so it is vital to find out what is reasonable at the particular phase of the market in which you are seeking funds. Securing an experienced lawyer, who has done plenty of venture deals, is crucial – and still a fairly rare commodity in Europe. Try to compare notes with other entrepreneurs, too, to understand what they have been seeing, and what they have successfully negotiated. In these circumstances, knowledge is power. At the height of the bubble, when investors were shovelling money into companies as fast as they could, some pretty strange agreements were signed. Supposedly professional venture capitalists were even investing in ordinary (rather than preference) shares. At the same time, while this was the period when the entrepreneur was supposedly in the driving seat in terms of negotiating power, some quite draconian terms were happily agreed by inexperienced founders racing towards their sure-fire multibillion winners. The Clickmango term sheet produced by Atlas, famously signed and completed in eight days, is the reverse of sloppy, including as it does some pretty tough terms.

As the public markets tumbled from March 2000, venture firms began to introduce ever more punishing clauses. By 2001 the Frankenstein term sheet started circulating in the Valley – a collection of the most egregious possible set of terms favouring the VC investor, and certainly very far from the traditional US style of friendly partnership. Today, venture capitalists justify these terms by saying they were trying to bridge the still high valuation expectations of entrepreneurs, although it is only with hindsight that it is clear just how unrealistic the valuations paid continued to be. It was certainly only later that investors saw the very divisive effects of the Frankenstein terms, and the better operators have learnt from the experience.

With the reams of tougher terms introduced since the bubble (see below) the gap is in some senses narrowing between the US and European philosophies as American VCs put in more harsh clauses, and Europeans incorporate US structures (such as anti-dilution, and so on). At the same time, I have encountered plenty of (often less sophisticated, or more domestically focused)

European investors who appear almost viscerally hostile to the basic American term sheet structure of convertible preferred shares which they regard – wrongly in my view – as a bubble phenomenon. The old loan-based structures are certainly making something of a come-back in Europe. But then the US way has always been a good deal more favourable to the company – and it may be that, in tough times, many European venture firms will again be able to get away with their model.

As a rule, European term sheets from all but the most sophisticated firms still tend to be short on detail. A short term sheet that barely scratches the surface is dangerous because the first (or indeed much later) draft of the shareholders' agreement from the lawyers will then pitch up containing a whole raft of terms you will have never seen before – some of which could be deal breakers. It is also worth remembering that an aggressive-looking term sheet may be nothing more than the product of amateurism and bad drafting. The less reputable venture capitalist may be trying it on, but equally he may just have an inexperienced lawyer. Bastardized structures – which end up being meaningless – are common. 'I have seen things called convertible redeemable shares,' says one lawyer, 'that are neither convertible nor redeemable' (because to be so this has to be spelt out in the articles of association). Simon Darling, who started a text messaging chat software business called Fonepark, remembers being issued with a very aggressive term sheet during the bubble period: 'It didn't need to be. Someone had just pulled it off the shelf. It was badly drafted. The negotiations took much longer than they should have done.' His lesson would be: Rather than attempting to negotiate every crass term, try and persuade the investor to start with a fresh document.

The basic aim, from the entrepreneur's point of view, is therefore to secure as 'clean' a term sheet as possible. If you push on valuation, you will get unattractive terms. 'You can't agree on price, so the VC adds a bunch of bells and whistles,' says one venture capitalist. 'That is how we get comfortable, by adding all this stuff. It becomes a negotiation on trade-offs to reach an artificially high price. The entrepreneur thinks everything will go well so they don't care.' With less reputable firms it may not be as scientific as that – they may simply be trying it on.

Controversy then arises when the next round of funders come in, and try to renegotiate away existing investors' rights in areas such as protection against dilution. So clean is good – clean but detailed. As well as averting frantic last-minute negotiations on seminal points, detail facilitates comparison between term sheets – for those fortunate enough to have more than one offer. A VC offering a higher valuation may not be offering, overall, nearly as attractive a deal when all the other terms are considered, so it is crucial to know what those terms are. One particular trap is set by firms that simply send out a short letter, containing references to 'our usual provisions'. Pin them down. You want as much set out as possible – a seven- or eight-page draft term sheet being reasonable.

Capital structures

Equity

Ordinary shares (common stock in US parlance)

The simplest class of shares, they are generally held by founders, friends and family investors, angels (though angels may sometimes invest via preference shares) and management, often through options. Ordinaries, which carry one vote per share, are the riskiest security in the capital structure, ranking behind absolutely everybody else in any form of pay-out ranging from sale of the company to distribution of dividends to liquidation.

Preference shares (preferred stock)

Preference shares are typically issued at a higher price than the ordinaries and rank ahead of them. Investors can basically attach whatever raft of rights, privileges and protections they like to prefs, which is what the term sheet is mostly about. If a company needs multiple rounds of financing, it is likely to issue new classes of preference – in the USA labelled alphabetically from A onwards. These will be issued at a different price and have different rights attaching, calibrated to reflect the stage the business has reached, and, of course, external market conditions.

They come in a fairly confusing variety of forms, but they all carry the same basic preference right, which means holders of prefs get paid back – in a sale or liquidation – before the owners of the ordinary shares. This is very significant and 'multiple' preferences, denoting the right to several times the amount of the investment, are one of the more contentious parts of the term sheet, as will be explained in further detail below.

There is a good reason, beyond arrant greed, for investors wanting at least a simple preference. Imagine a venture capitalist had invested €5m in a company at a pre-money valuation of €5m, €10m post-money. In exchange for his cash, he receives half of the company, while the entrepreneur has half in 'sweat equity', namely for his idea, plus the time and effort he has put into the business. Suppose the company is sold almost immediately for €5m. If the VC had invested via ordinary shares, he would be entitled to just €2.5m and the entrepreneur would also get €2.5m, leaving the VC looking somewhat foolish having lost half his initial investment. With a preference, he gets his €5m out – and the entrepreneur of course gets nothing in this instance.

Convertible preference shares (convertible preferred stock)

These are the most common instrument in US-style agreements, and carry the right to convert into ordinary shares at various key points in the life of the company, such as when new stock is issued, or at exit. In the above example, if the company is sold for €10m or less, the investor would not convert – at €9m he gets back his €5m, but if he converts he would only be entitled to his 50 per cent of the business, now valued at €4.5m. Convertible prefs generally carry voting rights as if they had already been converted into ordinaries.

Convertible participating preference shares

This represents an extra layer of jam for the investors, allowing them to get their cash out first, and then to participate in whatever is left, according to the size of their stake, as if the prefs had converted into ordinaries – a double dip once thought to be faintly unethical, but now fairly common. In the same example, if the company sells for €9m, the investor receives €5m plus another €2m, namely 50 per cent of the remaining proceeds.

In a hot market where management feels – probably foolishly – confident of an initial public offering, they may object less to this highly dilutive instrument which converts automatically into ordinary shares at an IPO. As an entrepreneur, your pushback on this is to argue that, if it is structured as a fully participating preference, the VC and founders are simply never in the same boat. However well it is going for you, it will always be going better for the VC. (A compromise might be to put a cap on the participation right; after the VC has earned two or three times their investment, his participation right goes away.)

Geared equity instruments

These terms reflect the dominant effect of the buy-out mentality on European early stage deals, in the sense that they are mechanisms for creating a more predictable return. In theory investors get their money back sooner, and may also receive a regular dividend or interest payment. Their potential upside comes in the form of a layer of preference or so-called A ordinary shares in which they also invest.

The basic geared structure consists of some form of loan note and a thin layer of preference shares, A ordinaries (a preference share-like instrument that has fewer rights) or a warrant to subscribe for shares at a predetermined level. The advantage to the investor is that he receives an interest coupon, gets the loan repaid at a specified time and, in the event of a default, ranks as a creditor, ahead of preference and other shareholders. The fact that it is a loan means that the company does not need distributable reserves to repay the loan or to pay a coupon (by contrast with a preference share dividend where it does). Also, the investor exercises the warrant only as and when there is any value in the equity.

Any advantage to the company? Well no, frankly – and it makes the balance sheet weaker into the bargain – unless you count the fact that there is tax relief on the interest (which is, of course, irrelevant for a loss-making company).

The loan may or may not be convertible into equity. If it is, the investor is clearly even more in the position of having his cake and eating it. If the company does well, he can participate in the equity upside; if not, he gets the benefits of the loan (namely status as a creditor, rather than shareholder). From the entrepreneur's point of view, this is clearly the worst of both worlds.

The interest coupon is usually set, at around 8%, rather than at any market rate, mirroring the hurdle rate of return VCs pay to their investors – although sometimes it may be set as a sliding rate, starting at zero and moving up. Repayment will typically be in instalments after a certain date, perhaps three or four years after the investment is made.

Entrepreneurs sometimes think they spot a silver lining in the loan structure in that if they repay it, they will no longer have an investor with control rights hanging over their heads, as they do in the preference structure. However, this is simply not the case. Some of the rights attach to the loan, but many will be attached to the prefs or A ordinaries (and there seems to be no great rhyme or reason as to what goes where).

The other nasty trick about loans is that the valuation is treated more or less as if it were equity – although obviously this comes down to negotiation. Suppose the VC has agreed to put in €2m at €6m pre-money, (€8m post) of which €1.5m is as a loan (and the rest in A ordinaries). The VC will try and argue he should still have 25 per cent of the company. It may be *called* a loan, he will say, but it is 'at the bottom of the stack' of creditors and he really does deserve 25 per cent – despite the fact that the company is paying interest.

Term sheet terms

Below is an explanation of some the terms you may encounter and their implications (but, given the confused state of the market, it is inevitably far from exhaustive). It essentially reflects a US-style term sheet for convertible preferred shares, with references as to how European geared structures would be implemented. And throughout the process, it is as well to remember with whom you are dealing. One lawyer told me he thought entrepreneurs were often a bit naive as to just how cut-throat VCs can be. "'Oh they wouldn't do that," people say to me. I say to them, "Oh yes they would".'

Hold the front page

The term sheet kicks off with the basics of the agreement including the names of the investors, the amount to be invested, the instruments (Series A convertible preference shares), the number and the price of the shares (or outline of the loan) to be issued. As valuation at this point is very much a moving target, the investor will often enter the pre-money valuation as 'to be determined' when the initial draft term sheet is presented. Or, the firm may outline its 'thoughts'. Clearly by the time you sign the term sheet, you want the valuation nailed down and clearly stipulated.

There should also be an appendix to show the capital structure both before and after the investment – on a fully diluted basis, including all outstanding options and warrants and any new employee share option pool. At draft stage the latter would obviously be left blank, given the preliminary nature of the valuation discussions.

Liquidation preferences

A liquidation preference gives the investor a 'first right' to any cash available to shareholders in a liquidity event. Somewhat confusingly, 'liquidation' refers not just to the winding up of the company but to any 'liquidity' event, such as sale to another corporation, or an initial public offering. Liquidation preferences climbed vertiginously as the bubble burst, with a five or six times multiple not unheard of, particularly in later rounds. A German investor told me he had seen a ten times preference. All this is clearly preposterous. A five times multiple means the preference shareholder receives back fives times his initial investment before other shareholders see anything. In multiple rounds, different classes may have preference over each other. Take the example of a company that has raised three rounds of financing, series A, B and C. The holders of series C shares may get all or part of their money out before the B holders, who in turn have preference over the As (with the ordinaries of course at the tail end of a very long queue).

A high multiple can render the size of the management's shareholding and the latest valuation virtually irrelevant, so this is a clause to scrutinize most carefully. Suppose $4m has been invested in a series C round, carrying a three times preference. That means that $12m is owed to that class of investor before anyone else sees a cent. So if the company finds a buyer for $8m, neither management nor earlier investors will make a cent. Preferences can easily be set so that, even if the company does tolerably well and is sold for $20m or $30m, nobody gets paid out except the last class of investors. Multiple preferences where the investor has convertible *participating* preferred are clearly all the more unattractive from the company's point of view. How do the venture capitalists justify it? Well, they say, a three times return on their money over three years is 'only' an IRR of 44 per cent. And that is before fees are subtracted.

But the fact is some investors, nervous about their exit options as the public markets fell, have been trying to nail down a financial return through these structures – rather than doing their job, which is to help build a company. While the one times preference does make sense, as we have seen, a six times liquidation preference is clearly ludicrous. Very often they are a negotiating ploy and part of the power play between early investors and management in a down round when the valuation has fallen and early investors and management are fighting dilution (see Chapter 17). Needless to say, the liquidation preference affords absolutely no protection if the company collapses and there is no cash at the end.

It is vital to make sure these preferences are explicit in the draft term sheet. Even the professionals can get caught out. One venture capitalist looking for a large follow-on funding for one of his portfolio companies had received one of those pithy letters from the new investor where many of the terms were simply left as 'subject to our usual terms and conditions'. At the eleventh hour, as the lawyers were negotiating the final details of the transaction, he found there was an onerous liquidation preference buried in the documentation which effectively meant the company would have to be sold for more than €200m before management saw a penny. The *Spiel* from the new investor, a leading European firm, was: Well, look how much everyone makes if the company is worth €1bn (or some other irrelevantly large figure). Of course, if everyone is wildly successful, arguments about how the pie is split are going to evaporate. In this case and many other cases the proposed liquidation preference was so high that the valuation became irrelevant. The company walked away, and was able to find alternative financing.

The good news is that some venture capitalists have learnt just how divisive these instruments can be. Says Adrian Beecroft, partner at Apax: 'In my mind they were legitimate when you were investing at valuations no one really believed were sensible. You gave the entrepreneur the choice. But when valuations are more realistic, what is the justification for the ugly venture capitalist to get three times? They don't appear to have been a great invention.' The more sensible VCs have, for one thing, witnessed the problems these terms cause when introducing new management. A new chief executive, offered stock options, might well point to the fact that the options were over ordinary shares – and hence ranking behind the multiple preferences. 'This is the sort of deal an entrepreneur would do,' he might say, 'because he is betting his life on the company. But I want a sensible risk reward profile. I don't want nothing at $50m and the world at $200m.' In some circumstances, incoming senior management may be cut into liquidation preferences by receiving options over the preferred shares.

Again, incumbent management have sometimes successfully negotiated the creation of a special class of E (employee) share, which, say in a C round with a three times liquidation preference, would at least rank alongside the A and B investors. Then of course it is the ordinary shareholders (founders no longer around, angels and so on) who get shafted.

The effect of a multiple liquidation preference can be achieved in the loan structure – which is effectively a one times preference – in a somewhat cumbersome fashion by attaching a 'redemption premium' of, say, two or three times. But that raises legal questions as to exactly how enforceable it is, which you should certainly point out if any investor tries to pull that one on you. (The liquidation preference may of course be attached to the A ordinaries or warrants in which case this argument does not help.)

Dividend rights

Young companies need cash to grow and do not by and large pay out dividends to shareholders. Their main effect, with a convertible preferred structure, is in the event of liquidation. The primary distinction is between cumulative and non-cumulative, the former being clearly more onerous from the company's point of view. In the non-cumulative case, if the company is unable to pay a dividend (because it is has no distributable reserves) or decides not to do so in any one year, that is the end of it. If it is cumulative, however, the obligation to pay accrues even if the company does not have the resources. This then effectively adds to the liquidation preference owed at the end. The dividend would typically be set around 8 per cent per annum. Look out also for whether the dividends have preference over previous classes of shares, namely the ordinaries and any earlier prefs. It is clearly more onerous if they do.

Conversion/automatic conversion

At the heart of the US structure is the concept that preference shareholders have the right to convert their holding into ordinary shares, typically in the ratio of one to one. However, that ratio may be altered (as for example because of anti-dilution protection, see below). On conversion, the stock obviously loses its rights, such as liquidation and dividend preference and anti-dilution protection. The prefs will convert automatically at various points, including an IPO under certain conditions ('a qualifying IPO'). The purpose is to clean up the capital structure. Automatic conversion may also be triggered by a set percentage of the votes of the affected class of shares.

A qualifying IPO will be defined by investors as one in which the company raises a certain minimum amount of capital, and at a certain minimum valuation for the company. Clearly the entrepreneur wants as low a threshold for both these amounts as possible, as it is in his interests to see the preference shares convert. As throughout this process, temper your natural optimism as to the size of exit you think you will achieve. Bubble era entrepreneurs have been stuck with investment agreements specifying ludicrously high qualifying IPO thresholds.

Anti-dilution protection

This is a one of the principal ways in which investors seek to protect their downside risk, and mitigate dilution of their position if the value of the company has fallen by the time it enters a future financing round. It is achieved either by a retroactive adjustment to the conversion ratio, or, much less satisfactorily, by the issue of new shares, and can be very divisive in its most extreme form.

At the height of the bubble, 'down rounds' were not something any entrepreneur contemplated. But as the bear market set in, chief executives soon needed to get to grips with whatever form of anti-dilution mechanism was lurking hitherto undetected in their shareholder agreement. As it came to the new financing, it turned out either that the previous round now looked overvalued, or the business had not proceeded to plan – or both.

The horrors of the down round – and to a lesser extent a flat round at the same value as the previous round – are all about dilution. Investors who do not 'follow their money' or buy shares in a new financing round in sufficient quantity to maintain their pro rata stake get diluted anyway, but anti-dilution protection changes the maths dramatically. The mechanism by which both full ratchet and weighted average anti-dilution protection should be achieved is via an adjustment to the conversion ratio at which the prefs are converted into ordinaries (for example by changing the conversion ratio from one preference: one ordinary share to one preference: three ordinaries). Traditionally UK lawyers will try to achieve this by issuing more shares. Both routes are fraught with legal problems.

Full ratchet anti-dilution is by far the more aggressive form. It effectively applies the lowest share price of the later share issue to the prior round, so that the investor with this form of protection sees his entire holding adjusted as if he had invested at the lower price, regardless of how many new shares are issued. It is therefore triggered even if only one single new share is issued – with the new price applied to the entire holding, which could be millions of shares. All the shareholders who do not have the ratchet – the founders and the management team (who would be likely to be option holders) – will be heavily diluted or 'flooded' to the point where their holding is likely to be more or less worthless.

Weighted average anti-dilution is somewhat less draconian insofar as it takes into account the relative sizes of the respective financing rounds, and involves some dilution for the holder. Again, a new conversion price is calculated at which the prefs will convert to ordinaries. The fewer new shares are issued, the smaller the adjustment to the conversion ratio, and hence the less the dilution. To further complicate matters, there are different versions of the formula – broad-based and narrow-based. The broad based is more favourable to the founders; the dilutive effect is less because it does the calculation on a fully diluted basis (including the effect of the option pool, anti-dilution measures and so on), whereas the narrow-based formula works only with shares in issue.

A full ratchet clause is often a negotiating ploy. One VC, when asked how many times he got a full ratchet, answered: Always. And the number of times he implemented it? The answer was never. It may be a tool, either in negotiating the term sheet in the first place (he will drop the full ratchet in return for X off the valuation), or in giving him influence over negotiations with new investors in the next round. Clearly, if things were going really badly, it could be used as a bargaining chip in removing founders and/or management.

You should certainly aim to obtain the less punitive weighted average option. In the end it all comes down to negotiation. One well-known European venture capitalist tended not to have anti-dilution rights in its early rounds, but would threaten to veto the next round unless it was granted anti-dilution. More often, later round investors will refuse to put in cash unless the earlier round waive their rights. What is never on the menu, unfortunately, is anti-dilution for the founders.

Pay-to-play

This provision, which appears at bearish points in the cycle when follow-on funding is uncertain, says that if investors are to keep enjoying their preference privileges, they must participate pro rata in subsequent financing rounds. If they do not, they either forfeit their various rights such as liquidation preferences and antidilution, or their preference shares convert to ordinaries (and lose all their rights). This is one of the few clauses that is clearly in the interests of the entrepreneur.

Redemption rights

Investors need an exit, and want to avoid the company becoming a 'lifestyle' business, run to afford the management a nice income but without the growth characteristics that will produce anyone a healthy capital gain. This clause sets a date by which you are forced to start buying back the shares purchased by the investor. The redemption clause may demand a multiple of what the investor paid – equal to the liquidation preferences – plus the dividends as if they had been cumulative.

It is another of those terms that the VCs are most unlikely to hold you to. But it becomes a negotiating lever to extract better terms, to put pressure on the company to cut costs, or, at worst, to enforce management changes. In an initial financing round, the date will be four or five years away, so it is easy to dismiss it as a distant proposition. But be sure it will creep up on you. Find out what is standard. Push it out as far as you can – seven years is a lot better than four years.

This clause is still less common in Europe than in the USA, which goes back to the differences between US and European law and the fact that in Europe companies can only redeem shares if they have distributable reserves. But it is certainly something to watch for – US investors sometimes insist on it. Aim to negotiate it away, or at least to dilute it heavily. In addition to the legal point, you can also bring up the undesirability of being forced to make a hasty decision simply because the redemption deadline is just round the corner. Says one entrepreneur: 'This is very contentious. You don't want a gun to your head. You could consider agreeing that, if after five years the company has not been sold, you recognize some of the dividends. That would mean you are in profit so that is good news. Or agree that the board will appoint an investment bank to look at exit options.'

Registration rights

This applies only to companies seeking a public market listing in the USA – but then most investors will want to keep that option open. It is a rather confusing concept, which comes about because, in the USA, the *sale* of shares – in an IPO or in a subsequent secondary offering – has to be registered with the Securities and Exchange Commission, the US stock market regulator, or exempt from registration. In Europe, once a class of shares is listed, all shares in that class are freely tradable (subject to any lock-ups, see below). In the USA, only those shares that are registered or exempt can be sold.

The two most common forms of registration rights are demand and piggyback. A demand registration right allows the investor to force the company to register the venture capitalist's stock with the SEC, whenever it demands. In theory, and occasionally in practice, the demand right could include a provision that, if after a certain period, say five years from the date of investment, there has not been an exit, it can force an IPO. This is a strange concept given that, if a company is not ready to go public, a venture investor's right to demand a listing will hardly make this any the more feasible. No underwriter will take out a company where the chief executive is against the IPO in the first place. It is therefore most unlikely to be invoked, and so, like many of the other clauses, it becomes a negotiating tool. It should be resisted.

The piggyback right enables the investor to be included in a share registration that is already being done, allowing the VC to piggyback on the company's preexisting registration (and the company, of course, does all the work and incurs the very considerable fees). This is much less problematic than demand registration rights.

Lock-ups

This may be included in the registration rights section of the term sheet; it may not crop up until discussion of the main shareholder agreement; or it may not be included at all. Lock-ups specify how soon after an IPO the founders and venture capitalists can sell their stock. These are heavily negotiated in the run-up to the IPO with the underwriting investment bank, whose aim it is to make the company as attractive as possible to the investing public.

But a general reference to lock-ups in the shareholders' agreement is a good idea. The last thing you want is for a VC with a 25 per cent stake in the business not agreeing to a lock-up at the last minute. The wording would be to the effect that the investor agrees to a lock-up of, say, 180 days, as long as the founders and management are locked-up for at least the same period. In practice, founders and management would normally be locked up for a year in Europe.

Transfer rights

Pre-emption

Pre-emption means the right to purchase in preference to someone else, and comes in two flavours. Pre-emption on issue refers to the right of existing shareholders to subscribe to new shares issued by the company in a way that does not dilute them (and is incidentally statutory under UK law); pre-emption on transfer, which is what concerns us here, allows current shareholders the first opportunity to purchase shares from a departing shareholder. It is essentialy there to discourage the transfer of shares to unfriendly or awkward outside parties (and is in practice rarely used).

There are two form of pre-emption on transfer – the right of first refusal and the right of first offer.

In the former case, the selling shareholder has to give the rest of the shareholders the chance to match the terms of an offer from a third party (initially in proportion to the size of their holding). The latter means that a shareholder who wants to sell must approach other existing shareholders first and give them the chance to make an offer (in advance of an offer from a third party). Whichever form appears, this is generally not a clause on which to waste energies negotiating, though the shorter the period during which other shareholders may take up their pre-emptive rights, the better.

There follow two additional transfer rights, drag along and tag along. It is worth remembering that any relevant pre-emption on transfer will apply before the drag or tag comes into force.

Drag along

The drag along is designed to prevent small shareholders from holding a company hostage. If the venture capitalist wishes to sell out to a large corporation, the drag along allows him to bring the rest of the investors with him.

Look carefully at the voting structure. Suppose the drag along kicks in if 85 per cent of the shareholders in a certain class of stock are willing to sell.

But if one venture capitalist has 20 per cent of that class, that in effect gives him a veto – and hence a negotiating lever. As one entrepreneur says: 'Two of our investors had effective vetoes and that meant [in a merger that in the end went through] they diluted less than other investors [in the final deal]. They came up with every bullshit reason in the world not to do the deal, saying we were doing well growing organically and so on, but it was basically just a negotiating ploy.'

Tag along

This is designed to ensure that, if the founder for instance does a sweet deal and sells his stake to Microsoft, then the other investors, namely the venture capitalists, can 'tag along' on the same terms. From the entrepreneur's point of view, this affects how many shares he is allowed to sell; shareholders with the tag along right can sell shares in proportion to their holding – hence reducing how much the entrepreneur can sell. A point to understand rather than negotiate on.

Board composition

Most venture capitalists will regard a presence on the board as pivotal to the partnership that is being built. A reasonable deal would be two seats for management, two for the investors and one for an outside director. Clearly if you are four founder directors, this will be extremely tricky – but in the end you should be considering what is the best board structure for the company and hence what will create the most value for your shares. Of course, board seats are, from the VC's point of view, another device by which they leverage their minority position. A later round investor may have only 18 per cent of the business, for example, but 40 per cent of the voting power of the board. You should push for a structure that keeps the financial investors in a minority. If the numbers are even, then consider getting agreement that an independent chairman has a casting vote. Clearly, if it comes down to a board vote itself, the company is in deep trouble, but at the same time, the tone of the board discussions will directly reflect the power around the table.

Look carefully at observer rights too. 'Observers are not observers,' says one entrepreneur. 'Well, not unless you fit a glass wall down one side of the board room. Voting is not the issue. How often does it come to a vote? If you start voting you have a serious problem.' Corporate investors will often ask for observer rights. This means they do not have a vote, or even, technically, the right to speak. They often take observer rights in the hope of avoiding the liabilities associated with being a director – although of course it is not as simple as that, and they may be deemed a shadow director anyway. But the right to participate in board meetings means that they will inevitably be party to sensitive discussions, and may in practice hold not inconsiderable sway. 3i is unusual in preferring observer status for its own staff. It will, however, seek to appoint a director, often the non-executive chairman, who essentially represents its interests. A lead investor may well ask for observer rights as well, to allow him to take lawyers or a junior associate to meetings.

Consent rights

There will be a laundry list of things over which the investor will seek veto rights. His aim is to ensure he has control – and is involved in all the critical decisions – even though he does not have a majority of the shares. These are decisions which require consent at either shareholder or board level and are also a mechanism to deal with investors who are not represented on the board. The less scrupulous investor may use them to force a restructuring, by exercising veto rights on hiring key staff, buying essential items of equipment, and the like.

The items would be likely to include the issue of new shares in future fund raisings, the issue of new options, changes to the budget, wider changes to the business plan, borrowing levels, the recruitment of senior executives, mergers and acquisitions activity, sale of the company, an IPO, and the circumstances surrounding bankruptcy. It depends how controlling the venture capitalist wants to be. Their mantra, is of course, that they do not want to interfere in the day-to-day running of the business. So the consent rights should not shackle the company. You don't need to be asking permission to buy the next box of paperclips.

This is obviously an area where there is also plenty of scope for debate. For instance, the venture capitalist might try to set a borrowing limit before approval at €100,000, while the company might endeavour to raise that to €500,000. Clearly, in a financing structure with multiple investors, the fewer with consent rights the better.

In the case of corporate investors, it is very important to make sure they have not slipped in a clause that effectively stops you from making sales or entering a partnership arrangement with a competitor of the corporate investor.

As with the drag along clause, look at the percentages carefully and check out who has a veto that, for instance, might be exercised to try and block a new fund raising – and if necessary, negotiate.

Information rights

These are fairly straightforward and are likely to require the company to send monthly (unaudited) management accounts, audited annual accounts, the annual budget and so on. Make sure you have confidentiality agreements in place. Some investors may try and include additional requirements, such as sight of the auditor's letter to the company regarding the audit and any problems it encountered, or the right to look at the company's books at any time. If you have a very large investor base, you need to be particularly careful. For instance, some angel groups may sign as one entity, but you could be sending the information to scores of people around the world, which is clearly undesirable.

Warranties

Founders unfamiliar with term sheets tend to be alarmed by the concept of warranties. At first sight, they do indeed look fairly intimidating. At the same time, the venture capitalist wants to make sure he is not investing in a bunch of crooks. His argument is that he is simply asking the people who know the business best to provide relatively straightforward assurances about factual matters. Does the company own its intellectual property? Is there a secret class of shares such that the VC only has 2 per cent of the company when he thought he had 20 per cent?

This is another area where US and European practice differs, incidentally. In the USA, it will only ever be the company that gives warranties, whereas in Europe both the founders, directors and the company will be expected to do so (it is viewed as easier to get money from the founders). In a technology company, intellectual property, for example, will be viewed as pivotal and the investor will want assurances that it does not infringe someone else's IP – that it is not, for instance copied or otherwise pirated. The trick is to work out what is reasonable and what is not. Laurence Holt, chairman of Quidnunc, says that one set of investors tried to get him to warrant the company's forecasts. 'I said: But these are *forecasts*. What exactly are you asking us to guarantee here?'

As regards financial information, what is reasonable in a raw start-up will be different from what might be expected from an established business nearing profitability. Warranting the business plan of a start-up is clearly entirely unreasonable – this is after all a set of projections, arguably puffed up by the company to get financing. In another case, a company lost a major client shortly after the venture capital deal. Did it know this was going to happen when it signed the agreement? No says the entrepreneur, we did not. 'But we could have been in trouble if we had signed the stringent warranties the VC was trying to get us to sign.'

Breaches of warranties

The investor will seek either indemnification or contractual damages for breach of warranties. Suppose you have given a warranty that the company is not involved in any litigation, when in fact it has agreed to settle a case for €100,000. With an indemnification, you would be forced to reduce the value of the company by €100,000 and compensate the investor; if you were liable for contractual damages, you would pay nothing if you successfully argued the shareholders suffered no loss. You should clearly establish an upper limit for your liability for breach of warranty. Some formula based on a multiple of salary is reasonable – perhaps 18 months salary. Investors will sometimes try on something much more stringent. One lawyer tells of a former management consultant raising $15m from an investor during the bubble, and the investor trying to insist he produced a warranty on the full $15m – which was clearly absurd. In very late rounds where founders are no longer involved, it would be likely to be the company, rather than the new chief executive, giving the warranty, and then up to the amount invested.

An alternative to a multiple of salary is for the investor to receive extra shares – returning him, he would say, to the position he was in if the warranties had not been breached. Say the investor deemed the company was only worth $10m (pre), not the $15m pre at which he invested his $5m. In order not to see his $5m devalued, he would now want 33 per cent of the company.

One thing to avoid is joint and several warranties. 'If my co-founder lied I didn't want to be responsible,' says one entrepreneur. 'We are not brothers who signed in blood.' Against any really unreasonable warranty, the push-back to the investor might consist of a delicate reminder of the need for trust between the two parties.

Vesting

Vesting can be one of the most emotional parts of the discussion from the founder's point of view. This is *his* company, and yet when the deal closes, he finds he will not really own his shares at all. They are now subject to a so-called 'reverse vesting' schedule. From the venture capitalist's point of view, he wants to make sure the founder or founders stick around.

Vesting in Europe works the opposite way round – reverse vesting – from in the USA. In America, entrepreneurs earn the right to keep their shares, according to a vesting schedule. Typically they would earn a quarter after the first year and the rest might vest monthly in equal proportions for the next three years. Hence, if you leave after four years, you would generally get to keep your shares, because you have earned them. In Europe, you have the shares, but you lose them if you leave – perhaps 75 per cent after the first year, 50 per cent after the second, and so on. (There is an almost infinite number of ways in which vesting schedules can be constructed.) The European attitude is again the product of the dominance of buy-out thinking. In a buy-out, the private equity shop is very much backing the management – it is after all called a management buy-out and it would be most unusual for the team to leave. So, as in a buy-out, the attitude used to be that, if you leave, you lose your shares – which is clearly nonsense in a technology company where the founder or founders may well move on, possibly indeed with the venture capitalist's encouragement. Today this is generally modified by a good leaver/ bad leaver distinction whereby a good leaver retains his shares and a bad leaver loses them.

So who counts as a good leaver? The joke in the industry is: Only someone who is carried out feet first. However, you should try and ensure the drafting is such that unless you are fired for cause – theft, fraud or such like – you count as a good leaver. But then comes the question if, after the fourth year, when you have earned all your shares, do you keep them if you leave (as you almost certainly would in the USA) or do you still have to sell them back to the company – at the higher of fair value or cost if you were a good leaver, or the lower of cost or fair value if you were a bad leaver. (Fair market value is of course a slippery concept too.)

There are also all sorts of variations. I have seen some draconian ones. For instance, the practice notes to one term sheet defined good leavers as 'dead, sick or retired and possibly those wrongfully dismissed'. Bad leavers were everyone else, including those unfairly dismissed. It is very much a question of what you can negotiate. Make absolutely sure the good leaver definition covers you if the venture capitalist decides he wants someone else running the company at any point in the future.

If the company is sold before all your shares have vested, there may be partial 'accelerated' vesting, meaning that the founder gets a larger chunk of his stock back. But the venture capitalist is likely to resist this – certainly complete vesting – because, he will argue, the company then becomes less attractive to a prospective purchaser who may be very interested that the founder sticks around (if he is still running the company, of course). However, sometimes the boot is on the other foot. One venture capitalist tells the story of a health-care start-up with two founders – one a serial entrepreneur with a record of making money for venture capitalists before, and the other a heavy hitter from a large pharmaceutical company. Six months after the investment was made, one founder came to see the investor and said he couldn't stand being in the same room as his co-founder, who duly came in later saying the same thing. One had to be fired, but the investor spent six months in the legal dispute. The fired founder successfully argued that the bad leaver provisions did not cover the founders falling out. So he counted as a good leaver and walked away with half the company (which, not very long afterwards went bust).

Option pool

The term sheet should agree the size of the employee option pool – the percentage of the equity reserved for new options for existing and future employees. It might range from between 15 and 30 per cent of the company. The option pool affects the valuation, which is why it is so important to have it sewn up prior to the investment. From the entrepreneur's point of view, the pre-money valuation ideally excludes the option pool, particularly in early rounds. The argument is that it is not logical that existing shareholders should be diluted by the creation of the option pool which is crucial to developing the company (retaining key staff and recruiting new senior people).

Milestones

These are a way of staging or 'tranching' the investment – another set of terms which largely went away during the bubble, only to be revived later as the greed/fear seesaw lurched. From the VCs point of view they are partly a risk management tool (giving them more control and reducing their exposure), and partly a device to keep the management team focused. They should be scrutinized with great care because they can easily become divisive.

Milestones come in many forms, all of which essentially measure technological and/or commercial progress. They can range from completion of beta testing of the product, to the recruitment of a professional chief executive to replacement of the founder. The big problem is that technology companies are Protean creatures, changing so rapidly that it is pretty hard to set sensible milestones. The danger is, furthermore, that the company's efforts are entirely directed at hitting the milestones – landing one particular customer, for instance – rather than doing what is best at the time to build the business. To hit a tight sales milestone a company might hire three more sales executives and exceed the revenue milestone with ease, while adding even more to the company's losses.

They also have the effect of pitting VC and entrepreneur against each other. If there is a board disagreement about strategy affecting the milestones, that becomes tricky for investors as well as the team. If the milestones are not met, investors will gain extra influence in determining a cut in the burn rate, for instance, and will be likely to try and renegotiate terms and/or valuation. In the worst case, clearly, they will refuse to put in the further tranche of funding. Milestones are very much part of the negotiation. Think hard about what is achievable. Temper your natural optimism (again). Consider what might happen if there is a change to the business plan which might make the old milestones meaningless. And make sure the targets are clear and not open to undue interpretation. One start-up that had hit its milestones in terms of revenues was told by the VC; Yes you have hit the milestone but not in the way we'd like (in other words the right sales total, but accounted for by too few customers). If they are tied to profits, there is clearly all sorts of scope for disagreement regarding accounting treatment.

At the same time the more developed the company, the more venture capitalists can expect an entrepreneur to be confident in meeting his plan. If you stick out with undue intransigence against any form of milestone whatsoever, the venture capitalist may legitimately become suspicious.

Conditions precedent

These are a company's milestones for getting the deal done, between the signing of the term sheet and completion of the investment. They will always include satisfactory – from the VC's standpoint – completion of due diligence. Other conditions could include cost cuts such as staff reductions. In the worst case, they can be so onerous – securing a very large new customer – that they make the term sheet virtually meaningless.

Confidentiality/exclusivity

While everything else may be up for grabs, there are basically two binding aspects to the term sheet. The first is confidentiality – both parties agree to keep confidential the fact that talks are happening, as well as not to divulge any information supplied. The second is exclusivity. Once you have signed, you are prevented from talking to other venture capitalists for a certain period. In the USA, an entrepreneur will rarely agree to exclusivity. In Europe, investors seem to expect it and often ask for 30 days or more. The most a US company would be likely to sign up to would be a 'no shop around' provision; namely that he would not use the signed term sheet to generate *new* interest.

But it would not prevent him talking to other venture capitalists who were already interested.

It is of course in the VC's interest to have the company signed up to exclusivity for as long as possible because it puts the company out of circulation as regards other VC firms. At the extreme, it means it is forced to accept terms because it needs the money and does not have time to seek another VC. Again, it comes down to negotiation. If you are forced to take exclusivity, consider slicing it into different tranches – 15 days for the completion of legal due diligence, 15 days for the completion of accounting due diligence and so on, so that you are renewing exclusivity, not granting it for the whole period.

Fees

Many venture capitalists earn huge management fees on the funds they manage, but prove extremely tight when it comes to spending money on anything other than salaries and office space. Hence the custom of charging everything to the company, including due diligence costs and so on. Make sure you put a cap on due diligence and legal costs, for example. Be clear who pays if the venture capitalist backs out. They should pay their due diligence costs and legal fees if they decide not to proceed.

Some venture capitalists will charge the company for taking board seats – 3i has the unattractive habit of charging for the non-executive director it appoints. Many venture capitalists do not, though once one in the syndicate levies a fee, the others tend to as well. You could try insisting they took any fee in options. A few European VCs also charge a deal fee for doing the transaction – which very much reflects the buy-out mentality and seems, frankly, unjustified.

Links

Both these books address US entrepreneurs, but are very helpful.

Term Sheets and Valuations   www.aspatore.com
An inside look at the intricacies of
term sheets and valuations (by
Alex Wilmerding, Aspatore Books
Inc. 2001)

The Entrepreneur's Guide to Business Law
(Constance E. Bagley and Craig E. Dauchy. Published by West Educational Publishing Company)

www.westbuslaw.com

14

Negotiations

Come live with me, and be my love,
And we will some new pleasures prove
(John Donne)

DURING THE NEGOTIATION PROCESS, entrepreneur and venture capitalist are laying the early building blocks of a relationship that could last seven or eight years. It is important to get it right and not to rush in. Make sure you have begun to connect with your potential investor before you start. Certainly do not attempt any form of negotiation in the first meeting. Entrepreneurs who have been successful at fund raising say they categorize the person or people with whom they are dealing in fairly straightforward terms, and adjust their demeanour accordingly as they look for ways to start building trust. Venture capitalists come in all hues. Is this investor a spreadsheet aficionado? If so, bombard him with endless Excel calculations. Does the individual seem particularly risk averse? If yes, show him you have thought through the worst case scenarios, how you are a 'tight bastard' focused on cash management. Meanwhile a point-scoring, tough negotiator may invite an equal and opposite response from the other side of the table, but recognize that such an individual probably also attaches more than average importance to feeling he is winning points. On the whole, the more experienced the venture capitalist, the less he will get a buzz purely from playing hardball on the deal. At the same time, the investment transaction climate seems, counter-intuitively, to be more adversarial than it is in the USA, including among the lawyers. 'You feel people are for ever trying to sneak unfair terms in there,' says one British adviser. 'It is much fairer and more open in the US.'

Entrepreneurs start off on an uneven footing. Arguably, there are few business situations in which there is quite such an imbalance. You are likely to be

negotiating a shareholder agreement for the first time, while the venture capitalist gets to practise in multiple situations. Entrepreneurs can level the playing
field a bit by getting as much information as they can (see later in this section
on comparing notes with other venture-backed CEOs). At the same time, it is
worth considering that the VC is also in a somewhat unusual position, playing,
as he is, multiple roles. First you are pitching to him and bringing him round
to your idea. Once he falls for the deal, he is then firmly on the entrepreneur's
side, pitching enthusiastically to his professionally sceptical partners. Then he
is back on the other side of the table, sparring with the entrepreneur to get
the best terms he can for himself and his partners before, if all goes well, signing on the dotted line and striking a partnership to build the business. Understanding his position may help in interpreting his stance as the negotiations
progress.

Bargaining effectively while building trust is a delicate balancing act. Neil
Rimer, general partner at Index Ventures in Geneva, says he certainly wants
the teams he backs to be tough negotiators: 'We expect that, because it also
means they will be hard negotiators with customers, suppliers, future
investors and so on. At the same time, there is a fine line between tough and
ruthless, reckless or insensitive. It comes down to the issue of trust, and arriving at a deal that everyone senses is fair. You want a feeling that risk is shared
and that there is upside for everyone.'

Laurence Holt, chairman of technology consultancy Quidnunc, agrees:
'Negotiating the terms is a big part of the dance. But a good VC will respect
you if you push back. Tell them that it is in all your interests that this company is well run. Things that slow you down or even prevent you from
making the right decisions are just silly. The VC will see this as a sign of a
strong management team.'

In one of the many signs of the immaturity of the European scene, one
venture capitalist recalls that a mere few years ago he would spend most of the
negotiations 'teaching' entrepreneurs – in other words, initiating them into
the black arts of ratchets, liquidation preferences, and the like. While that individual was probably pretty fair, it is clearly preferable to learn the ropes not
from the practitioners of the black art themselves, but by tapping into the
experiences of other teams who have been fund raising recently. Full Moon in
Cambridge is an example of a club where founders and chief executives of
high technology and biotechnology businesses can network and exchange
advice. Negotiations to sell a stake in your company are in this regard somewhat akin to buying a house in the UK. You need to know the techniques
appropriate to the stage of the cycle (which in the case of house purchases, get
discussed at British dinner parties with relentless monotony).

Likewise, founders and CEOs can learn a lot about the precise state of the funding market from their peers. As is already clear, the balance of power between entrepreneur and venture capitalist shifts dramatically with the cycle – sometimes within a matter of months. In a hostile environment, when few venture capitalists are active, the issues will be quite different from a period when VCs are falling over each other to get into deals. Find out as much as you can concerning the reputation of particular firms. Does the house have a habit of nickel and diming, or of overpaying? Is an individual partner a particularly hard negotiator? Well-networked CEOs tell me that during a downturn they are much more open with each other, discussing details down to the level of each other's option pool and sharing, blow by blow, the discussions they have had with their venture capitalists. In an upturn, there is less camaraderie and more competition and people become reluctant to divulge anything useful about valuations or sensitive terms.

Power levers

Given the apparent imbalance in the negotiations, it is worth identifying the entrepreneur's principal levers of power, in order to figure out how these can best be manipulated.

Time

Time is never on your side, but the closer the company is to hitting the wall and running out of cash, the weaker is your position. Start as early as you can. Paralysis grips the system during a downturn. Deals can be stalled for months; investors play for time while entrepreneurs hope that the environment will improve, when in fact it gets rapidly worse.

Less scrupulous VCs will pull any number of tricks when they know you are close to running out of cash, from dropping the valuation dramatically, to turning the deal from pure equity into a debt structure.

Competition

The venture capitalist will be quick to sniff out whether the company is desperate for cash or has a fistful of other offers tucked in its back pocket. So it is a priority to aim for more than one term sheet. In a difficult funding climate, that is clearly a tall order. It is also trickier in Europe, because the venture capital community is a lot smaller and less competitive than in the USA.

At the same time, on account of the lemming characteristics of venture capitalists, term sheets do beget term sheets. Even in the worst environment, some deals become 'hot'. Nor is another term sheet on the table the only mechanism for injecting a sense of competition into the air. In a bear market, it often seems that the companies who get cash are the ones who do not need it – or perhaps create the illusion of not needing it. Think hard about other options, the most obvious being continuing to build the business without outside funding.

Remembering the ultimate harsh term sheet push-back

Keep in mind that, in the end, sensible venture capitalists recognize it is fruitless to impose punitive terms which thoroughly disincentivize the management team. The tougher the environment, the more true that should be.

Being prepared to walk

As in any negotiation, if you are willing to tell them the deal is off and to walk away (see 'Competition'), your power increases dramatically.

Negotiating styles

Negotiating styles are highly individual and it would be unwise to be prescriptive. Be alert, however, to the games the venture capitalist will be playing. The 'good cop, bad cop' routine is seemingly a fairly common technique. The bad cop seeks to drive a hard bargain on some term or other, or by constantly demanding extra pieces of due diligence. The good cop will then try and make the peace, saying that he thinks he can bring his partner round if the valuation is dropped by a further half million. As one jaundiced entrepreneur says: 'Of course, they are both basically bad cops.' Another common technique is hiding behind the lawyer and being 'unavailable'. Do not allow this to happen; make sure you negotiate directly with the venture capitalist.

Nor will every venture capitalist be handling the situation with perfect aplomb on their side; the younger ones out of inexperience or arrogance; others because they are under pressure elsewhere, perhaps with other investments going sour. 'In negotiating, people hugely overinterpret the other side's actions,' says one senior venture capitalist. 'Is the meeting in the morning or the afternoon? Is the [venture capitalist] late for the meeting? The kind of signal you send is very important. We want to be seen as open and friendly. It is something our young guys are not necessarily good at.'

Pivotal to a successful negotiation is the question of timing, and when to bring up the matter of valuation. Like any complex sales negotiation – whether it involves a big piece of machinery, enterprise software, or consulting services – price must be set in the right context. The venture investor will want to introduce valuation early. In a downturn, their aim will be to start damping expectations as soon as possible. Your game, meanwhile, is to reel the venture capitalist in, lead them in the dance. It is all about the art of seduction.

The VC may have dropped his heavy hints early on, but the hard core discussion should be left until you have finished making a thorough case for the investment proposition. Unlike a normal sale, though, the audience's reaction will tend to be one of extremes. In most cases, a venture investor will either be very excited or not much interested (the latter, as we now know, without actually saying no). In a sense, this makes matters easier. An opportune time to negotiate might well be the moment that you sense the VC is starting to sell to you as well. That means each side is warming to the other, and finding common ground.

Alain Falys did not have the luxury of multiple term sheets, but as he began to negotiate with the VC that ended up leading the transaction, he was also in discussions with a Swiss investor, who was engaging in preliminary due diligence. That was the point at which the lead venture capitalist started to bite. 'They knew I had a couple of alternatives, though of course they did not know what they were,' Falys explains. The VC partner in charge proved canny at selling himself and his firm. 'He established empathy. He stressed that he knew and understood service companies, and that his expectations were different from a pure technology start-up investor.' Falys found that particularly refreshing after a string of meetings with venture capitalists preoccupied by the latest fad (then, nanotechnology). Unusually, the VC firm also offered an advance of £500,000 – in effect a bridge loan – in the event that the 'contractual crap' took longer than expected and the company was stuck. Normally it would be the existing investors who put up a loan, and demand it be convertible into equity, generally at a discount to the share price of the next round. 'That gave me a very warm feeling. That may have gained them a couple of percentage points on the equity participation,' says Falys.

Just occasionally, the discussion can be delightfully straightforward. Lennart Ramberg was fund raising for Altitun in Sweden in a healthy market in 1998. The venture capital partner pitched up with a young analyst fresh from business school, sporting reams of Excel spreadsheet detailing free cash flow years hence – for a company that had not made a krona in revenue. The partner kicked off: 'We have worked out it should be a pre-money valuation of SEK20m. That's a nice round simple number.'

'Well,' Ramberg replied, 'we propose SEK40m, which is also a nice round simple number.' So they opted to split the difference but 'let us win a little' by settling at SEK31m. Ramberg agrees there was no logic to it. 'It was one meeting, then we agreed on the phone the next day.'

Even in an up market, that is the exception. Giuseppe Zocco, general partner at Index, reckons that on the whole the valuation debate is trickier in Europe than in the USA. 'It is all: "Look, my company is worth x because my brother-in-law raised x at a pre-money valuation of y and told me I should not accept less." It is a really uphill battle to bring [founders] round because they are really convinced.' Venture capitalists will of course talk their own book, but at the same time entrepreneurs do need to be realistic in their expectations. A pre-revenue or small revenue business is essentially worth what people are willing to pay. There *is* no other yardstick. If you are in a boom market and you are lucky, of course you will end up with a much better valuation. But even in a bad market, if you are a good company, you know you are good and you are realistic, you will get a fair deal. Again, get as much data as you can on the valuations of recent comparable deals, and keep an eye too on trade sale and IPO valuations in your sector, or adjacent sectors.

Creating the necessary competition without annoying investors is another delicate business. In the bubble, term sheets flew around like confetti and start-ups would be juggling a dozen offers. The trick in that environment is to secure commitment letters that are as detailed as possible so that you can compare the deals in the round, not just valuation but the terms too. The valuation might be higher in one, but because of the nature of the liquidation preferences, or the way the investor has set up a forced exit, the overall deal may be worth less to the founders than an alternative offer at a lower valuation. Not that anyone did this of course. Everyone was single-mindedly concentrating on pushing up the valuation, on getting the deal done and on dreaming of the 'upside'.

In more sober times, venture capitalists get distinctly shirty if they think they are being dragged into an auction. Pond Ventures, a UK early stage investor particularly committed to the notion of providing a real service to its investee companies, likes to make out it is above any kind of bidding war. 'If an entrepreneur says he has got two term sheets and asks us to make him an offer, we won't. The view is, if he is just taking us for our money, we don't invest,' says Charles Irving, Pond co-founder.

You should still seek as many alternatives as possible. All the guys want the girls with lots of dates, and in venture capital it is no different. Rather than rushing to pick up the gavel, though, consider more subtle approaches such as flattery – telling the investor how you have another term sheet on the table, but would prefer their firm as your backer because of their fabulous network. Clearly it is acceptable to use one firm's term sheet if you are building a syndicate, which you will be likely to be doing in partnership with that investor anyway.

While creating the sensation of lots of other interest, beware of bluffing. If you say you have another term sheet when you do not, and are later caught having to mumble something about the other deal having fallen through, you obviously lose credibility fast. Stuart Evans of Cambridge-based Plastic Logic, closed a deal in the spring of 2002 which he concedes, even in that bear market, got to be 'hot'. He explains how 'market forces take care of the price. It is nothing as crude as having an auction. The price floats to its natural level. We got a 70 per cent uplift [on a previous seed round] but I hope we left something on the table. I don't want [the lead, German, investor] to think they got screwed'. His advice is, when faced with the luxury of choice, do not go for the highest price, but rather focus on the quality of investor.

The clean deal

Each negotiation is a trade-off between valuation, investor quality and terms, as Chapter 13 stressed. Quit worrying for a moment about the extent to which your stake in the multihundred million company is being diluted. Concentrate instead on how much of the loot you and your team will see in the event of a modest sale of the company where onerous liquidation preferences kick in.

Some venture capitalists will be inclined to start to negotiate on valuation alone, and only bring up the terms much later. Watch out particularly for those firms who insert references to 'our usual terms and conditions', which turn out to be punitive clauses that only rear their heads at the last minute in the shareholders' agreement. By the time you see the draft term sheet, you should have discussed, at least in broad outline, all those unattractive elements such as liquidation preferences, anti-dilution and vesting provisions. As already noted, harsh terms lead to ugly down rounds and tricky merger and acquisition discussions. There is a pretty clear correlation between the complexity of a transaction and the likelihood of breakdown in relations between venture capitalist and entrepreneur later on. When things go wrong down the road, as they inevitably will in an early stage business, you are going to need each other. If one or other side feels they were screwed at the outset, it will make for a yet more intense conversation about why things have not worked out.

Any good entrepreneur should therefore take a step back and ask the investor what the valuation would be on a *clean* deal. You may not much like the number, but at least it is a more balanced transaction, aiming to lay the foundations for a proper partnership rather than a set of acrimonious debates. Be on the look-out too for unusual terms in the term sheet. They may not necessarily be sinister, just a reflection of house style. But do understand, with the help of a good lawyer, how unusual they are and why they are there. Also avoid getting stuck on negotiating away one specific term and thereby neglecting the broader picture.

Winning negotiations

So what is negotiable? Mark Suster at BuildOnline highlights the dilemma: 'You want to push back against all the onerous terms, but you don't know against which, and you are worried that, if you push too hard, the deal will fall apart.' Each entrepreneur who ended up with a fair deal will have had his own particular triumph. Evans of Plastic Logic managed to negotiate away milestones, helped by the fact that he had enough term sheets to afford the luxury of drawing up a shortlist: 'Of course we *have* milestones internally. How else do we know we are making progress? But we argued that milestones [in the investment contract] were not appropriate at such an early stage of the business.'

In his $7.7m financing closed in January 2002, Falys at OBE ended up negotiating a fair deal from a lead VC (UK-based) firm and the corporate venturing arm of a US corporation, including a simple once times liquidation preference, in which the existing angel investors ranked alongside, rather than behind, the new venture capitalist money: 'We were very clear what we didn't want. We didn't want the VCs having some sort of guaranteed return,' Falys recalls. 'That defeats the purpose and screws my existing shareholders.' Nor was he having any truck with share vesting either. 'There was no way we were going to have the shares vesting. We have brought the company to here. It is our equity.'

Both concessions, it must be stressed, are unusual. How did he do it? Mainly, he argues, because his existing angel investors put up just over a third of the new round. From a pool of around 30 shareholders, only two declined to reinvest. 'I hate to use the phrase balance of power, but the discussion was reasonable because of that', says Falys. 'Normally people concoct a deal that makes sense for the VC, is not *too* bad for the entrepreneur and the angels are forgotten.' But he was determined his angel backers were not going to be squeezed. The new VCs wanted 'something over the angels' so we agreed to weighted average anti-dilution. 'None of this is black and white, which means you can barter; there is room for each party to give and take.'

Legal aid

Use your lawyer. If he is good, he will be able to point out a lot of potential traps not immediately apparent to you as well as the current trends in term sheet provisions. But you may need to be quite proactive in this regard. As mentioned before, every legal adviser will be used to sitting on both sides of the table; the last deal he did may well have been on behalf of a venture capitalist. He may have become a bit too relaxed as to what is normal and what is not. Keep asking how the term can be used against you.

Most people would also caution against leaving either side's lawyers to negotiate between themselves – except in matters clearly only of interest to other lawyers, such as which court of law disputes are to be settled in. It is much more powerful if you, as a non-lawyer, can say directly to your future investor: 'I don't think we should have this clause.'

Signing on the dotted line

So at what point do you actually sign a term sheet? If you agree to exclusivity (see Chapter 13), you accept you will not talk to other VCs, and you are also indicating that you are basically happy with the headline deal – even though of course it is not binding on either side. It is crucial to establish from the venture capitalist their ratio of term sheets signed to deals completed. A firm that has signed nine term sheets and made seven investments will be pretty committed. 'We take exclusivity very seriously,' says one investor of that ilk. 'The presumption is we are going to invest, provided we don't uncover fraud. If you drop out after 30 days it can really damage the company.' Contrast that with an outfit that has put out 17 term sheets and done two deals. Another indication of seriousness is that the firm agrees to pick up its legal and due diligence fees if it pulls out.

It is also very useful to establish where the decision has got to internally. More than slightly counter-intuitively, the production of a term sheet does not mean there has been any kind of decision by the whole partnership or investment committee. Often that decision may not be taken until very near to the final closing. One entrepreneur says he was shocked to find how late in the process the investment committee sign-off occurred: 'They didn't tell us they still had to do that. The good news, though, is that you are so far down the road that everyone wants the deal to close by this point.' It is worth understanding in greater detail how decisions are actually taken.

Decisions, decisions

In the centre of the boardroom table at London-based venture firm Elderstreet is a roulette wheel – a decision-making tool perhaps more appropriate to the venture business than a laptop full of spreadsheets, though not one that necessarily instils confidence in limited partners. But then Michael Jackson, Elderstreet founder, an early investor and director in Sage the accountancy software firm, is a bit of a maverick. He has a reputation for saying both yes and no on the spot (apparently without the aid of the wheel), something highly unusual in the venture capital community. The no always comes with reasons, which is something entrepreneurs admire, and his technique may owe something to his own entrepreneurial background building Sage.

Each venture firm is different in the way in which it reaches its decisions, but it will help in the negotiations if you understand as much as you can about the process at the firm or firms to which you are talking. A few basic principles apply. As has been argued earlier, the venture capitalist's main decision-making technique seems to be prevarication. Venture capitalists rarely say yes, and take even longer to say no. There is no end to the ingenious ways in which they will keep your hopes up – so that you don't go to the competition, so that they can negotiate down to the wire as you become desperate – or because they are running scared after a series of bad investment decisions. 'We need to do some more due diligence', 'We need to get the rest of the partnership on side', 'We're fund raising right now'. And so it goes on.

The decision-making process certainly seems to speed up a bit once other firms have shown interest, most particularly after the investment has closed and the money has hit the bank account. Says one CEO in the latter happy position: 'We have suddenly now become much more interesting to VCs. People had wind of something after we signed the term sheet. And now [the deal is complete] they are calling. We are thinking, maybe we will need $20m or $30m in the next two or three years. It is quite clever of the VCs and it is stupid for us not to keep a link.'

Styles differ immensely. *eBoys* [Stross 2000] captured the trust-your-gut, shoot-from-the-hip, we-are-all-frat-boys-together ethos at Benchmark, even if the partners viewed the book as a less than full and fair treatment. Within the small Valley-style partnerships, approaches to the business vary from those

driven primarily by gut feel to the more rigorously analytical. Some partnerships combine analysis and instinct under one roof. Hermann Hauser and
Anne Glover, co-founders of Amadeus, are a study in contrasts which, while
ever a delicate balance, can work well.

Anne on Hermann: 'He's incredibly strong at a conceptual level. He is a
classic physicist, everything has to hold together logically. He is incredibly
demanding, and won't accept a sloppy explanation of how something works.
He pushes on the architecture. It comes from his having headed the research
labs at Olivetti for years. But he will accept a rather sloppier answer about the
market. It's big – OK. I push on other levels.'

Hermann on Anne: 'Anne is very disciplined,' he says, citing her training
at Apax. Hauser says he became a venture capitalist – achieving what he calls
his 'evolutionary niche' – precisely because he wanted 'more discipline on my
own behaviour'. As an angel, he had had such a vast deal flow that he could
not assess the quality properly and so needed a more structured process. He
was also spread very thin. 'Investors in the first fund wanted to know how
many boards I sat on. I had never counted. The answer was 24.'

Plastic Logic, a spin-out from Cambridge University, is an illustration of
the differing styles at work. Glover describes the business as 'so early stage it's
not even a sector'. Pivotal to the deal being done was Hauser's relationship
with Prof. Richard Friend. They had taken their physics PhDs together and
Hauser had invested in Cambridge Display Technologies, an early spin-out
from Cambridge University which Friend co-founded and which, despite a
bumpy ride, was proving a successful deal. 'The day Richard made the phone
call [Hermann] did the deal,' says Anne. 'I said what are we doing? An associate did a lot of the work about precisely what we could spin out. I said we
need a CEO. "Oh that's a good idea," said Hermann. The difference is that in
the old days, there would have been a business angel investment. No one
would have worried that the IP [intellectual property] was all messy. And no
one would have known what was happening, and there would have been no
leadership. Hermann was happy as a clown because he got to do the deal. But
the fact is, it took three of us to complete it.'

In a small firm, where all the partners sit round a single table, the procedures will always be somewhat more informal and flexible than at a larger,
more institutional organization, where the process involves separate committees. Executives at Apax, which is famous for the analytical rigour of its investment committee, reacted with particular mirth at the *eBoys* portrait, but either
extreme is open to criticism. Some would argue that Apax is prone to overanalysis in an area where there are no answers and that, as a consequence,
some of the firm's people judgements have been weak. Investors who spend

too much time ripping the business model apart may fail to answer some of the basic questions, such as: Do I trust this person?

Most venture firms stress the consensual nature of their decision making. Kevin Comolli, managing partner of Accel in Europe, says the US firm, like most of its peers, does not have anything as formal as an investment committee: 'We have Monday partners' meeting with 20 people round the table. It's a consensus. That means there are no heroes in good times, no scapegoats in the bad times.' (Well, that's the theory.) But what exactly does consensual mean? 'Lots of people say their investment committee is consensual. But it ends up being a case of you scratch my back if I scratch yours,' says one private equity specialist, who needless to say avers his firm's committee is 'truly' consensual. In other firms, some partners are more equal than others. 'It is a true partnership. We agree or disagree in unison,' says one, before immediately contradicting himself: 'People listen to and really trust the two senior partners.'

Consensus

Consensus is mostly achieved adversarily. A former associate in another small partnership says he could tell when the VC's natural state of prevarication transmuted into proper interest in the business. 'You could tell when the partners were starting to engage because they would begin tearing into the proposal, ripping it apart.' This is helpful for an entrepreneur to remember. The slew of extra due diligence questions you have suddenly received may reflect the objections of partners you have never met (and may never meet).

The idea is that the consensus builds slowly. A venture partner newish to one London VC complained to the firm's managing partner that he could never pinpoint when the decision about any individual investment was made. The response was: 'Good, that is how it is supposed to be.' The process in that firm is described as follows: 'One partner – who may have been introduced to the idea after a meeting with an associate – champions the idea. The rest of the team throw rocks at it, until the risk is reduced to a size that is manageable. If the champion is under too vicious a tirade of rocks, he withdraws. The idea is that it should not be be turned down at the final meeting. It should have received the necessary criticism along the way.'

In larger institutions with formal investment committees, one set of executives is inevitably attempting to second-guess another set, which makes the dynamics yet more opaque and unpredictable for an outsider. An important question to ask with an international firm is whether decisions are taken locally or at headquarters. Entrepreneurs backed by Intel Capital used to complain of the painful process of securing approval at European level and then being told they had to await the decision of a higher authority in Santa Clara, California. Interestingly, Benchmark and Accel adopted opposite approaches in setting up their European operations. The former devolves decision making to the European team; the latter invites its companies to the seat of the partnership in Palo Alto. Cape Clear, the Irish web service, flew to Palo Alto three times. (The partnership was still learning about a then brand new sector and probably, equally important, there was the reputational issue of the firm's first investment in Europe.) 'The idea is we apply the same standards in Europe as we do in Palo Alto,' says Jim Swartz, one of the founders of Accel as well as an architect of its international expansion. 'But it is not easy to do. Can we apply the same standards? To be truthful, we are still learning.'

Building a syndicate

As negotiations progress, you may be working with the prospective venture investor to build a syndicate. In bull markets, venture capitalists are often keen to hog an entire financing round. Conversely in a downturn, they tend to be keener on syndication from the outset. It becomes another mechanism for limiting risk. They want extra minds around the table and access to wider networks that, for example, a mix of European investors from different countries can provide. They may also want to feel the existing syndicate can fund the company through to the point when it reaches profitability if necessary, without having to rely on other investors at a later stage.

Investors tend to syndicate with particular individuals they know and like as much as with firms. With many syndicates disintegrating into querulous chaos in the downturn, VCs are trying to be a good deal more professional in the partners they select. Is this individual from a firm that has money? Does the outfit have staying power? Are they overexposed in a certain industry sector? How does the individual behave when the going gets tough? Does he keep his word? It is very much down to individual partners' records.

Assembling a syndicate has all sorts of hidden pitfalls, with multiple possible sources of tensions between other investors to which entrepreneurs need to try and be alert. In BuildOnline's case, one large private equity investor (whom Suster did not in the end select) was adamant that it did not want the private equity arm of a well-known investment bank in the investor group, while Suster saw the bank as lending 'a huge sign of credibility'. The large investor was arguing that it could send all sorts of potentially awkward signals as and when BuildOnline came to do an initial public offering. If you don't choose the bank as your underwriter, or the bank doesn't choose you, the market will be asking questions, was their line.

Suster also inadvertently set fur flying among the investment bankers himself. Morgan Stanley contacted the company on its own initiative shortly before the funding round was set to close. BuildOnline's founder knew, and rated, the organization's real estate sector expertise. After a series of furtive Sunday meetings in discreet London hotels, Suster then went to the first investment bank and suggested that BuildOnline enlarged its funding round and brought Morgan Stanley in. 'They went through the roof.' The team tried to argue they did not want Morgan Stanley to fund a competitor. The argument did not impress, although that was exactly what Morgan Stanley did, leading a $70m round for Buzzsaw of the USA. GRP, by contrast, the US investor that Suster chose, was proactive in introducing the company to other possible co-investors across Europe.

The game, VCs sometimes like to say in ugly management speak, is about co-opetition. Certainly the emphasis on the co-operation or the competition varies with the state of the cycle. But to most entrepreneurs, it is the collusion that stands out. It is a clubby business. VCs collude to get into deals in an up-phase of the market – and to share risk at favourable prices in more uncertain times. As already mentioned, venture capital gatherings (such as the Chemistry Club) can often end up being quite alienating to entrepreneurs.

At the same time rivalries can be intense, for instance regarding deal attribution, either within a firm, or particularly when one partner has moved elsewhere. During the bubble meanwhile, jealousies flared when partners quit for seemingly more attractive billets: Eric Archambeau, who moved from Atlas Venture to Benchmark Europe, left behind some green-eyed colleagues. (Today it is more apparent just how difficult it has been to extend the Silicon Valley firm's brand to a new European operation – and Archambeau has anyway left Benchmark to set up a seed fund.) For entrepreneurs, the motto is to be aware of such sensitivities and to avoid as far as possible getting caught between clashing egos.

The VC bear market has also caused plenty of investors to fall out with each other. Tensions have flared particularly in follow-on financings, when one syndicate partner has gone back on their word at the eleventh hour and ruined confidence in the rest of the syndicate. A particular problem has been large institutions which have suddenly decided to pull out of private equity altogether, or heavily reduce their exposure to technology. Some companies with the backing of three or four large institutions have been left high and dry when all more or less simultaneously closed down their operations. Picking the right syndicate partner has become much harder for VC and company founder alike – and the lack of a deep pool of competent investors is being acutely felt.

Breaking the deadlock

Most negotiations will reach some sort of impasse – a particular clause or term that the VC wants and you are resisting. Falys suggests putting the investor on the spot by asking a few simple questions: 'What purpose exactly does this clause serve? Let me understand why you are insisting on this. What is the situation you are really trying to protect yourself against?' If the venture capitalist cannot articulate a strong commercial reason, that puts him in a weak position. Equally, you may also be prepared to concede a point yourself because you realize it is something that has less impact on you than you thought.

As time goes by

One of the problems of a fund-raising process that extends over many months is that conditions change and you may well need to be constantly adapting your business model. Investors heartily dislike companies changing their story. The business may well be right to do so, yet the partner may have presented the proposal to his investment committee and be reluctant to explain new changes. Within reason, investors should value an entrepreneur's flexibility, but many will need more than a little persuasion to see it that way.

References

Stross, R. E. (2000), *eBoys*, The true story of the six tall men who backed eBay, Webvan and other billion-dollar start-ups. Crown Publishers, New York.

15

Close

It ain't over 'til it's over
(Yogi Berra 1973)

THE DOOR TO MARK SUSTER'S OFFICE at BuildOnline had been shut for two weeks; the only sound to emerge had been the occasional bout of shouting during heated exchanges down the telephone. He and his general counsel shuffled around 'like zombies', dark shadows under their eyes. The rest of the team felt they were walking on eggshells. At 2.30 on Monday afternoon Suster called the staff together. He arranged his features in a suitably funereal pose. March-First, had just filed for bankruptcy, he reminded them. Etoys, the toy retailer, was poised to go under: 'This is a tough market, it's not just BuildOnline.'

He harked back to the 'very difficult process' they had been through the previous month when the company had shed 18 of its 78 staff as part of a sweeping cost-cutting exercise. 'Today is a different process,' he said enigmatically. After months of poker playing with the venture capitalists, he was allowing himself the brief indulgence of a mind game with his staff – one in which he was, for once, in control. As a trolley of champagne was wheeled in, the staff learnt that, far from representing another bout of dire news, the 'new process' was one of celebration. BuildOnline had just raised £10m of fresh funding, securing one new investor as well as the support of existing VCs.

This was only about a third of the sum Suster had originally been aiming for. With the Nasdaq at 1600 as opposed to its peak of 5000, he had had to accept a much lower valuation and the exercise had taken about nine months. But with so-called business-to-business e-commerce companies as unfashionable among investors as last season's catwalk triumph, it was something of a feat nonetheless.

The closing occurs when you sign the final legal documents and the money is transferred to your bank account. There would appear to be an immutable law of nature which dictates that signings take place in the lawyers' offices at about 4am, often when the company is down to its last €100 in the bank. One entrepreneur describes the process as like climbing one of those hills where you keep thinking you see the summit, only to have whole acres more hillside open up before you. In any transaction, the closing always gets put off at least once. Needless to say, it is in the lawyers' interests to string things along.

The two most important final documents are the investment agreement, which is the contract between the shareholders and the company, and company's charter documents (the articles of association for an English company). If there is a loan involved, there will be a separate loan agreement. The various clauses you negotiated in the term sheet reappear in these documents (see box), though what appears where seems to be remarkably flexible in Europe.

Investment agreement
◆ Subscription obligation (investors' agreement to subscribe for the shares)
◆ Conditions to subscription
◆ Consent rights
◆ Information rights
◆ Confidentiality obligations
◆ Provisions regarding exit
◆ Warranties and indemnities
◆ Restrictive covenants (preventing the managers leaving and competing with the company. These are included in here because they are more enforceable than if they appeared solely in the employment agreements.)

Charter documents
◆ Details of the share capital breakdown
◆ Rights of the shares, including:
  – Dividend rights
  – Liquidation preferences
  – Redemption rights
  – Conversion rights
  – Anti-dilution rights
  – Voting rights (that is one share one vote, or on an as-converted basis)
  – Transfer rights (drag-along, tag-along)
  – Pre-emption rights
  – Good leaver/bad leaver provisions

You may still be negotiating down to the last day, but the trick is to make sure you have negotiated the large points over which either side could fall out before the term sheet is signed.

The more investors are involved, the more complicated it becomes, with multiple sets of lawyers arguing about minutiae. Nick Kandola, chief executive of a now defunct e-business IT trading hub, detailed to me the woes of clinching an agreement even at the height of the bubble (*Financial Times* 2000): 'The company and investors would get together and agree a point that made sense. Then the lawyers would go away and suddenly one of the lawyers would say: "That's not what we thought my client agreed" and everyone would go back to the drawing board.'

As already noted, there is an unfortunate tendency in Europe for each party to be trying to outsmart each other, trip each other up. The importance of setting a cap on both sides' legal fees (Chapter 13) is clear. The more investors and lawyers are involved, the more the process can drag on. In all cases, it is up to you to drive the process. Make sure you have the names of all the lawyers involved (if it is a large syndicate) so that you can personally hassle the foot-draggers. You alone can keep the momentum going. One entrepreneur reckons:

"Completion means the negotiation is complete, and unless something forces it, that could be 16 years away. At some point, though, you have to stop. What stops the whole thing? Tiredness mostly [or, of course, the company running out of cash]. Everyone is worn out. Because you are worn out, it makes you prone to listening and really trying to find a solution. At the same time you both realize all you are doing is putting money into the lawyers' pocket. That is when you come to the quid pro quos. I gave my VC something he was very keen on – that made him look good to his investment committee (relating to a modified forced exit). He gave me something that I was very keen on – that would have shafted my existing shareholders (provisions were changed so that, in the event of an IPO, angel investors could sell their shares at the same time as the VCs)."

The other immutable law of closings is that everyone is so exhausted that the exhilaration of deal completion generally passes them by. That comes a day or so later. Suster's celebration was on the Monday following a Friday signing.

Reference

Campbell, K. (2000) 'A sour taste of success', *Financial Times*, 23 March.

PART THREE

Working with venture capital

16

VC on board

The two extremes appear like man and wife,
Coupled together for the sake of strife.
(Charles Churchill, *The Rosciad*, 1761)

SO THE MONEY IS IN THE BANK. Time to forget the venture capitalist? No, now comes the real work of cementing an effective relationship and ensuring the nascent love affair blossoms, rather than sours at speed.

First, your new status as a venture capital backed company makes it a good time to work on the board structure. During the bubble when normal business rules were suspended, building an effective board seemed an irrelevance. Many entrepreneurs were running their first start-up; boards were slung together and few did the job properly. Indeed, one could argue that one of the many reasons why Europe has produced so few successful international technology companies is the preponderance of ineffective boards.

An internal study by Apax in May 2001 identified as many as 150 publicly listed technology companies across Europe that had at one point reached a market capitalization of more than €1bn (and were still extant at that date). There were whole swathes of pretty obscure names on the list of former high-flyers, and the total was certainly a surprise, even allowing for the still inflationary after-effects of the bubble. About half were still capitalized at over €1bn. While any link between fallen angel status and board incompetence is more surmise than evidence, it is certainly a lot harder to find instances of effective boards than of the reverse.

Dysfunctional boards include those where the entrepreneur dominates. One former chief executive of a software company admits he spoke '95 per cent of the time' in board meetings. 'It was pretty much me presenting –

updating people and getting approval.' Or the board may be decorated by a non-executive director or chairman put in by the venture capitalist, but this character is heartily resented, usually with good reason, being as he often is a big company type who is clueless about the company's industry generally, or because his experience, while appearing relevant at first glance, is not (a retailer, but of cheap clothing when the company is an upmarket furniture designer). Still a common sight in the UK is the top-heavy board filled with the great and good – Sir Archy Featherstone and his polo-playing cronies. 'The VCs don't want anyone on the board who will show them up,' says one cynic, 'so you end up with the great and the good because they supposedly have good governance skills – when what a young company most needs is contacts that can help it grow its revenues from $3m to $6m.'

Cultural and legal obstacles abound too. In France, says one investor, small company boards are taken still less seriously than the UK. The concept of a portfolio director, for instance, going 'plural' in a second or third career and holding several non-executive positions is virtually unknown. Says Gérard Tardy of Sitka Partners, a specialist adviser: 'People would find that bizarre, certainly for anyone below retirement age. They would want to know what your real job was.' French non-executives are paid too little, about €4,000 a year, he says. 'It is seen as really greedy if you are asking for more than €10,000. People will ask: Who is this guy?' Meanwhile French chief executives mostly take exception to a venture capitalist imposing a non-executive director: 'The immediate reaction would be to see it as a threat. Indeed maybe rightly so, precisely because people don't have portfolio careers. "Why aren't you more frank with me, why don't you tell me if you want to replace me?" they ask. It sours the relationship immediately.'

In Germany meanwhile the two tier Vorstand/Aufsichtsrat (management board and supervisory board) structure certainly complicates matters. To put it mildly, German corporate law is not set up with small companies in mind. The Aufsichtsrat is selected by a company's shareholders and would normally meet just four times a year. So the VC really wants to be on the Vorstand, but that is there for the day-to-day running of the business. In practice the supervisory board becomes the board in an Anglo-Saxon sense. 'Actually people behave as if it were a normal board,' says one VC from a pan-European firm. 'Every now and then someone puts up their hand and says: But you can't do that. There is a lot of legal process. It's very rigid about who speaks when and so on.'

While a raw start-up clearly does not need a huge unwieldy board, even a pre-revenue company can, if it is ambitious, assemble a fairly heavyweight line-up. Nexagent for instance (see Chapter 7), while still a pre-revenue proposition, had assembled three senior non-executives in addition to the two venture investors on the board. It is an area where venture capitalists can add real value, by making introductions to suitable non-executives from their wide network, but in Europe too few have been focused on the issue – beyond insisting on their own one or two seats at the boardroom table (which they may or may not inhabit to good effect).

US venture capitalists have tended to approach the matter very differently. They generally wish to control the board – either by number or de facto in the sense that they assume the non-executive(s), who they may well have introduced to the company, will vote their way. As on public boards, there will often only be one executive from the company; on the grounds that filling a seat with an executive is a wasted opportunity when it could be used to secure valuable outside input. This position on control has a lot to do with the fact that, historically, US venture investors have paid far less attention to the details of the shareholders' agreement, although since the bubble's bursting that is changing. In Europe, by contrast, investors were not much bothered if the board met once a quarter; they exercised their control via the list of 27 items in the agreement for which the company needed to seek specific shareholder approval. Since the downturn, European investors are becoming more proactive with their companies and, with more US venture capitalists in Europe, US-style arrangements are more common. One experienced US lawyer in London cited a UK company that had recently rejigged its board to contain the chief executive, three non-executives representing the VCs, one independent industry figure, and one individual who is representative of, but independent from, the founders.

Entrepreneurs are often pretty unenthusiastic about the very concept of a board, especially one that shows any signs of being prescriptive. What is the point anyway? One European founder who combines the role of chief executive and chairman, says the company is too small and young (staff of 30, two years old with a large group of angels and first round venture capital funding) to bother with independent non-executives. 'We are too young to have a buffer [between management and shareholders]. The shareholders will come to me.' He concedes a chairman could be useful in time, but sees non-executives as a waste of space. 'How would a non-executive help you resolve an issue? It all comes down to power. And where does the power lie? With the money.' He has already rejigged and slimmed down his board, including removing a director representing an angel syndicate. 'I felt they were professors looking at my copy and marking it. I don't need that.'

The trick is to think of the board not as a necessary evil – an audit committee in disguise – but as a constructive resource that challenges you effectively. Resist the temptation to recruit a passive board. Just as chief executives need to come to terms with hiring people better than themselves, so they should be seeking strong board members, not a bunch of compliant friends. Unlike a public company, a private company board can still largely be assembled with an eye to genuine utility, rather than to compliance with rules, regulations and form (although, following the run of US corporate scandals, there are fears that small private as well as large listed companies may be caught up in the waves of draconian legislation affecting non-executive directors).

Some venture capitalists will insist on taking the chairmanship themselves, which shows a degree of confidence that may or may not be well placed. But in a five-man board with two VCs, a good balance might be two company executives and an independent chairman. It is desirable to have at least one genuinely independent director, given the venture capitalists, however much they *should* be acting as directors, will inevitably have as their priority the best interests of their own funds. It is a time consuming job if taken seriously and non-executives should not have more than four or five directorships. The dearth of good candidates will also have been made the more acute as people become increasingly nervous of the legal implications of such responsibilities in the current climate.

What is a chairman for? You don't need the rock star industry figurehead, but someone who nevertheless, ideally, has deep industry knowledge and who can preside over a rational, valuable board discussion – and yes, not let you the chief executive dominate. Among a multiplicity of functions, a strong chairman can help build trust with investors. Graeme Minto, founder of inkjet printing company Domino Printing Sciences, who has worked extensively with VCs, says:

"Venture capitalists *are* human. They want to have trust in the people they have invested in. They don't want to be second guessing what is going on. One of the ways to build trust is to have them confident the business is well run. For instance, that it is managing growth from five to 50 people. A business savvy chairman can be useful in this sense. It avoids VCs grousing behind the chief executive's back. If done delicately, the chairman can be a middleman between VC and entrepreneur."

A genuinely independent chairman can also on occasion be useful in counterbalancing the venture capitalists. Lennart Ramberg of Altitun explains how he and his team wanted to establish their own manufacturing facility for the tuneable laser company: 'The VCs resisted it, complaining it was very expensive. Let's build a product line, not a production line, they said. As it turned out, in 1999, access to manufacturing capacity was what counted. There is no outsourcing, there is nothing like a fab in this industry. You can't be fabless. The VCs said, 'Bah, engineers, how typical, they don't realize customers count.' The way it was resolved? 'A very senior industry guy joined the board. He had physical gravitas, and was from Uniphase Europe. He said, in this industry we need to manufacture. He said it once, everyone agreed. That's what it took. He said it, it was right.'

Board effectiveness is generally inversely proportionate to the number of people around the table. A board of nine will be a circus – more ill-informed bodies to ask silly questions and waste time. In due course, a full complement might be seven, including three non-executives, ideally providing a balance of financial monitoring, business development and technological expertise.

Another problem in Europe is that boards tend to be domestic in their composition – a French board in France, a Swedish one in Sweden. Yet if the business (and competition) is global, one of the biggest challenges will be managing international expansion. Hence the desirability of an experienced, multicultural board. At the same time, finding these individuals has always been tough. In the aftermath of Worldcom and Enron, many executives will be additionally nervous of taking a board seat in a country where they do not understand the local legal system and so are unsure what extra liabilities they may be assuming.

As already noted, many European investors lack extensive networks in this regard, and there is anyway the dilemma that you may not want your VC to handpick your 'independent' director. One option to consider is forming a technical advisory board, where individuals do not have the liability of being directors, but can still act as useful sounding boards on industry developments.

VCs as board members

'VCs are incredibly impotent. They don't have enough information. They are very sensitive as to whether they piss off the chief executive. They don't dig beyond what he says. Our company was moving very fast, the VCs had to rely on the personal judgement of the chief executive. They didn't question if we could do things better, whether we were really building a world class business.' This is a typical rant from a young, opinionated entrepreneur. Other complaints include incompetence even after the company has floated. One US investment banker in London says too many VCs just do not know how to behave on the boards of public companies (on which they may remain for years). He says he has seen 'blatant violations' of the UK takeover code – such as the investor who sounded out his investment committee about their view on selling a 20 per cent position in one of their public company investments. The open discussions immediately made insiders of the entire investment committee.

If you have chosen well, however, your investor will be a source of wisdom and strategic insight, as well as rigour and focus. While VCs may sometimes be prone to undue panic (see below), the better ones will be tough when tough action is required and will stop things being swept under the carpet.

Styles vary considerably. Pond Ventures draws a distinction between those investors with a large portfolio who are bound to err towards the investor/investee relationship – by contrast (of course) with Pond that aims for 'a more interactive relationship'. Says Charles Irving: 'We train our people never to call up and bluntly ask what this month's sales figures are. You must always call up with new knowledge. This company is doing this – and by the way, what are the sales figures? You should be the first person the company calls if there is a problem. You don't get that if you behave like a pompous ass from the City.'

3i by contrast has a rather different model – perhaps inevitable given its size, but not always effective for the companies involved. While the firm's executives will take a purely observer role, 3i will be likely to insist the company appoint a non-executive, probably the chairman, from a shortlist it provides. Part of the problem is that the quality is mixed. The indirect nature of the relationship is certainly another issue. Many entrepreneurs would feel they wanted the person who made the investment, and had the emotional commitment, to be on their board. Not only are they paying the non-executive director a hefty board fee, but questions arise as to quite whose side he is on – the company's or 3i's. When there is a problem, companies often find themselves talking *through* the chairman to 3i, which can degenerate into an unfortunate game of Chinese whispers.

Communication

However effective the non-executive chairman, the seminal relationship is of course between you and your investor. Be proactive in communicating with them – even, says one entrepreneur, if they don't sound all that pleased to hear from you. You do not want to be on the phone every day, clearly, unless there is a crisis, but they should be hearing from you once a week. It is very tempting not to do that. You have much more pressing day-to-day problems, especially when you have just raised the money and think you are 'safe' for another 12 to 18 months. It is always going to seem much more important to fix a problem or call a customer. But if the VCs haven't heard from a portfolio company for a long time, they are be likely to start assuming the worst. Trust is then lost and the penalty may be further irritating controls. When things do indeed go wrong, many investors have a habit of panicking and the whole thing goes off like a bush fire.

'The more they feel they are informed about what is going on – positive and negative – the more trust they will have in you,' says Mark Suster of BuildOnline, who advises getting to know them socially too – dinners with partners and so on. 'If a VC knows you, has a relationship with you, has worked closely with you, of course they are more likely to support you if things get rough. If they know you as an individual, they are less likely to make a tough decision based purely on a spreadsheet. Performance,' he adds, 'how you are evaluated, is a combination of metrics – and perception. Perception *is* reality, it's almost as important as metrics.'

Keeping your company at the forefront of the VC's mind can have certain not so immediately obvious benefits. Perhaps you are a few months away from doing a big second round of funding. Suppose your VC is talking to another large investor – about something else. He is more likely to bring you up in conversation if he is abreast of what you are up to.

Realism is also essential. If for five successive months you have been promising a particular sale is 'right around the corner', you will start to lose credibility. One venture capitalist tells wearily of 'a frank discussion' he had with one of his companies where the entrepreneur is described as 'extremely enthusiastic, with an element of naivety. I told him he was always *selling* to the board, which was beginning to discredit what he was saying; we were all starting to filter it.'

Another way to build the relationship is to help the VCs out on occasion – not something entrepreneurs necessarily consider. Remember they have personal issues within their own firm. Think about how you can help *them* be successful. One founder says one of his (relatively junior) investors was giving a presentation to the VC's global board on the subject of his most successful company. So the founder took time, in the midst of some complicated merger discussions, to help with research and more or less write the presentation.

Lies, damn lies and value add

As the weeks and months go by you will be discovering whether the 'value added' marketing spin you heard *ad nauseam* when you were fund raising is just that – so much spin.

Laurence Holt at Quidnunc, a technology consultancy, says that during the fund-raising process many investors promised help that was irrelevant to the company at its particular stage – such as hiring: 'We had been in the business ten years, we know how to do this.' What Quidnunc wanted was assistance with revenue generation. 'But that is not easy, spotting deals. Perhaps we have never trained our VCs sufficiently what a Quidnunc opportunity looks like. We possibly expected too much.' He adds that, rather than bringing deals, he would get 'these inane merger opportunities. They kept looking at their port-folio and asking, which two can we fit together? We have had the weirdest sug-gestions. At first we made the mistake of talking very seriously about each suggestion. Now we just say "Where is the logic"?' Holt acknowledges that perhaps the company did not train its VCs as well as it might have done. This correctly highlights the fact that, much as entrepreneurs love to gripe about how little 'value add' their VC brings, it is at least partly down to them.

Chris Ahlberg at Spotfire is an example of a CEO who has proved adept at using the resources of his backers, which include Atlas Venture, to the full, and hauling in help not just from the two partners most involved in the busi-ness, but from others across the firm. 'You can make people do amazing things if you ask,' says Ahlberg. In his early thirties, he is one of the few technolo-gists – he did a PhD at the Chalmers University of Technology in Sweden – who has made the successful transition from founder to CEO of a fast-grow-ing and now international business.

Areas where Atlas has played a seminal role have included recasting the marketing strategy from a horizontal to a vertical approach – moving from selling the software, which provides visualization software tools for data mining, selling to multiple markets simultaneously, to a vertical strategy, con-centrating initially on the pharmaceutical industry. The Atlas life sciences team provided market savvy and, later, powerful customer introductions. Like any ambitious European software company, tackling US expansion was also a conundrum. But that had been the way Ahlberg initially got to Atlas – ring-ing Philippe Claude, then in Atlas Venture's Paris office, simply to ask advice on internationalization. (Claude had been an early investor in Business Objects, one of the more successful technology companies to emerge from Europe in the past decade.) Atlas also played a big role in the far from easy task of recruiting a number two. And when Ahlberg was looking to expand the board he trawled the contacts of every Atlas partner (to secure David Yoffie, Harvard Business School professor and Intel board director).

Each entrepreneur will form his own view of where he can mostly usefully tap into his investors' resources. If nothing else, VCs have to be useful for follow-on financings, and here again the process will go more smoothly if everyone is getting on. (This subject is treated in much greater detail in the next chapter.) Stuart Evans of Plastic Logic stresses how crucial it is to get the existing investors on side because of the signal it sends to potential new sources of money. He had Amadeus and Dow Chemical in his seed round, with Hermann Hauser of Amadeus on the board: 'You develop the business plan, discuss it with the board which includes Hermann. If Amadeus thinks it's stupid they will say so. They will never *promise* to invest, you can never take it for granted, but they will say yes, it looks all right, here's our support, off you go [and make introductions]. Amadeus always did what they said they would. Other people find VCs supportive early on, and then not later. Sometimes that's the world and sometimes that's VCs not behaving well.'

In a bear market an entrepreneur will be worrying about massive dilution of his position. 'Everything is stacked in favour of the investors. The only way to protect yourself is to be so valuable they can't afford to lose you. And maintaining good relationships with the investors is an important part of that,' says Suster.

Hitting a bump in the road

How much is it good for the VC to know? One entrepreneur, anonymous understandably, says he ended up running three sets of numbers: 'There were the forecasts that went to the board; the set we actually ran the business on; and a third set for senior individuals within the business. That way we had a buffer if we hit a problem. Most VCs do not ask a lot of questions as long as you are on plan, even if the plan is set quite low. They start getting interested when you have missed something.' The entrepreneur said he always had a winning rejoinder when he did miss forecasts or was otherwise confronted with a difficult question. He would enquire delicately: 'Well what are you doing for us?'

What investors least like is surprises, so keep feeding them information. If there is a piece of bad news to be communicated, get it out early. Pick up the phone, don't wait for a board meeting. Plenty of people will instinctively hide bad news from investors. They lose a major client, but they pretend it hasn't happened. (Not that VCs are necessarily any better themselves, incidentally, in terms of reporting bad news to their limited partners, who dislike surprises equally intensely.) Anne Glover says she knows one US venture capitalist who works on the principle that if the management team is not meeting the plan, it means one of three things: They *can't plan*, or they *can't execute, or both*. All of which are a problem, in the eyes of this VC. She believes attitude is more important – a good explanation of why the numbers have not been met and how the problem will be fixed is what she wants to see.

When venture capitalists get nervous, they tend to ask for ever more data. It can become a vicious circle. You give them more data, which prompts requests for more data. 'The whole thing becomes very silly. At some point you have to say to them. Hang on who's running this?' says one entrepreneur. 'We learnt to use PowerPoint slides rather than Excel. It forces you to present at a higher level. The push-back is: We don't have a full-time person dedicated to churning out spreadsheets for you.'

When the facts change I change my mind. What do you do, sir?

(J. M. Keynes)

How understanding will the VC be if it comes to a major modification to the entire business plan? This depends. Investors say they like their management teams to be flexible, but you may suddenly find some limits to that particular penchant. Bear in mind that if they are essentially keeping track of the business simply from what they glean from the monthly board meeting, the business plan itself may assume disproportionate importance. There may be additional resistance if the VC has to go back to his firm and explain major changes (especially if he is more junior).

One French VC tells the unhappy story of a syndicate of international investors, of which he was part, which had backed an internet business. A few months after the fund raising, the entrepreneur realized the plan was wrong – there had been a big clue in the failure of its US equivalent. The venture capitalists divided into two groups: those that agreed they were backing the entrepreneur himself, and those that were furious: 'They said, "This is the business plan I backed. I want to get out." My attitude was, he is a great entrepreneur. He will find a way to do something in this space. Their attitude was not so laid back. It was extremely surprising. In my view the entrepreneur was doing the right thing. He was frank enough to tell it very bluntly. Some of the most successful VC investments have changed models countless times.' The supportive investors bought back the stake of the unhappy investors 'who left money on the table', while the entrepreneur, needless to say, took further dilution.

Another French venture capitalist says he tends to be more worried by the opposite problem: 'In France sometimes an entrepreneur is out to prove the business plan is right. The market is *going* to be there. Customers who find his product stupid are themselves stupid. These people are very dangerous, they have cost me personally a lot of money. In the end of course the market is always right.'

Founder transition

The prospect of someone else succeeding you as chief executive of your business is probably the hardest thing to come to terms with in this entire process. Yet the founder who stays on to preside over a multibillion dollar company is rare indeed – Microsoft, Oracle, Dell, or in Europe SAP, Autonomy and Business Objects, are very much exceptions. Founder succession is also one of the most delicate and difficult parts of a venture capitalist's job. The great irony is that, while venture capitalists spend an awful lot of time trying to persuade other people of the necessity for such transition, they are generally hopeless at managing succession within their own firms.

Renoir , a headhunter specializing in assignments for venture-backed technology companies in both the USA and UK, claims that, on average, a start-up will change its chief executive two or more times before it reaches initial public offering. Naturally given its line of work, Renoir argues that the most successful companies employ at each stage of their development CEOs with certain distinct traits and skills, finding as many as five categories of leader to manage different stages of growth, ranging from the 'inspirational visionary' in the early days, to the 'general' presiding over the army at IPO and beyond.

My feeling is that venture capitalists reach for the lever of changing management far too frequently, particularly when things go wrong (see below). I also think they are frequently less than clear on the matter at the outset, leaving plenty of scope for misunderstanding. After all, the mantra of backing 'management, management and management' hardly seems consistent with founder transition. In that context, management actually turns out to be, you could say, a dynamic rather than a static concept; the investor looks for the best management available *for that particular phase of the company.*

Perhaps you are someone who believes you can genuinely grow with the job, learn how to delegate, identify your strengths and weaknesses, and find others to compensate for those weaknesses. In that case, if you have picked a good venture capitalist, you may succeed in making the transition (and not everyone, after all, is on the path to building a multilbillion dollar corporation). Says Gerry Montanus at Atlas: 'Most changes are foreseen when we invest. Unlike some VCs we never say, let's invest and deal with it later.'

Ahlberg describes how Claude gently probed his attitude to founder succession before the investment was made. 'I only realized that was what he was doing with hindsight. It was very clever.' He had been asked for his view on management, and had given what Claude obviously thought was a less than satisfactory answer. 'OK,' said the prospective investor, 'let's go through a scenario planning exercise.' Ahlberg was asked to write a memo with as many 'what-ifs' as he could come up with. Claude then helped him think through certain possibilities. For instance, the Swedish company planned to move its sales and marketing operation to the USA early and would need to hire a president and COO. What happened if it proved impossible to hire a sufficiently high calibre individual into the number two slot? What happened if, as Ahlberg puts it, 'Ahlberg turned out to be a nutcase'? Six years into the company, Ahlberg is still very much in charge (having hired as his number two an American who is 15 years his senior and been involved in four previous start-ups).

A big difference is often noted between US and European attitudes in this regard, though that does not mean the process proceeds without acrimony in the USA. Sandy Lerner, co-founder of Cisco, had running battles with Don Valentine of Sequoia and was eventually forced out in 1990. As a rule however, (as has been noted, Chapter 7), US entrepreneurs are more focused on how much they will make, not whether they control the business. So they will recognize more readily the need for transition if they can see that is likely in the end to make the business, and hence their stake, more valuable. A US founder will think more about protecting his economic interests. At the same time, Christopher Spray at Atlas is among those who believe attitudes in Europe are changing: 'It used to be frustrating for everyone because people were determined to hang on at all costs. But that happens less frequently these days. Yes we have had to have a few painful conversations, we don't think you are the right guy. Sometimes of course we say no to a deal because it is clear that the founder intends to run the business indefinitely.' When transition is managed properly, the way is prepared, and a few positive words are said. 'The company has reached the next level, you have done an amazing job, now we are looking for someone who is good at X.'

Do venture capitalists always get it right? Clearly not. One venture capitalist involved in a deal where one of the milestones specifies finding a new chief executive rightly views the process as being 'as delicate as an organ transplant – will the body reject the new organ?' But entrepreneurs can be stubborn in the extreme – and of course egos get in the way. A former colleague of one founder resisting the inevitable says: 'He is utterly ruthless in many ways, but not in this case. He just can't see it is in the interests of the company for him to step down.' For those who can manage to be realistic about their own weaknesses, the process is likely to be smoother. If it comes to the inevitable, it is then a matter of negotiating the best possible deal. Work out what leverage you have got, what value you can continue to provide. Find a new role such as CTO, VP of engineering or VP marketing, or push to retain a non-executive board role.

If you leave you have to be prepared to see your stake whittled down (that is even assuming your shares have vested and the investors count you as a good leaver, see Chapter 13). In future financings or mergers and acquisitions, there is unlikely to be anyone to protect the dilution of your ordinary shares. Mark Suster at BuildOnline was unusual in this regard: 'The biggest fight in our latest round was over Brian [the founder who had handed over to Suster in the very early days]. I threatened to walk. I got him cash. Not millions but he was low in the pecking order and low on leverage and in the end he would have got zero.'

At the same time, hanging on can create tension. One venture capitalist, who says he had been told by his mentor 'never to leave the king to roam the kingdom' nearly found out the hard way the wisdom (from his point of view) of such an approach. He had brought in a new international chief executive to run the company, which was based in Sweden, and moved the founders to other positions. The new man had, as planned, changed everything in the business on its route to internationalization. A few months later there was insurrection. The founders wanted to kick out the new chief executive and buy back the venture capitalist's shares. For 48 hours, crisis reigned. In the end the non-executive chairman, who was also Scandinavian, was brought in to mediate.

The worst situation is probably when the issue is fudged and the founder stays on – but in some corner office lacking a clear title. This is hard for him, and can be confusing in the extreme for employees who have been used to him as the boss.

Bad calls

Venture-backed companies made a lot of very bad hiring decisions in the bubble. They would bring in a VP EMEA of a multinational software company to run a business that was still at the stage of needing product development skills, when the individual was accustomed to selling against a sales proposition devised elsewhere in the business. Plenty of big company types simply did not make the transition to a start-up environment.

Spray argues that it is a misconception that venture capitalists are trigger happy at firing management: 'The general inclination is actually to try and make it work. Once you have made the decision, the reaction frequently from people inside the company is, "What took you so long? Why didn't you get rid of him months ago?" Compared to someone working with the CEO every day, it will not be as obvious to the VC [that things are wrong]. If they are good at spinning a story, they can hide the problems.'

Pace Spray, some venture capitalists in recent years do fall into the trigger-happy camp – and it may be that the larger, institutional firms are more open to the charge. When the whole portfolio is suffering, there is a great temptation to change the management simply in order to be seen to be doing something. One country head of a pan-European VC firm advanced to me, as evidence of incontrovertible progress, the number of chief executives and chief financial officers he had changed in the previous six months.

Investors are prone to panic, says one former chief executive who has witnessed such behaviour at first hand: 'We were not making the sales. But we didn't have an open dialogue. Maybe they detected I was having doubts, that I had figured out it was going to be a marathon and not a sprint and that I didn't necessarily have the legs. But instead of helping, they went in for the kill.' The largest investor decided something had to be done, and it started out as an exercise to change the chairman (who had been appointed by the investor). Two days later, the chairman was asking the chief executive to leave: 'There had been no indications in any of the board meetings. There was never a conversation about any of my weaknesses – "you may need to think about this, work on that" – none of that sort of thing. It was all back-room stuff. Afterwards everyone blamed each other. The board was saying it was the investors, the founder [who had brought in the chief executive] was saying it was the chairman, the chairman was saying it was [the largest investor], the investors were saying it was the board.'

Apax did a study which found that 'defensive follow-on' financings, with or without a change of management, hardly ever paid off. The quality of people who can be hired into an ailing young company is not high. 'It is a perpetual debate when to follow your money and when to let a company go,' says Adrian Beecroft, Apax partner. 'We found that in defensive follow-ons, we made one and a half times our money, compared with three and a half times in companies that were doing well. If we were changing management at the same time, the returns were yet worse. Everyone's experiences of defensive follow-ons tend to be poor. But you have to take into account the human factor. People want to give it another go, you don't want to recognize your mistakes. Also in terms of reputation you can't be seen to be off at the first sign of trouble.' Some venture capitalists will put in another partner to assess the merits of a follow-on investment to provide objectivity in case the partner on the board has 'gone native'.

Under pressure

When everyone is under pressure, the strains between entrepreneur and venture capitalist can be at breaking point. Danny Chapchal, a technology turnaround specialist, says: 'VCs never understand the entrepreneur's need for advice and encouragement rather than constant criticism.' VCs, for their part, think entrepreneurs are often stubborn and unwilling to listen to anyone when things go wrong.

Sir David Cooksey of Advent says there have been endless problems with unrealistic CEOs since the bubble deflated: 'People raised a lot of money at ridiculously high prices. It has been very difficult getting them to stop dreaming, to batten down the hatches and make sure they survive. They have been flattered by the high valuation, and, having frequently come out of a huge corporation, are anyway used to very deep pockets. You'd be amazed how resistant some people are to facing reality when they have got money in the bank. It's a much bigger battle than you would believe.' At the same time, the VC who in a crisis remains accessible and supportive while still being effective is rare indeed.

Remember, of course, that there may be stresses and strains within a partnership affecting your investor – forcing him to act, to 'take a gutsy decision' that will take the personal pressure off him. Plenty of entrepreneurs complain that VCs panic. Says one entrepreneur who was facing a big dip in sales: 'The board observers suddenly started turning up to board meetings. We were getting calls once a day instead of every three months. If the investors' panic comes across, it is difficult for the CEO – who is trying to keep up employee morale. The pressure transmits, and everyone starts making mistakes.' Given the nature of the job, one might question why investors are not more inured to trouble and failure. At the same time, if everyone was unduly laid back and philosophical, the limited partners who supply the capital would have grounds to worry.

Sometimes VCs can be more than a little insensitive into the bargain. One entrepreneur, who was flying around Europe on easyJet and staying at bed and breakfast establishments as the company went through a vicious downsizing, was suddenly presented by one of his investors with a large bill for attending board meetings – first-class flights and nights at the Berkeley Hotel in London. Some of the expenses were 12 months old. 'They want you to succeed, they beat you up to make you cut costs, yet they stick you with the bill for the Berkeley, keeping up their great VC lifestyle.' He decided he would attempt to engage in some public shaming by bringing the subject up at the board meeting. His line was that the VCs should be taking some of the pain.

It was a shareholder not a board issue, he was told. In the end he met with the investors individually – and got them all to settle at 50 per cent of their expenses.

Pressure can also manifest itself to exit the business. Spray argues that it is another misconception that the VC will force you to sell: 'The evidence from the US is that in general entrepreneurs want to sell sooner than VCs.' The latter are more inclined to continue, he argues, because they are taking a portfolio approach, whereas entrepreneurs have all or almost all their net worth riding on the one investment.

Again, entrepreneurs sometimes tell a different story. Says the boss of one of Europe's larger privately held software companies: 'We can build a great company, I am convinced we can, but there is another view beginning to swirl around. I know it is being whispered by my investors. "You have had a great quarter, someone will buy you, we will flip you". My attitude is, do you want me to build you a good company or a great company? Because I can build you both. You decide.' The business could be acquired for a few hundred million Euros. The VC firm has recently had a few large write-offs and, like everyone else, few exits to show to its limited partners. 'It's a dilemma, I understand all sides.'

Holt of Quidnunc tells of another side to the exit pressure. The company, founded back in 1988, had grown organically for a decade before taking outside funding in October 1999 and again in November 2000: 'We wanted to expand in the US – which was wrong in hindsight – but we needed to be bigger and to be public. Our clients, particularly in the US, were saying 'What is wrong with this company? Why aren't you public?' What was not clear was that the company was then on a conveyor belt. 'A process starts in the mind of the VC. They may be prepared to wait quite a long time, but they needed to be able to tell their limiteds where the process was leading. It become difficult, then impossible to do an IPO. The VCs were much more frustrated than we were. They could no longer answer the question, where is the exit? A large part of the board meetings then became taken up with the question: Do we sell? Strategy discussions became narrowed down to one topic, achieving an exit. We keep having to point out that it is not a mistake by management, it is the environment.'

Being alert to the VCs' need for an exit, which will be more acute at particular points in the cycle, is part of the battle. It is also part of the original bargain. As in all aspects of the partnership, the more open the relationship and the greater the trust, the less scope there is for unpleasant surprises.

17

Down rounds

The language of complaint and reproach was in everybody's mouth,
and all the meetings were of the most stormy character.
(Mackay, on the bursting of the tulip bubble in Holland)

YOU MAY HAVE MET all the milestones, executed perfectly on the plan and have worked 18-hour days to achieve it. But when it comes to the next round of funding, investors are telling you it will be a 'down round'. All follow-on financing is potentially dilutive. But down rounds are by nature painful because the company is valued at a fraction of the level of the previous financing. The lower the valuation of the new round, the more dilutive it will prove. Down rounds become a feature of the landscape when public markets plummet and hobble the ability of companies to raise new cash at prices anywhere near those of their previous financing – regardless of whether they were performing to plan (which of course, as a downturn bites, many will not be).

With even less science than ever involved in reaching agreement on the numbers, the discussion essentially distils down to an assessment of how badly the company needs the money. Also pivotal to the balance of power is the willingness of existing investors to 'follow their money', in other words, put up sufficient cash to maintain their stake. It is gun-to-the-head time and the team's bargaining power is severely constrained. In the worst case, it can be a matter of swallowing hard and accepting the terms or facing bankruptcy. The arithmetic can be brutal. In one case I heard of, the founders had nearly 40 per cent of a company at a valuation of $54m post-money; following a down round, their stake was reduced to 0.4 per cent of the company at a valuation of $575,000. Such highly dilutive financings are sometimes known as cram-downs or washouts.

While the company is under extreme pressure, the venture capitalists are feeling the heat too, and the less experienced probably showing it. Missing the adrenalin kicks of carving exciting new deals, most investors are now locked into intense internal discussions about which companies they will continue to fund and which ones they must cull. For many, the post-bubble collapse in valuations was unfamiliar territory, the first time they had seen PowerPoint charts that did not rise inexorably from bottom left to top right . With a rare burst of wry self-knowledge, one venture capitalist explained to his limited partners at an annual meeting during 2001: 'We have liquidated all the start-ups with dumb business models so that we can concentrate on all those invest-ments for which we overpaid.'

One entrepreneur seeking follow-on funding describes how a punitive term sheet, highly dilutive for the founders and carrying a five times liquida-tion preference, arrived on the fax. The company had already been warned to expect tough terms 'because the limiteds [limited partners] are looking at our term sheets'. The term sheet was dependent, among many other things, on the company securing an ambitious contract from Cisco to buy its software. The entrepreneur was already worried that the hour and a half the venture capitalist had spent on the phone to Cisco at this delicate time had not helped its case. To make matters worse, no one from the venture firm had been in touch for two weeks following delivery of the term sheet. 'I just feel they could have managed it all more tactfully,' says the entrepreneur, who was gloomy about the prospects of saving the company. 'The management team is totally burnt out. Do the VCs understand? They are not giving on anything.'

Meanwhile existing investors with board seats are in an uncomfortable spot legally. Are they acting in the interests of the company or those of the fund? While the board has a duty to all shareholders, it is tempting for the VC to slip into doing what is best for his own fund. The chief executive needs to attempt to make the board behave like a board, rather than as a gaggle of squabbling shareholders (which is clearly easier said than done).

New money talks, and investors will insist on highly favourable terms if they are to put up cash. These may include full ratchet anti-dilution and high multiple liquidation preferences – all mechanisms to secure maximum down-side protection, and to force the hand of existing shareholders. Investors with a very good deal first time round, such as full ratchet anti-dilution protection, may well be forced by the incoming investor to forfeit those if the refinancing is to go through. It is a buyer's market for the new money, which can and will demand belt and braces protection – although of course the existing investor will at least have secured a place at the table by virtue of his own tough terms.

A steep liquidation preference can also be a device to deal with existing shareholders who are unwilling to stump up or have not got more money. It effectively tells previous investors they have lost their money and the new investor deserves all the returns. Interestingly, this may help the existing investors cosmetically. If the effective value of their investment has gone down because of the liquidation preference rather than because of massive dilution, they might well not report the former to their limited partners. (It has been customary to report changes in valuation but not capital structures to LPs.) In the end, though, it all makes for an impossibly convoluted spiral. Venture investors were perhaps determined to show they had learnt from overpaying in the bubble, but by seeking refuge in such structures simply created a myriad new problems.

Down rounds divide into two basic categories: those which attract a new investor, and 'internal' rounds which do not. If at all possible, entrepreneurs should endeavour to find fresh outside money. It means securing what is supposedly a fair market price. But in a climate when VCs have become excessively suspicious of each others' deals, this has become extremely hard. In choosing a new investor, incidentally, the same principle applies as in earlier, probably smoother, fund raisings. The idea is not to shoot for the best (or least unattractive) price but rather to hunt down a combination of the best quality of venture capitalist and the most favourable set of terms available. Be prepared, though, for plenty of acrimony. Tensions build, with at least three camps – new investors, existing investors and management – possessing very different sets of interests. Life is certainly easier if existing investors are prepared to 'follow their money', namely to reinvest to maintain their stake.

There has been no shortage of instances where a financing has foundered because early investors who were, for one reason or another, unwilling to stump up more cash, advocating bankruptcy in preference to heavy dilution of their positions. And why would anyone do that? Raw egos may be involved. Moreover a fund would generally adjust its valuations to reflect the most recent financing round and, in the eyes of its LPs, the difference between heavy dilution and write-off might be marginal. In the post-bubble era, countless other investors were unable to open their wallets again if they had wanted to. Many had frittered away the fund, put little or nothing aside to support existing investments, and had no prospect of raising a new fund.

Other categories of 'awkward' investor included the investment banks and corporate funds that pulled out of the market after the bubble. Seasoned venture capitalists have been kicking themselves for bringing supposedly deep-pocketed institutions into earlier syndicates without pausing to consider that deep but fickle pockets are pretty useless. Changes of policy at 'professional'

VCs are even more exasperating and, rightly or wrongly, a number of firms refused to deal with 3i in the aftermath of the bubble after the group fired 17 per cent of its staff, pulled back sharply from technology, and appeared to reduce its support for existing portfolio companies. Syndicates which included US investors who closed their European operations and limped back to America have faced similar problems.

Internal rounds

The price of the round is clearly in the hands of the venture capitalist. If there is no competition and only one or two investors, there is theoretically no floor on the price. Venture capitalists know that follow-on financings are extremely risky. One explains his – logically slightly dubious – thinking: 'Venture investors know that very few succeed but they require all that extra labour. That is why we feel justified in doing these cram-downs and wipe-outs.' It often comes down to cohesion of the syndicate. Plenty of otherwise sound companies have not been funded simply because the syndicate could not agree.

Take a company where the early investors put in a smaller amount of money, perhaps €5m, for 30 per cent of the business, while the later stage investors had put in €20m for 40 per cent of the business. The company is now looking for a third round and there is no external appetite. The two existing backers have very different sets of interests. For instance, the later stage investors may have a three times liquidation preference which means the early stage investors already see nothing if the company is sold for less than €60m. At the same time, if the syndicate is tolerably robust and the entrepreneur has genuinely been doing a good job, any reasonable VC would want to keep him happy. 'It depends how people have been treated along the way,' one venture investor points out. 'If you have a partnership with the venture capitalists, in other words the relationship has the right DNA, they won't want to screw you. But if the investors feels you have driven a very hard bargain in the past, and have resisted suggestions [for instance to make necessary job cuts] you will have a very different outcome'.

As an entrepreneur, the only real leverage you have is the value the investors place on you and whether you are prepared to threaten to walk if the valuation is punitive. In an internal round, in which existing investors each maintain their pro rata share, everyone is theoretically indifferent to the valuation because shareholdings have been maintained. But the founders are unlikely to have the cash to maintain their share, and so get diluted anyway. One way investors attempt to keep the management team happy when their ordinary shares have been diluted down to the ground is to grant them huge numbers of options.

CEOs should also fight to have the company's option pool increased in the interests of being able to hire strong members of the team in the future. In a heavily dilutive round, the option pool might have fallen from 25 per cent to 1 per cent, so the aim would be to try and negotiate the creation of a new pool. Watch the vesting provisions though. Options vest over time. Normally management would expect 25 per cent to vest after the first year; then perhaps 6.25 per cent every three months thereafter. Make sure the clock is not reset to the creation of the new pool, but stays as it was, as though it were the old pool. At the same time, there is the lingering problem that the options granted are still of course options over the (now nearly worthless) ordinary shares. A few entrepreneurs have managed to negotiate options over preferred shares or a special class of employee shares. Venture investors resist that, however, and insist any such discussions are left until any trade sale actually emerges. Of course other classes of ordinary shareholders – angels, founders no longer in the business and the like – have no levers at all, and, if unable to put up further finance, will suffer the most crushing dilution of the lot.

A bridge but not a pier

Internal rounds are sometimes a device to buy time in the search for an outside investor. One or more of the existing backers may then advance a bridge loan, which is likely to convert into shares at a discount to the price of the next round. The advantage is that it puts off the discussion about valuation and, in theory, by the time of the new round, the company will be worth more. Of course, if the next round is still a down round, then the bridge conversion becomes yet more expensive in dilution terms. In the past, bridges with discounts up to 30 per cent were seen. The venture capitalist would argue that it is risky from their point of view because the company may fail to raise future funds. But in a bear market any new lead investor would be put off by such a large discount and ask why the bridge provider should be entitled to pay so much less than him.

'Get a bridge and not a pier,' is the advice of one entrepreneur. In other words, be brutally realistic and make sure you really have enough money to tide you through. Falys of OBE advises: 'You don't want to be under pressure because you are running out of cash. You negotiate better if you are not under pressure. As the CEO, you need something up your sleeve. You can only trust your gut feeling as to how long it will take to get signed.'

As is becoming rapidly clear, down rounds are hideously complicated and there are multiple possible scenarios. Below are three tales from the front which attempt to illustrate how the perverse incentives of different shareholder rights from multiple rounds pit investor against company, and investor against investor in situations that can easily implode.

Politics

While securing an outside investor gives you a certain bargaining power, the process remains anything but straightforward. 'Dealing with investors is politics,' says one chief executive who has experienced multiple financing rounds. 'In my last deal I identified four different political constituencies.' These broke down as follows:

Management and executives.

The lesser investors [L]. These are seed investors, together with a set of firms who had not put up their pro rata share in later financing rounds.

The main investors. These included the lead investor from the most recent round [M2] and another earlier investor [M1] which had contributed more than its pro rata share to that round.

The new investor [N], which was putting up some cash as part of a merger deal with the company. Because the new investor's business is doing less well, it has less bargaining power than M1 and M2.

The entrepreneur, who is granted anonymity here given that the cardinal rule of playing political games is not to get caught, explains:

"As a politician you say to yourself, how do you win them over and give them what they want while getting what you want? Well, you work out who is aligned with whom. M1 plays the same game every time, they pretend they're the good cop. They must think I'm an idiot. They say: M2 won't approve this deal, they only invested a short time ago, how do we win them over? Perhaps they should have a larger stake, dilute less? Of course M1 wants the same deal as M2. And dilution has to come from somewhere – probably me and the management. So who am I most aligned with? In a funny way, the new investors. Perhaps I can whisper in their ear: You should ask for X – something that happens to benefit me and them, but something I can't ask for.

There are always secret discussions in these things. Everyone is talking to everybody, sizing things up, trying to strike deals, working out how to move the pieces on the chess board.

So I suggest to N that they ask for a lower liquidation threshold [the valuation of the company at which the liquidation preferences fall away. In bubble era optimism, this had been set very high].'

The entrepreneur had spotted that it was in N's interest that the liquidation preferences did *not* kick in. M1 and M2 had been in a stronger negotiating position, because N wanted the deal more than the existing company did, so they had negotiated hefty preferences over N. Under the proposed structure, unless the company was sold for a huge sum, M1 and M2 would garner all the proceeds. But if the liquidation threshold was adjusted down to, say, €20m, and the company were sold for €21m, the pie would be split equally according to percentage shareholdings. Guess who else benefits? The chief executive and management [with ordinary shares and/or options over the ordinary shares].

Among other concessions he managed to lower voting percentages on the consent rights, the laundry list of actions which investors could block – including new fund raisings. 'I said to [N]: "Do you want to have to get *their* permission if you want to raise more money in a future fund raising?" The percentage was lowered to 51 per cent – giving me a good deal more room for manoeuvre on all the consent rights.'

Good gReef!

Reef, a content management software company, is an example of a once high-flying start-up that expanded rapidly, fuelled by dizzying sums of finance (nearly €90m) from well-known backers, only to collapse just a few months after securing a €30m financing package. This was no story of Boo-type excess, but rather an instance of how a company can be undermined when the professional investors fall out with each other. What is more, the ambitious targets which management had failed to hit had almost certainly themselves been pumped up by the more than generous dollops of cash swilling in from the venture backers when bull market thinking reigned.

A regular feature on all the right lists of the hottest tech firms, Reef had been founded in 1999 by Belgian Philippe Brawerman, voted in June 2000 at number one in *Time* magazine's list of the 25 most influential people on the European technology scene. Brawerman, as former president EMEA of Cisco, impressed many people, and venture capitalists had clearly got over their usual aversion to backing family companies. (Co-founder, and vice president of strategy and business development was Cécile Féront, Brawerman's partner, while the company's chief technology officer was her father.)

Providing data management for non-technology specialists, Reef had attracted well-known backers, including Goldman Sachs, 3i, Viventures and Cisco. Like so many content management companies, the business had been encouraged to put its foot flat on the floor, building a vast cost base including a large US sales team. In mid-2001 it had a staff of around 340. But by the end of the year, unaudited financial statements showed a loss of more than $41m on revenues of around $11m, according to an internal document. In a memo to the Reef board and its shareholders presenting the accounts, revenues had fallen 32 per cent between the third and fourth quarters of 2001, which the chief financial officer blamed to a large extent on the diversions of the fund raising which had started in April. Reef appears to have ended the year with a cash balance of $2,526. But by the end of February 2002 the company was able to announce a heavy-hitting €30m series E financing round, raised with the help of advisers SG Cowen, and led by Carlyle, a US firm with one of the largest technology funds in Europe. (This included the repayment of a large bridge financing. So it was by no means all new money for the company.)

Michael Wand, a highly reputed former Deutsche Bank analyst, had run the deal from Carlyle's end. Brawerman waxed lyrical to me at the time about the 'company building' input he was hoping Carlyle would bring – even if the skills of a later round investor would normally be more immediately suited to the preparation of an IPO than to the operational tasks related to digging a company out of a fairly large hole. The series E financing carried full ratchet anti-dilution, a two and a half times liquidation preference, and a cumulative dividend, and the valuation, after conversion of the bridge financing, was a paltry $2m, the internal document suggests. Investors who chose not to participate in the round saw their holdings burnt to the ground. The D round investors, led by Goldman Sachs, appear to have seen their share of the company dwindle from 23 per cent to 0.5 per cent (with Goldman itself left with 0.16 per cent). Another day, another cram-down round, one might say.

By the beginning of July of the same year, however, the company had started wind-up proceedings. It appears that it required more cash and that, in the course of an almighty row between investors, it simply blew apart. It probably did not help that 3i, under pressure from its ailing technology portfolio, had heavily centralized its follow-on funding decisions in the meantime. (The local Amsterdam office, which had made the investment, had been singled out by Brawerman earlier in the year as having been especially supportive.) A French bank, a prospective new investor, is thought then to have grown nervous and to have pulled out, and the house of cards fell apart. Whether the company had prospects or not had become scarcely relevant.

Diary of a down round

Mark Suster, a former management consultant with Accenture, joined BuildOnline as chief executive in the summer of 1999. Unburdened by even a passing interest in the construction industry, his drive was to prove he could build a real business. Learning, as he did, what he calls 'depression era entrepreneurship' had not been part of the plan, but, unlike many others, he stuck at it.

Fund raising for series B, which had kicked off in July 2000, finally completed the following April. It could hardly have been more different from the preceding round, which had closed in early 2000 with Nasdaq nudging its 5000 bubble peak. By spring the following year, the US index had slid to 1600 and the mood was dramatically changed. 'In the first half of 2000, anything was possible,' Suster recalls. 'The idea that a business might not succeed just did not occur. An IPO was a right of passage. No one thought about failure. In the second half, the dotcom bankruptcies were piling up.' He had to go through two rounds of lay-offs, letting go friends he had worked hard to pull out of big jobs at GE Capital and BCG, and saw a procession of investors walk away as they caught the Nasdaq jitters. Here are his lessons from a roller-coaster ride (see box).

◆ *Be cynical*
'VCs [existing investors] say they're right behind you. You gradually learn that doesn't mean a thing. One of my investors was telling me: "We back you no matter what." "OK," I said, "put the money in now". "Oh, but we're waiting for [another investor] to make a decision. Then we can go to our committee and ask for more money."'

◆ *Enjoy poker*
'Figure out what cards you hold. Don't let anyone else read your hand.'

◆ *Don't be too proud about valuation*
'Lower the valuation, race around like hell and get some competition going if at all possible. If I had cut the valuation in September [early in the fund raising], I would have raised three times as much.' In the end he managed to achieve a price that represented 60 per cent of the first round valuation (which, in tune with the boom times, in turn represented a nine times uplift on the seed round).

▶

◆ *Know your worth*

'If you are a good chief executive and they respect and like you, there is some power in the fact that they need you. But this card must be played professionally. If you play it too strongly, they'll think you are an asshole and start looking at other options. It's an art.'

◆ *Start early*

'VCs delay and delay. The more they can drag it out, the more they can screw you because you become desperate. No one ever says no. In an up market you have a bit more control. In a tight market, the VCs have you. When it comes down to hard business they are not paid to be nice people and I think I was dealing with the nicest.'

In September 2000 Suster was in confident mood, believing he had secured fresh financing of between €35m and €40m, at a valuation 'a tiny bit up' from the previous round. The first intimations of trouble came the following month with a slide in the Nasdaq of about 14 per cent within two weeks. A Swiss investor that had been poised to contribute some $12m to the round backed off: 'This was a blow because they had been telling me the investment was already approved.' That still left three or four investors in the ring – or rather sitting on the fence: 'They didn't know what to do. Should they protect their existing investments? Should they do nothing? How about the price? The whole time they were fixed on their exit.'

It came to Thanksgiving and Suster was due on the first family holiday for at least six years; a party including his mother and brother and sister were off to Hawaii. At the eleventh hour he had to cancel. A corporate investor, pencilled in for around €18m, had started to waver. The company had done the due diligence and, Suster believed, the senior guy had agreed. But a more junior colleague had suddenly been introduced into the proceedings and wanted to negotiate terms. Says Suster: 'They wanted a lower valuation. I knew it wasn't going to happen.'

He flew to New York to meet the chief investment officer of ETF, a Lugano-based firm that was the strongest remaining contender: 'I said to them, "Look the market has changed, but we still have this great opportunity. We are near to a deal with Balfour Beatty. Our competitors are not going to get funded. We are starting discussions with iscraper [backed by Apax, subsequently wound up, with BuildOnline acquiring the German operation for nothing].'" I agreed to take the valuation down by 20 per cent. Would they do a smaller round? It was a very tense moment. [The chief investment officer] gave a verbal agreement – pending investment committee approval. I really think I saved the deal. It is always a risk when you go above people [namely the ETF team running the deal].'

He flew on to Paris to meet with a French company where he was also starting more serious merger discussions: 'Everything had to go on in parallel. You had to talk to the VCs. To strategic investors. And to your competitors – and with a brave face. Our fund raising is going great – but let's talk in case *you* don't raise funds.'

Meanwhile Suster had to handle rebellion among the investor group. 'It's a three-way battle between new investors, existing investors and the management team. New money talks, that is the basic principle.' But GRP, a US firm whose European investments included Lastminute, and which had led the previous round, played a pivotal role – illustrating how an investor may deploy his preferred rights as a crucial negotiating tool without actually imposing them to the full extent. The very early investors in BuildOnline were threatening to block what had now become a down round: 'If you are screwing your early investors and asking them for money at the same time, it's very difficult to do business.'

Suster still believes they were bluffing, but talks had reached something of a impasse all the same when Yves Sisteron, managing partner at GRP, took the initiative after a more junior partner left the firm. As a former lawyer he had experienced his share of tricky situations and possessed a real knack for disentangling seemingly intractible problems. Seniority and self-assuredness helped: 'Previously you had a room full of peers. But he had authority. He could deliver GRP. When you have guys from large investment banks [among the investors] they don't stand a chance [of pushing their case] ten levels up the organization when technology investing is no longer in fashion. When Yves got involved, we got momentum. He would sit there and push people and push people. The very early stage people didn't want to follow their money but they had the ability to block a fund-raising event, which they used as a bargaining chip to try and reduce their dilution. The later stage investors were saying Fuck You. Literally.'

Sisteron's strategy was to say: 'It is my right to [exercise anti-dilution rights]. But I will forgo those if you invest. It is put up or shut up. Would you rather have 30 per cent of company that is out of business or 0.5 per cent of a company that is worth something?' But we've brought the company to this point, the early investors would counter. Sisteron's response was: 'Look, the company is effectively worth zero. The reason it is worth something is because we are going to put money into it.' In the end the early investors supported the deal. 'I felt GRP were incredibly fair, they made tons of concessions,' says Suster. They were also supportive. While other investors did back-of-the-envelope calculations, GRP stayed in the office until the early hours of the morning, working countless spreadsheets to calculate the effects of variations in valuation, ratchets, options, warrants attached to an agreed bridge loan and so on. 'GRP knew the exact effect of every lever that could be pulled. In VC money is made on the details and GRP were incredibly detailed.'

Meanwhile the pressure was on. The valuation was continuing to drop as the general climate worsened, and the VCs were pressing the company to cut costs aggressively. One investor wanted a list of names of everyone who was going to be 'let go', which Suster, anxious not to have negative news out in the market before he had closed the funding, resisted as long as he could. Already drawing just a third of his Accenture salary, he went two months without being paid in an effort to buoy up the team. But even so the vultures were circling: 'We had gone from nine months to six months to one month of cash.' ETF was gaining power by the day: 'ETF started off with zero power because there were lots of investors. We were going to raise $40m. After the new investors fell away – twice – ETF started to realize the power they had. Then when GRP made the decision to put in more than its pro rata share, they started to team up with ETF and ask for harsher terms.' A liquidation preference of three times was proposed at one point, although Suster managed to negotiate that back down to 1.4 times.

Then came the day when he sat down and considered how he would deal with the liquidator. Suster had thought all the money was lined up and the deal very close to signing. Nasdaq continued to slide. Suddenly he was $2m short. One investor who had promised to commit more than their pro rata share ended up less than pro rata. The same day another small investor bailed. For the sort of sums no one would have got out of bed for in 2000. While he had set up a bridge loan as a back-up, this had to be approved by the investors: 'I did not believe they would vote.'

That evening Suster talked to Pierre Morin, GRP partner. 'I've seen much worse situations,' said Morin. 'The deal will get done. Do not lose confidence, that in itself is enough that the deal will fall apart. Mark, this is a poker game. Don't let people read your face. There are a few more cards to play. GRP loves poker.' Who else, asks Suster, would have given him that kind of coaching? After he finally closed the deal (Chapter 15) he returned to the theme about knowing your worth, with one rider: 'As chief executive, your only power is your performance. If you are a good performer, you can ask for things that are fair. If you are performing well, they will want to keep you. At the same time, even if they like you and they need to screw you to get the deal done, they will screw you.'

Reference

Mackay, C. (originally published 1841) *Extraordinary Popular Delusions and the Madness of Crowds*, (1995 edn.), Wordsworth Editions Ltd, Hertfordshire.

18

Exits

This parting was well made.
(Shakespeare, *Julius Caesar*, 1599)

EVERYTHING A VENTURE CAPITALIST OWNS is always for sale. The meaning of life is getting cash (or sometimes stock) back to limited partners. An exit is also an event that triggers carried interest, or the prospect thereof. Reaching the VC's exit is a very big milestone for the entrepreneur – even if it is not, as in the case of an IPO, necessarily your own exit. Below is an outline of what to expect, particularly from the point of view of relations with your investors. Each exit is given comparatively short treatment simply because by this point you will be surrounded by advisers (or indeed you may have handed on to new management in the business by this stage).

IPOs

Going public was once upon a time the seminal right of passage for a young company. It signalled that you had arrived. The widespread assumption now is that, in the aftermath of the technology bubble excesses and with the markets hobbled by accounting and corporate scandal, initial public offerings (IPOs) will be rare. But there will always be fashionable sectors again and the 'IPO window' will open for real companies. One of the lessons of the late 1990s is that those windows may not stay open for long. Seize the moment if that is really what you decide you want to do. The other even bigger lesson is that going public is extremely difficult to undo. Hosts of companies that went public during the boom should never have done so, and would have struggled even without the wider collapse of confidence in the stock market.

The IPO of Netscape in 1995 ushered in the period when the US public markets started behaving like venture capitalists, and started attributing multibillion dollar valuations to 12- or 18-month-old start-ups with zero revenues. As related by Michael Lewis (1999) the Netscape IPO only happened in the first place because co-founder Jim Clark saw a very large yacht he wanted and needed cash to build its replica. In similar fashion it was a single listing – that of Freeserve in August 1999 – that largely galvanized the much later and shorter dotcom frenzy in Europe.

At the same time, IPOs have always been the desired destination for venture-backed companies. The industry, at least in the USA, has made its largest gains from the IPO process, including poster children from Apple, to Cisco, to eBay. Even in Europe, where there has yet to be an established functioning market for growth companies, IPOs such as Autonomy (backed by Apax), Intershop and Brokat (both investments by Technologieholding) have produced big gains for venture investors. The biggest snag about the IPO market is that it is a most uncertain beast, unpredictable and never in equilibrium. It is always 'either too hot or too cold', as Jay Ritter, Professor of Finance at the University of Florida, has frequently pointed out.

In 1999, the average first day 'pop' – the difference between the price at which the stock is offered and the closing price at the end of the first day of trading – was 70.9 per cent. Priceline, the cut-price internet travel site, which listed at $16, climbed to $68 on the first day, taking it to a market capitalization of $10bn, more than United, Continental and North West airlines combined. Online grocer Webvan was initially valued at $8bn when it was projecting losses of $500m three years on from the date of the IPO. Of course we now know the array of unsavoury practices this overheated market brought with it, as analysts peddled internet stocks to flog to the public which they themselves believed were 'pieces of shit', and investment bankers handed out 'hot' IPO stock to favoured customers.

After the bubble, the window slammed firmly shut. In 2001, the once white-hot Neuer Markt in Germany saw the last of the year's 11 IPOs in July, after 133 listings during 2000. More new issues were pulled on Nasdaq during that year (160) than went ahead (92), according to Dealogic, an IPO data service. Illustrating the fading allure of technology already in 2000, Krispy Kreme Doughnuts was one of the most successful issues that year in the USA. Until 2000, venture-backed companies had a good record in the after market. In the USA, statistics show they outperformed non-venture backed companies for most of the 1990s. However, the crop of companies still in short trousers that venture investors forced on the market in 1999 and 2000 have, unsurprisingly, underperformed.

The most ambitious venture capitalists will still only back a company they regard as capable of an IPO. A business that makes it to today's market will however, be very different from the 'concept' IPO (a business with not only no earnings, but no revenue either) of yesteryear. When the window reopens the market will be looking for companies with significant revenues that are at cash break-even stage or are profitable, with the criteria clearly varying according to the sector.

Table 18.1 illustrates how software companies that went public after the bubble had a broadly similar financial profile to those from the pre-bubble era. In 1999 and 2000, by contrast, the figures reflect the ethos of rapid expansion in pursuit of 'land grab' – the revenues were much higher, and so of course were the losses. The notion that operating ratios could be brought under control when the land had been grabbed proved false. Costs were almost impossible to tame when disciplines had not been imposed early on.

Table 18.1 ◆ Software IPO metrics echoing pre-bubble period

| | Pre-tech bubble 1994 | Tech bubble years | | Post-tech 2001 |
		1999	2000	
At IPO				
Average NTM (next 12 months) revenue	$30.7m	$51.2m	$43.2m	N/A
Est. NTM net income	$2.3m	$(15.7m)	$(18.7m)	$8.3m
Percentage of companies with positive estimated NTM earnings	83%	27%	17%	100%

Source: Merrill Lynch

Going public makes looking for funds from a venture capitalist seem like a walk in the park in terms of the time and energy it will demand, as well as its complexity and cost. The following highlights some of the issues that are likely to arise between the management team and its venture capital backers.

Timing

As has already been noted in Chapter 13, the venture capitalist may theoretically be able to force an IPO, but it is impossible in practice if the CEO refuses to participate in the roadshow (the presentation to potential institutional investors) and to answer investors' questions. However, there can still be plenty of discussion about timing – as at Interactive Investor International (iii). An online financial services company founded by Sherry Coutu, iii had attracted venture funding from Arts Alliance in 1996, a year after the company was started, and later from Hollinger Digital. By the dotcom summer of 1999, Hollinger was pressing to do an IPO as fast as possible to capitalize on the 'hot' stock market. Unlike some of the flakier specimens already lining up to list, iii, although loss-making, had the merit of being a real business, built on pre-bubble fundamentals. But members of the management team, with their heads down concentrating on running the company, were unenthusiastic at the prospect of this immense distraction. Even in a company whose very line of business was financial services, they were not at all sure about the longer-term implications either. One of the directors, who was replaced shortly afterwards, was to be heard at a management offsite meeting calling for the company to 'stop pursuing an IPO for an IPO's sake'.

Coutu herself could see the logic of an IPO perfectly well, and set about selling the notion to the rest of the team explaining the desirability of raising a war chest to help fight cash-rich competitors such as Charles Schwab.

Investment bank

Choosing the investment bank to handle the process can be another issue for lively debate. In iii's case, the company had held the traditional beauty parade, with five investment banks pitching. All had pulled out the stops, which included phone calls from the then star New York analysts such as Mary Meeker of Morgan Stanley. Indeed the latter was the bank iii favoured – only to find Hollinger, 40 per cent shareholder in the business, was 'extremely clear' they wanted CSFB, with whom they had worked in the past. Morgan Stanley and CSFB refused to work with each other, so iii was taken public by CSFB, DLJ (before it merged with CSFB) and SSSB (now Citigroup).

The investment bankers set a pricing range of 120p–150p. There had been higher bids at around 400p, but iii had resisted the temptation to plump for the best offers. These were from the smaller investment banks and, based as they were purely on publicly available information, would have been subject to heavy downward revision once they got into the process.

One issue on which all the banks which pitched were in agreement was the wisdom of doing a dual listing on Nasdaq and London – and they were all wrong. Only about 300 of the 88,000-odd shareholders traded the stock in the USA. Coutu says going through the US rigmarole added about four months to the process – including the period from December to mid-January while the company waited for the SEC to clear its IPO backlog, in the midst of which an entire week went by while the sole woman who seemed to be able to progress matters was off work with a 'cold'. Worse, it added about £4m in costs (taking the total to £12m, about 7.5 per cent of the capital raised, then the going rate for a dual listing). As well as being exhausting, the process is bewildering in its technicalities, even for Coutu, with no less than three business-oriented degrees to her name. She says she frequently turned to one of the angels on her board, himself a veteran of 20 IPOs, as she tried to make sense of the roles of the dozens of lawyers, accountants and investment bankers involved in drawing up the prospectus.

Lock-up

Meanwhile, as always, the lock-up – the period during which founders, employees, venture capitalists, angels and others are restricted from selling their stock – was the subject of protracted negotiations with iii's investment bankers. In any IPO process the banks are seeking to ensure an orderly after-market and so want the various parties to stay 'locked up' for as long as possible. Arts Alliance argued that, as an early investor, it should be able to sell immediately, while the investment bankers were trying to insist that Hollinger and the founders were tied in for a year. In the end, a deal was struck with Arts Alliance and the angels were able to sell after three months, Hollinger after six months and Coutu and the management team after a year. She herself was philosophical: 'I took the view I was tied up for ever anyway. As the founder you can't just sell shares; that kills the company because everyone assumes you know something terrible that they don't.' In fact she was able to sell some stock in the IPO, which in the end went out at the height of the frenzy in February 2000. The issue was 33 times subscribed, and Coutu and Hollinger sold stock in the so-called 'green shoe' – an over-allotment device which investment bankers say allows them to smooth demand, by releasing some extra stock. Green shoe or no, the price had more than doubled on the first day, to 338½p, causing complaints at the time because that order of 'pop' indicates the company could have valued itself higher. (A year later the shares had slumped to 24p.)

From the venture capitalist's point of view, IPOs are a mixed blessing precisely because of the lock-up problem. Brian Larcombe, chief executive of 3i, has complained on a number of occasions that the group would have sold much more of its technology portfolio during the bubble had it not been constrained by lock-ups. Indeed the public markets constitute an imperfect exit route for VCs in other ways too, which is worth understanding in order to appreciate some of the possible simmering tensions, including between fellow members of an investment syndicate.

For instance, much of the rest of the VC community appears to think that Apax Partners made a fortune from its investment in QXL, the European version of eBay founded by Tim Jackson. In fact, the private equity firm never sold a penny. Apax partner Peter Englander, who now chairs the firm's exit committee, had remained on the QXL board after it went public. But the pace of QXL's activities was so frenetic in the initial post-IPO period, he relates, that there was always some deal or set of results around the corner that prevented Apax from selling. Reeling off the numbers without need of reference, Englander says the stock floated at 65p, climbed to 744p (briefly) and (at the time of our conversation) was down to 5½p with Apax still owning all 62m shares of its pre-IPO stake: 'Those who didn't do the work and rode on our coattails did very nicely. A lot of people made a lot of money. We worked very hard,' says Englander.

Investors get understandably heated in such situations. A senior Apax partner was overhead at an industry conference in the autumn of 2000 berating a venture capitalist at another firm, to whom Apax had introduced the deal, for selling out. 'It is one of the issues of staying on the board,' says Englander. 'A lot of other investors did sell because they weren't on the board. But at Apax, that's our history, that's what we do – though we are reviewing the policy.' At Autonomy, by contrast, he says, having Apax partner John McMonigall continue on the board meant that Apax knew the firm was making progress and so held on to its stock longer. Autonomy proved to be Apax's best investment ever, netting it an estimated £1bn.

As you and your investors contemplate the process, it is worth reviewing a brief summary of the pros and cons of an IPO (see box).

IPO pros and cons

For

◆ Huge gains in status and visibility for the business, including in the eyes of customers, suppliers and future employees. One giant ego trip for the chief executive as the boss of a publicly listed company.

◆ New cash at a good price – in exchange for floating, typically, between 20 and 30 per cent of the business. The idea is that you can raise money at a more attractive price in the public markets because of the simple fact of liquidity. Investors, in other words, will pay more for a share they can sell tomorrow than one that is held indefinitely in a private company. A better valuation for the company means less dilution for the management.

◆ The prospect, in time, of a lot of cash for the founders/management team as well as the venture capitalists. But this and the previous point only apply if the environment is right. One of the big complaints of those listed on the Alternative Investment Market of the London Stock Exchange and other junior markets is a lack of liquidity, meaning that founders and investors have neither been able to sell out nor to raise more money when they needed it. The collapse in stock market values mean that even many companies on the main markets have suffered the same fate (see Against).

◆ Acquisition currency. Having shares trading at some multiple of the business's earnings, or even of its revenues, means the company has an attractive form of currency, namely its paper, with which to buy other companies. In buoyant markets, stock options over public paper also constitute an important incentive for recruiting talented new employees.

◆ The discipline of all the public company reporting requirements. Depending on how you feel about it, this could be either a plus or a very big minus.

◆ Less interference from the VC, as their shares convert to ordinary shares. Except, of course, after a moment's thought, this is clearly an impostor. The rigours of the public market will make the venture capitalist seem positively cuddly and long termist (see Against).

Against

◆ Time. Taking a company public is an utterly exhausting process that takes many months and is far more time consuming even than raising private finance. One entrepreneur describes it as a 'life-changing' experience.

◆ The cost of the exercise. Underwriting, legal and accounting fees can account for 10 per cent of the money raised. At the same time, when there is a dearth of IPOs, there is room for negotiation with investment bankers whose offices are full of highly paid individuals twiddling their thumbs. Underwriting fees used to be a standard 7 per cent, but in slack times may be negotiable down to a much lower level or to a success fee.

◆ Performance pressure, which is unrelenting, and onerous directors' liabilities, particularly in the USA. Quarterly or six-monthly reporting of numbers to public reporting standards is required, as well as statements on significant developments at the company in between. Once you are public you will be expected to produce constant earnings growth (without being creative with the accounts). If you do not, investors will sell your shares. Extra reporting requirements and stringent new directors' liabilities were hastily introduced in the USA in the Sarbanes-Oxley legislation promulgated following the WorldCom and Enron scandals.

◆ The goldfish bowl effect, including requirements to disclose your salary and options. The chief executive of a quoted UK company was once heard complaining how his wife's mother was so indignant when she saw how much he was making (not excessive compared with many of his peers) that she had threatened to change her will so that all her money would be left to the wife's sister.

◆ Lack of liquidity. This can range from problems for small growth companies which even at the best of times cannot get the attention of large institutional investors to the difficulties suffered on a much wider basis in a bear market, especially by those who went public with insubstantial businesses during the previous boom. A few companies turn around and attempt to go private again, but that is not for the faint hearted.

◆ The possibility of a hostile bid for your company (though that is rare for a technology company).

◆ Time spent on investor relations and the press – infinitely more onerous than when you were a venture capital backed company.

◆ Uncertainty as to whether the whole thing will happen at all. Having gone through the entire gruelling and vastly expensive process, the market may move against you, forcing the company to withdraw its

IPO at the eleventh hour. Sometimes investment bankers make that call as late as the day before the issue is priced. If that is not traumatic enough, the company is likely to have been counting on the proceeds of the offering and so, with the IPO pulled, will be forced to go through a punitive 'cram-down' private financing round.

While the list of cons runs longer than that of the pros, the truly ambitious will always seek public company status and the possibility of growing in time to be a large multinational business.

Trade sale

A sale to a trade acquirer is the most likely exit route for most start-ups. This can range from a highly successful deal at a hefty valuation, to a distress sale which is effectively an alternative to liquidation. From the venture capitalist's point of view, a successful trade sale has certain clear advantages because he receives cash, or cash and stock (that should be relatively easily sold for cash), by contrast with an IPO where he is likely to be locked up and unable to sell most of his position for at least six months, probably much longer. For the entrepreneur, the position is rather more complicated.

Lennart Ramberg, co-founder and chief executive of Altitun, a Swedish company specializing in tuneable lasers for broadband networks spun out of a contract research company affiliated with Stockholm's Royal Institute of Technology, was in the shower one morning when his mobile phone rang. It was the business development director of ADC Telecommunications, the quoted US telecoms equipment maker. 'Is it all right if I fax you a written bid for your company?' the voice on the other end of the line enquired. 'Sure sure,' said Ramberg, less than enthusiastically, as he attempted to get dry. 'Can I put you on hold?'

After a while it dawned on him that early morning in Sweden meant the guy on the other end of the line had been working very late. 'This seemed pretty extraordinary.' In a slightly otherworldly way, the former research scientist says he chided himself for the 'disrespect' he felt he had shown. The fax duly arrived. It was sufficiently long to convince him the company was serious, and he duly leafed through the pages to get to the 'big figure': 'It may be ego fulfilling or whatever. But as soon as you get a serious bid, you become very vulnerable. If you don't accept it and then you hit hard times – as we would have done – other people might accuse you of being an ego-driven maniac. The original solidarity is gone. The others [members of the team and shareholders] aren't your great buddies any longer.'

A problem where the numbers are that order of magnitude – Altitun, a pre-revenue company whose investors included Innovationskapital, Swedestart and Kennet Venture Partners, was sold to ADC for $872m in stock in May 2000 – is a nice one to have and not one that is likely to recur for a very long while. (ADC closed down Altitun in November 2002.) But every trade sale will bring its own dilemmas.

Certainly history is replete with companies which spurned or otherwise failed to clinch a lucrative deal. Pointcast, the internet news service, turned down an offer from News Corporation of up to $450m, only to go under the gavel two years later for less than $10m. In Europe, Sportal, a much hyped sports internet company eventually sold for a nominal sum, had been in advanced discussions with French media group Canal Plus involving a bid of around £250m. Conversely, alando in Germany, which was bought by eBay for $50m when the business was just four months old, was criticized at the time for selling out too early and held up as yet another instance of how Europe was incapable of growing its own indigenous companies to any sort of size. In retrospect, given the long period that ensued when venture capitalists achieved no exits from their portfolios at all, the sale looks rather smarter, at least from the VC's point of view.

While an IPO is a highly uncertain quantity, there is no lack of unpredictability with a trade sale either. The acquirer may suffer a last minute change of heart, the stock market could fall precipitously, or the sponsor within the organization may fail to push the sale through. There are any number of reasons, which may well remain opaque to you, that could cause the acquirer to pull out and possibly force you into a new financing round. Altitun had already had one false start. Founded in 1997, the company had been poised to sell to a Nasdaq-listed company in spring 1999. Everything was in place, Ramberg had explained to staff why the sale was such a great thing and he was preparing a private housewarming party – the most extravagant bash he had ever had with hired steamship and orchestra on the Archipelago. At noon that day he received a phone call to say the deal was off. He then had to troop into the office to explain to staff all the structural reasons why Altitun was so much better off as an independent company – and go straight into a new (second) funding round. Because the market was strong, the valuation he obtained in the next funding round was around $27m, close to the price the Nasdaq business had been offering. (In a bear market the result would have been very different.)

When ADC called, the company was poised to start its third funding round and heavily courted by investment banks . His board, which included a former Goldman Sachs investment banker, was pressing to hold an auction. Ramberg was less than keen: 'To me an auction was very, very alien.' Ironically, the company's first big order, of $10m, was in prospect. But the market was red hot and the subsequent telecoms collapse unimaginable. Nortel had just paid $1.43bn for CoreTek, a New England MEMS tuneable laser company. A week later Swedish Qeyton Systems was sold to Cisco for $800m. The auction was duly held and it came down to two companies, each of which had sent its top brass to Stockholm. Ramberg raced between the two for an entire week, trying to remember what he had said to whom. In the end, Altitun, which had raised just $13.5m in venture funding, went on the block to ADC. The lock-up was short and Ramberg sold half his stock, which had continued to climb three months after the deal closed. 'It was just standard risk diversion. Of course I couldn't imagine things would crash this badly, which puts me in the mainstream of thinkers,' he says laconically.

Trade sales have their complications insofar as the interests of entrepreneur and venture capitalist are far from perfectly aligned. While both parties want to extract the best possible price for the company, the transaction represents a complete exit for the venture capitalist, but of course does not for the company. From the point of view of the entrepreneur, most especially if he is still the founder, he will be concerned as to whether the acquirer represents a good cultural fit for his business.

Unlike the venture capitalist, the CEO does not get all his loot out at the exit. For instance, much of his potential reward may be in the form of options in the acquiring company's stock. If there are liquidation preferences for some classes of preference shareholders, and the management team stands to make nothing from the sale, then the debate becomes all the more intense. Finally the venture capitalist will be worried that the management does a side deal with the acquirer (involving options in the new company's stock, perhaps) that he does not know about, so that the management is happy to proceed with what is a poor deal for the company and its shareholders (including the VC). To try and avoid that, the VC will normally insist that the board appoints a committee to handle the sale, including one or two VC board members as well as the chief executive. But before looking at some of the conflicts in a bit more detail, here are a few basic principles (see box).

A few basic principles

◆ **Hire a good adviser**. Many merger and acquisition advisers have no idea how to handle small companies. 'They charge loads of money for doing no work,' says one indignant UK entrepreneur. 'They have no idea how to value small companies, and are even more exasperating than venture capitalists. You get some third son of a baronet who has no understanding where the value lies. You need people who understand the synergy of the technology, who see it is more than just a financial transaction.' Mocking the still sizeable contingent of European financiers who remain shy of technology, he observes: 'It involves being interested in technology and all that horrid stuff.' In his case he found a US adviser who was 'aggressive and on the case'.

◆ **Engender competition**. This is just like when you were raising money from the VCs, only more so. Even if you are selling because the business is failing – you have found the market simply does not exist, at least yet, or you are mired in a sick industry where no one is buying kit – you may be pleasantly surprised as to the range and number of people who might want to buy your company. 'There are all sorts of reasons why people will pay something for your business – for the team, for the technology, for a specific set of business relationships,' says one entrepreneur, who went through the process and got more for his embryonic company than he expected.

◆ **Continue to run the business as if the sale is not occurring.** Easier said than done, of course, not least because it is a time-consuming affair. But pay particular attention to cash consumption, and try to avoid being pushed into another venture capital round if it does not come off.

Among the potential points of disagreement with your investors may be the timing of the sale, such as the following example of a business that had already floated. The stock market had slumped and one of the investors, representing the venture arm of a large corporation, was convinced it was not going to recover for a long while (a point on which he was certainly correct). Moreover, because of the fall in the market, corporate venturing was very much out of fashion, so the pressure was on to sell as much of the technology investment portfolio as possible. The management, however, was firmly against a sale of the company. The business was going well, still growing at 30 or 40 per cent a quarter, was more or less profitable, and with a very solid customer base. There was also still £50m of cash in the bank following the IPO. Meanwhile the economic incentives among the various parties were quite different. Management's options were worth nothing because the price of the stock had fallen so sharply since the IPO. The corporate investor, as a fairly recent shareholder, could by contrast expect a good return on its investment in any sale. An earlier venture capitalist would see a much more modest gain in terms of IRR because it had been in the business for some four years. Two angel investors were poised somewhere in between.

From the point of view of the corporate this meant the possibility of a good return now, as opposed to an uncertain return if it waited. For the management, and to a certain extent the other venture investor, it was a case of nothing or the prospect of a modest return now as opposed to the chance of a significant upside in three years' time when the business had developed and the market had, with luck, improved.

What happened? The corporate forced the decision through by using its power as the largest (though not majority) shareholder to veto everything. With its two seats on an eight-man board it vetoed acquisitions, staff hires, investments in technology, anything that involved board approval. 'We tried everything,' says the founder who had remained chairman. 'But if we couldn't do this and we couldn't do that, the company was hobbled. They forced our hand.' The wrinkle is that the founder had fought hard to resist a trade sale that was clearly lucrative personally. When the sale went through it unleashed a torrent of ire from numerous retail shareholders who had bought the stock at the time of the IPO and who wrote in saying their lives had been 'ruined' and demanding compensation. 'Needless to say they didn't write to [the corporate].' Every member of the founder's family and a lot of friends had also invested at flotation so the plight of this category of shareholder had been more than uppermost in the founder's mind during negotiations with the corporate.

Disagreements over timing can also operate the other way around, as mentioned earlier. Christopher Spray at Atlas contends that it is often 'the opposite of what you would think. It is usually the venture capitalists who want to stay in and the founders who want to sell'. The founder, he explains, has 100 per cent of his net worth tied up in the business, and so has a different view from a venture capitalist with a spread portfolio. He cites the case of Solid Works, which naturally has a happy end for all concerned, that had wanted to sell out to a buyer at $30m. Atlas persuaded the founder to stay in and the business eventually went for $300m. Founders are particularly likely to be inclined to take what they can in a downturn, he argues; for example if there is the prospect of another round of financing which might be heavily dilutive.

Of course the existence of multiple liquidation preferences will make negotiations particularly acrimonious. In a merger or sale where the entire loot is destined to be distributed to the preferred shareholders, leaving nothing for the holders of ordinary shares, such as founders, management, and angels, the situation will rapidly become extremely tense. Investors will realize it will be very difficult to get founders to go along with the deal under such circumstances and provided the acquiring company wants the team, that team has a certain amount of negotiating power. 'People jumped ship from big companies [during the bubble] with the idea that $10m was in the bank. They can get very unhappy', says one adviser.

A lot of negotiating will follow. The acquirer will want to make sure the team is excited to come aboard, but will also be keen that any cash sum comes out of the price – in effect so that the VCs give up part of the preference to which they are legally entitled. Remember, the preferences are regarded as negotiating leverage by investors, who will not necessarily expect to get the entire sum. Alternatively there may be an arrangement whereby the CEO and maybe other senior members of the team get a package which gives them options in the acquiring company. If they have a large pot of options in the previous company, awarded in a punitive down round, this will strengthen their negotiating position, even though the ordinary shares have been rendered worthless by the liquidation preferences. Of course early investors such as angels and any founders no longer employed in the business will be big losers in such a transaction.

Some entrepreneurs have tried, in advance of any trade sale, to negotiate themselves some form of compensation that takes account of punitive liquidation preferences, which venture capitalists say they find 'very annoying'. The VCs have to acknowledge, however, that when it comes to the sale itself founders have considerable negotiating power. Most will anyway want to see the team compensated, regardless of what they are entitled to, provided they feel these individuals have lived up to their side of the bargain. On the other hand if the VCs feel they are being held to ransom, they will not be inclined to be generous.

Shareholder rows can come in all hues, such as this story of a pair of angels more or less holding a company to ransom. 'It has got to the hatred point,' says an adviser. The deal for selling the UK start-up to a US corporation had been agreed down to the equity and cash split – 65 per cent shares and 35 per cent cash. The angels were insisting they get all their proceeds in cash, despite the fact that their return was a more than healthy two and a half times their money within a period of just 15 months. There was considerable personal acrimony into the bargain. 'The major angel [a stuffy City figure] views the chief executive [a software developer] as the lowest of the low.' His advice to the chief executive was to call the angels' bluff.

Another sticking point between entrepreneur and investor can be the warranties. The venture capitalists will be out to give the bare minimum. 3i is felt by many to adopt a particularly intransigent position on this point. 'If you are selling to a US company, they expect all the shareholders to give warranties,' explains one UK entrepreneur. '3i always take the view, we don't do it because we are 3i. It freaks out the US company. They cannot understand why a venture investor wouldn't stand behind its investment. It is a real nightmare. It poisons the whole thing, damaging the price and doubling the amount of due diligence the buyer does because they think you are hiding something.' Smaller firms in the UK, such as those running venture capital trusts, which are often populated by individuals who once worked at 3i, adopt the same practice, which entrepreneurs find yet more annoying. '3i are too dominant. Half the industry is ex-3i and so follows all their bad practices.' Unlike 3i, which is investing in start-ups off its own balance sheet, independent venture firms do have something of an issue with warranties for structural reasons.

Suppose a venture firm has distributed cash (or a mixture of cash and stock) from a sale back to their limited partners, and six months later there is a breach of warranties. They cannot at that point return to their limited partners and ask for some of the cash back. This is normally settled by an amount being set aside and put in escrow as 'deferred consideration'. But it is inevitably a complex discussion, with a lively debate as to what proportion of the proceeds to place in escrow, and the VC worrying that his return will be impacted by the portion of cash held back. From an entrepreneur's point of view, you should press for the VCs at least to take equal responsibility with you, or to cap your exposure. The refusal on the part of the VC to give warranties is another reflection of the contractual, banking approach to the business in Europe. In the USA, no founder would dream of giving warranties in these circumstances.

In the worst case a trade sale will be from a position of distress. If you and the venture capitalist have fallen out to one degree or another, or have very different views of the future, it will be painful. One venture capitalist tells it from his standpoint: 'We are the largest investors in this business, which has missed its forecasts twice in two financing rounds over 12 months. We have extended a bridge loan but we are doing it on very aggressive terms [if the company cannot repay the loan, the investor gets a chunk of equity at 10 cents a share, when the last round was priced at $2].' He says he has grown weary of the entrepreneur's promises of improvement which never materialize: 'We have had enough of this "just round the corner" stuff. It is punitive on our part and is meant to be. We are saying to the entrepreneur, you sell the company or get another round. He may think he is going to raise another round, but as far as I'm concerned I'm just holding it open until an acquirer is found.' In such situations the main motto is that it is impossible to overcommunicate. Because if you and the investors are genuinely at loggerheads it will be most uncomfortable.

The other kind of exit

It is the easiest thing, says Gerry Montanus of Atlas, for a VC to continue to fund a company: 'The difficult part is deciding to cut your losses and admit you made a mistake.' Adrian Beecroft at Apax echoes the sentiment: 'These are truly horrible decisions.' He recalls an investment in the early 1990s in a company providing a mobile car mechanic service, which Apax had continued to support for five years: 'It was a real emotional struggle. Technically it worked, but somehow, something with management or the concept was wrong. It kept growing but it never quite got profitable. We kept putting money in – a total of £4m, which was a lot of money then. We kept thinking it was going to turn the corner. I remember going home [after Apax had pulled the plug] and sitting down at the kitchen table. I really liked the people. I thought I don't want to carry on, I'll go back to being a consultant.'

Being sucked into spending too much time shoring up ailing companies is a big danger for venture capitalists. They know it is in their interests, in terms of generating returns, to spend time on helping the promising candidates in the portfolio, not the stragglers. 'No business goes into liquidation too early,' says one investor wearily. If it is emotional for (a few of the more thoughtful) VCs, how much more for the entrepreneur of course, who will often be desperate to save the business when the venture capitalist has decided to call it a day. There is *always* a contract just around the corner.

Montanus recalls when Atlas decided Ready2, the shopping advice portal founded by socialites Trinny Woodall and Susannah Constantine, was not going to make it. 'Trinny and Susannah are extremely capable and smart,' says Montanus loyally, adding that Atlas backed them when it saw 'Village.com and Women.com bubbling away in the US', at a time when there were no similar businesses in Europe. But the climate changed and attempts to raise outside funds had failed. 'We said: You worked extremely hard, there's no criticism, it is just a mistake, it simply didn't work. They were desperate to continue, it was very emotional.'

Not all entrepreneurs are necessarily like that, however. Rolf Dienst, senior partner of Wellington in Germany, tells the story of the scientific founder of a biotechnology company coming into his office with a piece of paper, which he handed across the table. Dienst read it and then slowly tore it into 100 pieces. It was the founder's letter of resignation. 'I told him he couldn't do that, it was *his* company, he had better get straight back there and sort it out.' Which he did – although the business did not survive in the end. Meanwhile, the less reflective or the more ruthless VCs will have no trouble in shutting down the 'problem' parts of their portfolio.

The VC's main aim is to put the company into liquidation well before the company is insolvent. He wants an orderly and quiet winding up in order to keep reputations as intact as possible. The objective is to pay off the creditors including employees in full and so the priority will be to call a halt while there is enough cash to do that. Almost all VCs will prefer to go through the process without appointing a liquidator. If there is any cash left after creditors have been paid, this will be distributed according to the liquidation preferences, which means that you are even less likely to see anything than the investors. 'If you are piloting an ocean liner, it is hard to slam on the brakes hard, but in a small company it should be easy to do it in an orderly manner,' says Richard Irving of Pond Ventures. If the venture capitalist is doing his job, he should have plenty of warning that things are going badly: 'We are never in the situation where we turn up at a board meeting and someone drops a spreadsheet on the table and says: We are in trouble. At any one time we know exactly when all of our companies will run out of money, and when they will be technically insolvent.' Well, that is at least the theory.

Strategic investors march to a particular drum, with internal political sometimes distorting decisions: an executive whose bonus is affected by how many companies are written off may be keener to string one or two along if he can. Damage to the brand is also highly sensitive (not that venture capitalists don't have brands to worry about, but failure is part of their game in a way it is not for a corporation). For instance, Bernard Arnault's decision to put more money into Boo.com shortly before it collapsed may not have been unconnected with the fact that he was planning to take Europatweb, his internet investment vehicle, public and wanted to avoid a big blow-up immediately beforehand (in the end Boo went bust and Europatweb did not float). Venture capitalists will also often be considering the portfolio as a whole as much as an individual case. The weaker ones are more likely to string companies along if at all possible in a bid to hide some of the damage from their investors for a bit longer.

At the same time, everyone involved will be very conscious of directors' liabilities – including the VCs themselves of course. Get the best legal advice you can. In the UK, directors need to make sure they keep on the right side of the Insolvency Act, under which it is the directors' responsibility not to trade insolvently. Directors are personally liable if they are later deemed to have breached the Act which carries heavy penalties from disqualification as a director to prison. Unlike in some European countries, however, the UK Act does essentially allow a business to continue to trade if the directors have a reasonable belief of raising further financing.

In France the issue of personal liability tends to make venture capital investors particularly nervous. Says one French venture capitalist: 'The perception is that if you push the ball too far, non-executives can be accused of having been *de facto* managers of a company that went into improper liquidation. As a VC they can come after you personally and after the VC firm if there is deemed to have been an improper liquidation.' He says that makes investors much more cautious and inclined to close the company 'way before' the cash runs out: 'That is bad when the company cannot explore full opportunities for further funding because the board and or the investors are afraid of financial exposure. At the same time, it does make board members very careful.' Another investor says he believes it makes French investors much more reluctant to help their companies when they are in trouble: 'French VCs would rather let the company die than do something and be deemed *de facto* managers. There is less direct action because it is more risky in a purely French company.'

In the USA it is rather more common to close down a company when there are still millions in the bank – so that the VC can return to its limited partners say 20 cents on the dollar. Management, says one investor, is also perhaps a bit more realistic that the company is going nowhere: 'In Europe, management teams are much more emotional than in the US. They argue that there is still a chance to turn around the business.' There are certainly advantages for the entrepreneur in going gracefully and not digging in his heels. 'The CEO can garner himself a huge amount of goodwill if the investors think he is doing his best to sort out an unpleasant situation,' says one US venture investor.

Richard Irving also advises enlightened self-interest: 'In Europe the stigma of failure is much less than it was. People need to understand it is not the end of the game. We will back people again who have failed, even from our own portfolio.' He also adds that, given the percentage of companies that really make it is so small, the rational thing to do is to extract yourself and move on to the next opportunity with the benefit of everything you have learnt during the process. Rational, but tough to do.

As a coda, there follows a liquidation story with a rare happy ending. Wax Digital is a supply chain software company which had received an investment of £3.2m from 3i in the bubble era. Like most businesses at the time, Wax Digital was encouraged to embark on a hiring spree ahead of a possible flotation. 'We went up to [a staff of] 70 people when it should have been 20,' says Mike Bowes, now chairman. Bowes had initially been introduced to the company as a consultant on behalf of 3i, called in when sales were taking longer to close than expected, and the loss-making company needed further funding of about £1m. However, the bubble had well and truly burst, 3i was reorganizing, its tech portfolio was looking terrible, and it was in the process of centralizing decision making. Everyone at 3i was nervous, anticipating a large round of its own redundancies – which would be the first time anyone had been let go from the group for at least a decade. Bowes was asked by 3i for his opinion as to whether the firm should reinvest – something he had done for the institution many times before. For once, he said yes and the local Manchester team of 3i was also very keen to proceed, believing Wax Digital to be one of its best investments. But the investment committee in London had other ideas. 'If we had claimed we had a cure for cancer, I don't think anyone would have dared reinvest at the time simply because the portfolio as a whole looked horrible,' says Bowes.

Because the local team had been so supportive, Wax Digital had not taken steps to cut its burn rate. The investment committee's negative decision came like a bolt out of the blue and the company went into liquidation shortly afterwards. The day the plug was pulled Stephen Ross, chief executive of Springboard and a former head of 3i's office in Manchester, got a call from Rothschild, who had been advising Wax Digital, asking if he wanted to take an informal look at it. Ross liked the business and had, back in his 3i days, invested both in another of Bowes's businesses (which had made money) and in a successful company belonging to one of Wax Digital's non-executives. So Springboard, which likes to back managers it knows who have a proven track record, invested £0.5m and the management team and angels put up a matching amount – and Wax Digital was back in business.

Reference

Lewis, M. (1999) *The New New Thing, How some man you've never heard of just changed your life*, Hodder and Stoughton, London.

Links

US-centric site tracking growth   www.ipo.com
company financings

Some official stock exchange sites
www.nasdaq.com
www.londonstockexchange.com
www.londonstockexchange.com/aim for the Alternative Investment
Market, the UK market for smaller growth companies
www.euronext.com (merged Paris, Amsterdam, Brussels and Lisbon
exchanges)
www.nouveau-marche.fr French stock exchange for emerging companies
www.deutsche-boerse.com German stock exchange
www.stockholmsborsen.se Swedish stock exchange
www.borsaitalia.it

PART FOUR

The future

19

A European industry matures

The report of my death was an exaggeration.
(Mark Twain, 1897)

WHEN BENCHMARK PARTNER Bruce Dunlevie became a venture capitalist in the late 1980s, friends told him he had missed the boat. Everything had been invented. Similarly when David Beirne joined Benchmark in 1997, people shook their heads and said he was too late. Yet his first partners' meeting consisted of a decision on an investment in a small company called eBay – one of the biggest hits in venture ever. As the industry endures its worst shake-out in history, it is important to keep some sort of perspective. True, the fall-out from the bubble is unprecedented, and wider geopolitical instability makes for hugely uncertain times. But downturns will always provide the best opportunities to start businesses. Periods where everyone agrees on the identity of the 'next big thing' in technology are, almost by definition, nascent bubbles.

The next five or ten years are pivotal to the creation of a robust venture capital industry in Europe. The region's advantage over the USA is that the descent has not been as vertiginous because the highs were nowhere near as exaggerated. But there is a long way to go to build the very delicate ecosystem that sustains the venture business. The best European VCs know this. While a number of their US counterparts are spending more time on the golf course (their past track record allowing them to sit out a downturn), VCs in Europe appreciate they have to work harder than ever now to ensure their industry's survival. There is plenty to be done.

In performing the research for this book I was struck by the endless anomalies of this business. In no particular order, these included the degree of hostility towards VCs by entrepreneurs who, rightly or wrongly, felt they had been well and truly shafted – and the extent to which the VCs themselves seem largely oblivious of this; the damage that has been done by ill-thought out but explosive terms in investment agreements (clearly helping stoke that hostility); the comparative naivety of many entrepreneurs regarding their approach to the venture process, and the lack of any great urgency to repair that ignorance (suggesting that when things go wrong it is not *always* the fault of the big bad VC); the opacity of the system (compiling Chapter 13 on term sheets was a very special nightmare, as I waded through a mass of ignorance and idiosyncrasy); and finally, the vigour with which the VC industry turns the funding tap on and off according to the state of the cycle. It is misjudged at both ends of course; overinvestment at the top followed by starvation of the stars of tomorrow in a recession. 'You don't get it' was the accusation levelled at those who did not fall for internet hype. Now it means 'you are not being gloomy enough'.

So there is no shortage of challenges – some shared by European and US investors alike. One of the most urgent is how to furnish effective seed financing when success in venture capital is defined by the size (big) of the pool of money you manage. Obviously, if seed financing is not available, the whole of the rest of the chain breaks down, but not enough VCs seem to be losing sleep about this. Ideally, a few experienced venture capitalists who are personally wealthy already will tire of wielding large funds and ache to return to involvement at grass-roots level to complement the activities of business angels/private investors. Or perhaps large venture funds should simply look at seed investing as sensible large companies once viewed research and development – easy to cut now if you want to increase short-term profitability, but hugely unhealthy for the pipeline of future products. This would lead them routinely to devote a certain proportion of the fund to seed financing anyway. And the answer to the argument that small deals are as costly and time consuming to pull off as later stage deals? Someone can do a study as to whether flipping a coin achieves the same rate of success in selecting investments at their very earliest stages as does the performing of detailed analysis. If it does, the answer is simply to make sure you do enough investments to be diversified.

Europe, underdeveloped as it is, has many specific additional issues. The challenge is how to develop a model that takes the best from the USA but also accounts for European diversity, while compensating somehow for the lack both of a single cluster called Silicon Valley and of a homogeneous market with 290 million customers. There is a tendency at present to indulge in *schadenfreude* at the travails of US VCs. (The Hyundai coupé ad 'disappears faster than a dotcom company' was inspired by the prevalent European view that dotcoms were a 'silly American idea that didn't work'.) But it would be blinkered in the extreme if Europeans concluded they had little to learn from three decades of venture experience the other side of the Atlantic. The spirit of partnership that has characterized the US industry for much of its history has been a crucial ingredient in past successes, whereas the deal-centric banking mentality lurking at the heart of the European way of doing things continues to constitute a considerable obstacle to progress. When I asked a European-based, first-time fund whether its difficulties in extracting cash from investors – the team had talked to 600 and were still going – made them more empathetic with entrepreneurs, the reply was, without irony: 'No it makes us more ruthless.' That the venture industry is headquartered in California is also noteworthy, its informality contrasting starkly with the temples of finance that VCs seem to want to build in Europe (even US VCs).

Lacking a Silicon Valley (and duly appreciating the futility of trying slavishly to ape such a cluster), European VCs need to work on creating and oiling the links in the virtuous circle of success (Chapter 2). This circle is where the best VCs attract the best entrepreneurs, and then, by virtue of the doors they can open to the best suppliers, customers and intermediaries, help to build successful companies, which are assured successful 'exits', which in turn burnish the brand of the VC. Almost every link in this chain is weak at present – partly, of course, because it is much harder to achieve across a diverse continent than in an almost self-sustaining ecosystem like the Valley. What Europe also still needs, and this is a matter of time, is VCs of the stature of a Vinod Khosla, who create markets almost by the sheer force of their personalities.

Exit routes are clearly one of the chief concerns of VCs around the globe, but the problem is particularly acute in Europe. The brief flowering of the European technology stock markets in the late 1990s has ended in tears and it is not clear how they can be revived. Sensible investors recognize they will have to devote much more time to building 'real' companies (as opposed to prepping start-ups for an IPO), and a few of these will qualify for listing on main markets. Meanwhile it may be that, as in the early 1990s, VCs have to rely more heavily either on a Nasdaq listing (assuming the US market recovers in due course), or on profitable trade sales. This in turn has important implications for company structuring.

The silver lining in enduring bear markets is that they eventually winnow out the weakest players. But when the sources of money for venture firms say they believe there are only 15 or 20 outfits of 'institutional quality' in Europe, that sends dire warning signals that the winnowing has gone too far. At the height of the bubble, there were at least 400 European VC firms; a quarter of that number is probably about right. And there needs to be diversity of stage (seed through late stage players) as well as a range of national players (the initial funders) through pan-European firms, to transcontinental operators. At the moment, too many firms are stuck with funds that are too big to be effective nationally, while lacking the networks to operate effectively across Europe. Moreover, while VCs liaise increasing well with their peers offering similar stages of funding, the links between the stages, particularly seed funders including angels and private investors and the next funding stage, are somewhere between fragile and non-existent. The role of US VCs present another interesting dimension. Having looked down on Europe for years, a number arrived with the bubble – and departed in short order. Only a couple of firms seem serious in their attempts to build a real presence, and transplanting the DNA of a Californian firm into Europe is no easy matter. Yet the lack of interlocking networks between the USA and Europe deprives the European entrepreneurs and VCs of a vast pool of experience, as well as of a framework for helping portfolio companies make the all-important leap to the American market. The fact that, perfectly sensibly from their investors' point of view, the European-based VCs only want to back serial entrepreneurs who have been through the venture process before is another impediment to progress because the pool of those individuals remains too narrow.

While it is easy to dwell on the challenges in the European environment, it is helpful to consider some of the natural advantages. For instance, the very difficulty of operating in several languages, cultures and legal and regulatory systems breeds investors with an international outlook that compares very favourably with the Valley's tendency towards insularity and superiority. That should constitute something of an advantage in selecting and building truly internationally competitive companies. At the same time, the fact that the bull market lasted so much less time in Europe means that it infected the psyche to a lesser degree. I am convinced that the American recovery was in part postponed by too many dreamers still stuck in a false reality – such as the 29-year-old San Francisco dotcommer who blew out his birthday candles with the wish that he could wake up 'and it would be 1997 again'. Moreover, European diversity ought to function as a useful counterweight to the insidious herd mentality discussed earlier (Chapter 3). The hype did indeed get far more out of control in the Valley hothouse than in Europe, amply demonstrating the negative sides of the cluster effect. At the same time, European VCs still need to suppress some of their own well-developed herding instincts. Perhaps a prolonged downturn is the time to re-examine certain assumptions, including whether backing 'technology' companies is really the only way to make money in venture capital.

Meanwhile, the US VC industry may back innovation, but it has been totally uncreative in its own development, with the unquestioning dominance of the limited partnership that raises money from investors every three or four years. This, when you think about it, is a very odd way to run a professional services firm. European venture firms are already less homogeneous in their structure. This has yet to produce a really creative alternative – although I am eagerly awaiting results given that the entire staff at Apax seem to have been instructed to read the corporate history of Goldman Sachs. And if politicians wonder what they should do to further venture capital in Europe, what is needed is neither more money, nor extra government subsidies, nor additional tax incentives. The number one priority, from Germany, to France, to Sweden is to abolish anti-entrepreneurial labour laws. But these are all changes for a generation, not a couple of years. While the attitude to risk and failure is much more positive than it was, Europe still lags far behind the USA. As a French civil servant remarked: 'In Europe, we are not allowed to succeed. And we are not allowed to fail.'

So finally, where does that leave the entrepreneur in this flux? Well-informed founders are an essential constituent of a mature market. Canny institutional investors supplying money to venture firms know they will only make money if they pick 'top quartile' performers. As a first-time entrepreneur, you will not (unfortunately) always have the luxury of picking the very best VC for your first venture, but you need to know what a good VC looks like. The more you know about how the game works, the better the quality of funding you are likely to attract. If this book has helped at all in that understanding process, it has achieved its purpose.

Jargon buster

Below is a guide to some of the jargon that infests the world of venture capital. It is by no means comprehensive; for instance, if you are struggling over one of the many prolix terms lurking in an investment agreement, turn to Chapter 13. Nor, for obvious reasons, does it attempt to explain basic business terminology, such as ordinary and preference shares.

angels *See* business angels.

anti-dilution rights A mechanism by which investors try to protect their position if subsequent rounds of financing occur at a lower valuation. Beware – these can be a source of much acrimony in future funding negotiations (see Chapter 13: 207).

bridge financing A loan typically extended by existing investors to tide a company over until it secures further finance. The trick is to make sure it is a bridge, and not a pier – in other words, that the facility does not expire before the new money is in place. The terms are likely to include an equity kicker, allowing the investors to subscribe to any new round at a discount. As always, the more you need the money, the harsher the terms are likely to be.

business angels Wealthy individuals who supply cash – and often, entrepreneurial and business skills – in return for a stake in an early stage company. They are to be distinguished, in terms of their net worth and, with any luck, business acumen, from the alternative source of very early stage funding, namely the three Fs – friends, family and fools. The wider catch-all term private investors is probably more appropriate – these people are not in it for philanthropy, after all – but the angel moniker seems to stick.

buy-out Often called management buy-outs in the UK and much of the rest of Europe, leveraged buy-outs in the USA. The purchase of a mature, generally profitable, business, by a **private equity** firm, which then owns the company for a period of three to seven years before exiting it via a **trade sale** or an **initial public offering (IPO)**. These businesses are private, often orphan divisions of large companies, family businesses, or sometimes, listed businesses taken private. Drivers of returns include leverage. Substantial levels of debt will have been injected at the beginning. The management team will also be motivated to do a good job by being given an equity stake. This exercise, which dominates private equity activity in Europe in terms of scale, has historically also been referred to as venture capital, which is clearly nonsense.

captive A venture firm owned by a financial institution – a bank or insurance company. This has been particularly prevalent in continental Europe, although these teams are today increasingly seeking independence. Captives invest entirely using the balance sheet of their parent; **semi-captives** raise some **third party funds** from other institutional investors, to supplement balance sheet funds. This is often as a prelude to going fully independent. Captives can be rather bureaucratic and impersonal in their ways. Just try finding anything about the backgrounds of team members, or even their names, on the website.

carried interest/carry The locus of the jam – if you are a venture capitalist, that is. In the typical **limited partnership**, profits are divided so that 80 per cent go to the **limited partners** (institutional investors) and 20 per cent to the **general partner**. Carry has made a lot of venture capitalists very rich indeed. Its distribution within any individual partnership – according to carry points, typically allocated at the beginning of each new fund – can be the source of great angst, instability and ultimately, if it is felt to be really inequitable, the break-up of some firms.

cash multiple One measure of a venture capitalist's return. A $200m fund which eventually produces proceeds of $600m to investors who committed the original cash is said to have achieved a three times multiple. Or, at the level of an individual investment, $2m turned into $20m is a ten times multiple, sometimes known as a 10x. It is a very different measure of return from an **internal rate of return (IRR)** and an institutional investor assessing a venture firm's performance would look at both.

claw backs When it all goes wrong in the **carry** milch cow department. During the bubble VCs would take their share of the carry on individual investments, only to find that, following the crash, the fund as a whole was **under water** and the sums taken in carry were in fact owed to investors just to repay their initial capital (or the capital plus the **preferred return**). If the cash has been sunk into other technology stocks in the 90 per cent club, or time shares in private jets, this can be more than a little uncomfortable for the VCs. (This has been a much bigger problem in the USA than Europe.)

corporate venturer A corporation that takes minority stakes in other companies, which can take many forms. The most relevant for young companies in search of cash are corporate VCs with an in-house fund that invests in businesses external to the company (by contrast with those that incubate internally generated ideas). Unfortunately, corporates are some of the most fickle investors around, and disappear almost entirely in down cycles.

cram-down A particularly punitive form of **down round** where founders and existing investors find their shareholdings 'crammed down' to next to nothing by the demands of the new investors in a current funding round, who have the whip hand if the company is to survive.

down round A financing round where the valuation is lower than the previous rounds. Companies that raised initial funding in the bubble suddenly found that investors would put up further cash only if the valuation was greatly reduced. Drastic down rounds unfortunately leave founders, angels and existing shareholders with equity worth very little indeed.

due diligence A fancy word for research. If a venture capitalist is sufficiently interested in an investment proposition, he will perform due diligence, looking into everything from the backgrounds of the team to the solidity of the patents of a technology business. In bubble periods, this process is concertinaed down to a minimum. In a downturn, the procedure appears to drag on indefinitely, and can indeed sometimes serve as a handy cover for investor dithers.

elevator pitch A well-prepared elevator pitch is a necessary piece of an entrepreneur's armoury. A US concept, it refers to a chance encounter between entrepreneur and investor in an elevator; the former must enthuse the latter about his proposition before the doors roll open again a few floors on.

exit VCs only make **returns** as and when they exit, or realize, their investment. The most likely form of exit is a trade sale or, when market conditions are right, an **initial public offering (IPO)**. The latter tend to generate the really big wins – although, even if they actually happen, founders and investors will not be able to sell immediately, not least because of **lock-ups**.

first-time fund For VCs, as for entrepreneurs, there is always a first time. However, the suppliers of cash to the venture industry, the institutional investors, are notoriously reluctant to commit capital to teams who do not have a track record, which makes it hard to get started – except in a bubble, when people will put money behind an elephant with hay fever.

flotation *See* **initial public offering (IPO)**.

fund This is the investment vehicle of a venture capitalist. The salient points about it are its size (€100m); vintage (2001) and its number (Fund 3, namely the firm's third fund); generally organized as a **limited partnership**.

general partner (GP) In a limited partnership structure, the venture capitalists are general partners, or else own the company which is itself the general partner. By contrast with the **limited partners**, the general partner can be liable for a fund's debts – hence the attractions of forming a company in which the VCs are shareholders.

hurdle rate *See* **preferred return**.

initial public offering (IPO) An initial public offering is the means by which a business obtains a listing on a stock exchange, or 'goes public', enabling it to sell shares to the wider investing population. Something of a rite of passage for an entrepreneur, but only a few companies actually achieve it, and the IPO 'window' can remain closed for years at a time, when the bears hold sway and investors are simply averse to the idea of new offerings.

internal rate of return (IRR) A discount rate – the rate at which all the fund's cash flows (commitments by investors and disbursements back to them) are discounted so that the net present value of the fund amounts to zero. Together with the **cash multiple**, these are the two principal benchmarks of a venture capitalist's performance.

institutional investor As opposed to a private investor. These are pension funds, insurance companies, endowments, foundations, who are the primary source of capital for the venture industry. They do not by and large have the resources or expertise to invest directly in companies, so they invest via VCs' **limited partnerships**.

IPO *See* **initial public offering.**

IRR *See* **internal rate of return.**

limited liability partnership/limited partnership This structure, governed by a partnership agreement, is how US venture firms have been organized since the 1960s and 1970s. Many European VCs have also adopted this form. The limited partnership has a finite life, generally ten years. The idea is the VC invests the cash in the first three or four years (much more quickly in the late 1990s) and then harvests the proceeds in the remaining life of the partnership, which is then wound up (sometimes after an extension).

limited partner Institutional investors in a limited partnership. The LPs, as they are often known, are 'limited' in the sense of only being at risk for the amount of their investment – by contrast with the **general partner**.

liquidation preferences Another bombshell that may be buried in the investment agreement. This is a provision whereby the last round of investors get their money out before everyone else – and multiple liquidation preferences, where they are due a multiple of their investment sum, can wipe out founders and early investors in the event of even a fairly successful exit. Liquidation, by the way, refers not primarily to the winding up of a failed company but to any 'liquidity event' that generates investment proceeds, such as a trade sale (see Chapter 13).

lock-up A provision stopping founders, angels, VCs and others from taking their shares and selling at the first opportunity following an **IPO**. Lock-ups for founders typically last six months or longer. Their duration can be the subject of fierce negotiations with the investment bank underwriting the offering.

management fees VCs are paid a fee on the funds under management. The clever thing about this, from the VC's point of view, is that institutional investors pay a percentage of the sum *committed*, rather than, say, the sum invested, which at the beginning would be a tiny amount. The fees are supposed to cover expenses and so on, but the bigger the fund, the more is left over to pay high salaries and bonuses.

mezzanine round A pre-IPO financing round. A confusing term since mezzanine, in a buy-out, means a layer in the capital structure somewhere between equity and debt. In venture capital, a mezzanine round is an equity round like all the others.

multistage A multistage VC firm will invest in both young companies and leveraged buy-outs (LBOs) – and maybe everything in between. This is a phenomenon that is more common in Europe than the USA, and is arguably a function of the more institutional approach to venture capital and private equity in Europe. Detractors would say that the skills required to invest at these very different stages of a company's life are quite distinct, and that VCs and LBO specialists do not belong under the same roof. The large funds that multistage firms raise soon mitigate against real venturing because it is not cost effective to make small investments.

non-disclosure agreement (NDA) Something which almost all VCs have an aversion to signing.

post-money See **pre-money**.

PPM See **private placement memorandum**.

pre-money A pre-money valuation is the value of the business ascribed by the venture capitalists *before* the investment has been made. Hence an injection of €2m 'at €2m pre'. This gives a **post-money** valuation of €4m and the VCs a 50 per cent share of the equity.

preferred return A hurdle rate, generally about 8 per cent, which a VC has to beat before he starts to earn carry. So, for a €100m fund with an 8 per cent preferred return, he would need to return €108m to investors before carry was due.

private equity In its broadest sense, the provision of equity finance to unquoted companies. The terminology is a minefield. In the USA, private equity denotes the leveraged buy-out part of the business, as distinct from venture capital. Private equity can also, confusingly, be used as an umbrella term to refer to everything from venture to leveraged buy-outs (LBOs). American usage is becoming more common in Europe, although, historically, venture capital has been the catch-all term for private equity activity, including management buy-outs (MBOs).

private placement memorandum (PPM) The marketing document issued by venture capitalists when they go fund raising. In the highly secretive world of VC, this is the nearest you will get to lifting the veil on a venture firm's performance numbers. Although the material is of course carefully doctored, a PPM can give a useful indication of the health of a venture firm's portfolio. These documents are not easy to get hold of either, but there is something of an underground 'trade' through intermediaries, including lawyers and, once you have one, you have currency.

returns The cash generated by venture capitalists courtesy of their investors' money. Negative returns are what happen when VCs lose money. You may also hear VCs talk about realized and unrealized returns. Realized returns constitute real cash back to investors. Unrealized returns are estimates of the value of companies that remain in the portfolio and, given the unquoted and early stage nature of the businesses, a highly subjective matter.

seed The hardest form of capital to secure – €100,000 or so, or less, to develop a prototype product and the business plan. Venture funds have become ever larger in recent years – not least because that is how they make money personally – with a deleterious effect on the provision of capital to this utterly essential part of the venture ecosystem.

semi-captive *See* **captive**.

serial entrepreneur A company founder who has done it before – built and probably exited a previous business. A breed much beloved of venture capitalists, because they feel they are taking fewer risks with individuals who have been through the mill before.

series A (and subsequent letters of the alphabet) Series A is first round funding (after seed). The traditional US model saw two or three rounds of funding (say to series C) with new investors coming in at each round, paying steadily increasing valuations before the business is sold. During the bubble, when public markets were highly receptive to IPOs, companies would sometimes list with just series A funding. As the bubble unwound, financing rounds were done at steadily lower valuations – **down rounds** – and attracting new investors became difficult. Now VCs are increasingly syndicating investments at the outset so that they are not reliant on outside investors further down the road. This is more akin to the old European model, where a single investor would often fund a company to exit.

syndication The sharing of a deal by more than one venture capitalist. As well as providing extra pools of cash, VC syndicates can supply complementary sector or geographical expertise, a wider hinterland of contacts and so on.

term sheet The prenuptial agreement between entrepreneur and venture capitalist, containing the terms which will later appear in the investment agreement. Pivotal in the negotiation of any investment.

third party funds Money from outside institutional investors. For example, **semi-captive** venture firms invest partly off the parent's balance sheet, and partly with funds raised from other third party institutional investors.

trade sale The most common kind of exit; the sale of the business to another, often much larger company, for cash, cash and shares, or shares.

under water A fund is generally said to be under water when it appears it will not return investors' original capital in full. VCs do not survive long if they lose investors' cash.

VCT *See* **venture capital trust**.

venture capital The provision of equity capital to private young companies. For terminology confusion, *see* **private equity**.

venture capital trust (VCT) A UK-listed entity which offers tax breaks to retail investors. Designed to encourage start-ups, rather too much cash found its way into small management buy-outs. Some VCTs do still fund venture businesses, but if you are considering them as potential backers, beware that quality is very mixed.

washout *See* **cram-down**.

X As in 5x or 10x. *See* **cash multiple**.

Index